Dorothy, 56

The House That Dorothy Built

DOROTHY AINSWORTH

LUMINARE PRESS

WWW.LUMINAREPRESS.COM

The House That Dorothy Built
© 2016 Dorothy Ainsworth

Printed in the United States of America

Cover Design: Claire Flint Last

All photos taken by Dorothy Ainsworth with the exception of the burning house photo on the back cover by Denise Baratta of the Daily Tidings, Ashland, OR.
Editorial cartoon on page 18 by Don Childers, artist for *Backwoods Home* magazine.

Luminare Press
438 Charnelton St #101
Eugene, OR 97401
www.luminarepress.com

LCCN: 2016954350
ISBN: 978-1-944733-03-2

CONTENTS

I dedicate this book to the American Dream.
I had the good fortune of being born in America where anything is possible if you are willing to work for it.
This great country is truly the land of endless opportunities, where a person of humble beginnings can reach lofty goals.
Only in America could I have achieved what I have.

Dorothy's Work Can be Seen in the Following Publications:

Backwoods Home magazine (regular contributor)
Mother Earth News magazine (twice)
Log Home Living magazine
Cabin Life magazine
American Falconry magazine
Oregon magazine
Fine Homebuilding magazine
Tough Times Survival Guide (book)
Best of College Photography 1987 (book)
Best of College Photography 1990 (book)

Also, of note:
In June of 2001, actors Tobey Maguire and Kirsten Dunst (Spiderman) rented Dorothy's log house for a week for their vacation.

FOREWORD

I can't say enough about Dorothy Ainsworth. And believe me, I can talk.

Read her website, send her an email. She is real. That property she developed on a shoestring over the past thirty years is worth gold now. You will find, as I discovered, that Dorothy embodies the true meaning of persistence. There are songs about don't back down and don't give up, but she was the original inspiration.

I first learned of Dorothy's accomplishments while reading *Backwoods Home* magazine. I read about how a single mother working as a waitress moved her two children to a better part of the country to start her own life. She wasn't waiting for someone to rescue her or make her dreams come true. After settling in her new town, she finally found ten acres that no one else wanted and started a thirty-year journey to create a showplace.

How many other women would have the courage to live in a tent with a dog and a shotgun when the kids were off at college while slowly building her dream? How many other single mothers would put dating on the back burner and spend half their monthly income on a land payment? Dorothy did. Her story chronicles the early days of securing water and remodeling the chicken coop to getting the skill set under her tool belt to cut down a log, peel the bark, drag it into place, and drill and spike the thing vertically to create a wall in a music studio that she lovingly created for her son to use for his talent as a musician.

Read her work. You'll find yourself pulled into the story of a lone woman on a hill working slowly and methodically to build the studio, and later her dream home. She is not the Amazon woman. Her petite, pretty pictures will betray the powerful woman you will learn to love. You'll smile with her when you read about the love of her life that stumbled across her path. Like me, you will have tears when you see the fire that destroyed her home but not her dream or her spirit. Finally, you will cheer her through the finish line when the house goes back up. Read her work. You'll learn how to live happily.

Thanks to her contributions I developed a whole new outlook on simple foods, simple living, and self-reliance. I learned not to envy what other people had; develop who you are, and the rest of the story will fall into place. She's a breathing example.

Building a house sounds so easy from the perspective of an armchair reader. As another woman who is in the epicenter of her own build, I can tell you that reading and doing the thing are dramatically different.

I know what a log feels like when you need to move it to the other side of your property. I get it. I know a sixteen-foot slice of 2" x 10" is a workout all by itself when moving it into place. I know that around every corner is a man trying to tell her how to do what he's never done and she has completed. I know she had more critics than cheerleaders. I understand the math involved in designing stairs. I understand that nothing, absolutely nothing in construction is without some degree of straining muscles and mental horsepower to put it all together. Dorothy makes these tasks appear possible and consistently inspires people like me to find the enjoyment in the project and eventually finish strong.

Ms. Ainsworth embodies the meaning of courage and tenacity. I seriously doubt she will ever grasp how much of an inspiration she has been to me and to others who are fortunate enough to have discovered her.

Read her work; you won't regret it.

—MARYLYNN BROOKS

(A real lady in Mississippi living her own self-reliant dream.)

Dorothy, 22, waitress and mother of two

INTRODUCTION

I have compiled this collection of articles in hopes of inspiring people at subsistence-level incomes like myself to pursue their own dreams of building a house in the country and becoming as self-sufficient as possible. I've documented my journey of property development by writing articles and taking photos as I progressed. They have been published in *Backwoods Home* magazine over the years, and I continue to contribute articles when I can. It's an excellent magazine that emphasizes a philosophy of self-reliance and individualism (www.backwoodshome.com).

Some of the accounts are how-to articles, but for the most part I just tell how *I* did it, not necessarily how *you* should do it. Some stories overlap, some are recaps, and some are variations with a new wrinkle, but my objective is to show and tell by example what *can* be done—with very little money and very little previous experience. You pay as you go, and you learn as you go. The most valuable lesson I can pass along is that everything happens in tiny increments but they add up into huge results.

About Me

I've been called a workaholic but consider it a compliment. My philosophy is that there is only so much time and energy in life, and I choose to spend it wisely on many and varied projects. My main focus for thirty-five years has been to develop a bare piece of property (ten affordable acres) into a comfortable, self-sufficient, and attractive homestead on a $15,000 a year waitress's income ($12,000 when I started).

With no previous experience and very little help, I've

built a pump house, water storage tank, root cellar, two workshops, two guest cabins, piano studio, barn, garden tool shed, two storage sheds, two deluxe chicken coops, a greenhouse, a tree house, a large stud-frame house, and *two* log homes (the first one burned down, but with help, I rebuilt it).

I'm now semiretired but still in good shape and going strong. I have so many interests I'd need several lifetimes to pursue them all. If anything, I need to speed up in the next decade rather than slow down. I love to laugh, so I tend to find the humor in almost everything (even mistakes), thus my work is also my play. I balance out property management and construction labor with hobbies I enjoy, such as cooking, sewing, and writing. Photography has been a lifelong passion.

Closing Thoughts

From age thirty on, I was a single mom and waitress who reared my kids by myself, and from age forty on created the security and lifestyle I so passionately wanted—on a shoestring budget. I've written various articles to share what I've learned and to help others who are in the same boat—having little cash but lots of drive. I believe that lofty goals *can* be achieved with hard work and tunnel vision because *I* was able to do it. *If I could do it, anybody can!*

I wouldn't trade the satisfying feelings of accomplishment for all the money that could have *hired* it done. It has been an arduous process, evolving into a Jill-of-All-Trades while working as a waitress and a prep cook, but it has been so fulfilling that the journey was absolutely priceless.

"Goals are dreams with a deadline," so I encourage *you* to get started—NOW!

Dorothy Ainsworth

CHAPTER 1

THE PIANO STUDIO

Piano Studio

When I graduated from high school in 1960, my father wrote in my autograph book: "When you get married and have twins, don't come to me for safety pins!" His droll humor turned out to be prophetic. Culturally, my role in our large family was Susie Homemaker, and sure enough, by age twenty-one, I had fulfilled my destiny: two kids, two jobs, one husband; then, to lighten the load, no husband.

For fifteen years I had put myself on the back burner, where hopes and dreams of security and independence were simmering. A notebook entitled "Wants and Needs in a Home" and a filing cabinet stuffed with log and timber-frame ideas revealed my yearning. Being an apartment-dwelling single mother waitressing in a big city was not my idea of the good life. Something in my genes insisted on a massive medieval fortress decorated in early pioneer. I wanted a house that the wolf himself couldn't blow down!

This smoldering desire for a rustic home of my own flamed into passion when I turned thirty-eight. "Ripeness is all," said Shakespeare. "Send my roots rain!" (Hopkins 1875)

I had reared my two kids to teen-hood and had survived a lifelong career in waitressing by feigning a tough hide to protect my romantic soul. It was time for a change, so, down to the lint in my pocket, and with the North Star as a windbreak, I started out on the long road to freedom.

I diligently shopped around for a nice, culturally rich small town, secured a job and an apartment in advance, loaded up Eric and Cynthia (along with his piano and her horse), and we were off. Happiness was Reno, Nevada, in my rearview mirror!

It took a year in idyllic Ashland, Oregon, to find a suitable chunk of property I could afford and to secure a farm loan. As serendipity would have it, I found ten acres for $40,000, and only three miles from town. It took another year to drill a well and get electricity.

I was determined to have a big rustic house—never mind I had no building experience, no fat bank account, and no helpmate. What I did have was a piece of land, an old pickup truck, and a high pain threshold.

I cut my baby (saw)teeth on remodeling a couple of old racked outbuildings into storage structures. Fraught with nothing but parallelograms, I learned harsh rule #1: Plumb, Level, and Almost Square, and tricky rule #2:

Measure Twice, Oops, Cut Twice. That summer the hand tools used me. The dog would slink away when I donned my carpenter's belt and furrowed my brow in grim determination.

For a novice, there's no thrill like the tactile kinetic experience of driving a sixteen-penny nail home in three blows, then burying its head with two extra whacks for no reason. There was evidence of beginner's overkill everywhere. Electrical cord repairs looked like snakes that had swallowed gophers. A job wasn't finished until all the nails were gone. There were no gimmicks or shortcuts in the learning process. I sweated and strained and scarred. But the satisfaction of sawing a clean, square cut with a handsaw rivaled sewing a fine seam or baking a perfect loaf of bread, and eventually the results became just as predictable.

It wasn't long before I discovered power tools with my Sears charge card. Yikes, that could mean twice as many mistakes in half the time! My circular saw was a new force to be reckoned with. It came with two blades: ripper and shredder. When I braced myself with gritted teeth and squinted eyes, the dog scurried out of sight.

Once in a while I'd take a break, sip a cup of coffee (liquid motivation), and gaze upon my ten acres of star thistle and poison oak, envisioning a proverbial rose garden (without thorns) and a beautiful log home on top of the hill surrounded by fruit trees in Technicolor, and kittens playing all around. For now, though, I'd enjoy the red-tailed hawk circling overhead and coyotes kiyiying at night.

As a farmer creates his self-portrait in a freshly plowed field, I was driven to carve out an original relationship with this hilly, hostile chunk of land. There was no going back to the comfort zone.

I focused my energy, and lucky things began to happen. Someone told me about lodgepole pine logs available right out of the forest for 3 cents a lineal foot and only twenty miles away. This economical option prompted some new possibility thinking. It confirmed my decision in favor of vertical-log construction for minimal notching and for relative ease in handling and transporting. Inspired, I hastened down and bought a personal-use pole permit from the local ranger district of the USFS. I estimated enough linear footage for one medium-sized structure and paid the fee in advance. When I needed more I would go back and pay for more.

Vertical-log construction was the practical choice for a 125-pound woman with a strong back and a sturdy little chainsaw. Short logs would fit in my pickup. They would require minimal notching, so the walls would go up fast. Shrinkage in length is negligible, so settling wouldn't be a problem. Besides, Davy Crockett was my great, great, great, great uncle, and that's how he did it. Forts back then were erected in a day, stockade-style. Why not now?

Eric wanted an eight-sided piano studio (1,000 square feet) for good acoustics, and I wanted a barn-style house (2,000 square feet). The terrain dictated pier foundations. Big on ideas but short on skills, we decided to practice on the studio first. Flushed-faced with enthusiasm, we sketched his blueprint on a napkin in a restaurant. Two heads are thicker than one, so we got a book from the library on how to set up the batter boards and we staked out the foundation lines.

With common sense as my guide and a pile of how-to-do-it books, I drew up some plans, constructed a model, and proceeded to gather enough logs for his studio. In our family, classical music is a necessity.

One day Eric was playing a Bach prelude; the next day

his white knuckles were gripping a chainsaw and felling trees! After several excursions of terror and torture, we had stockpiled 180 logs for $43.20. Together we carried each 8"-10" x 8-foot green log 100 feet or more, stepping over slash piles, hobbling, staggering, grunting, and whimpering. As my grip weakened with every step, I kept mumbling to myself, "Only three cents a foot, only three cents a foot." We loaded fifteen logs at a time in the old Ford pickup and careened home, front-end floating.

Upon one visit to the lumberyard, I spied a huge pile of large timbers in the back lot, and my pulse quickened. It was love at first sight, and I bought them all as impulsively as a woman buys a pair of shoes. The salesman quietly wrote up my order for 10,000 board feet at $250 per thousand (all my savings), looked up with one raised eyebrow and said, "Lady, do you know what you're doing?" I said boldly, "No, but I know what I want."

The stack included thirty huge, heavily creosoted, pressure-treated pilings salvaged from an old railroad trestle. I just happened to need twenty-nine pilings for both foundations.

About a week later, a neighbor stopped by, curious about my timbers, and revealed that he owned a boom truck and giant auger bit. After a brief discussion of foundation plans (my favorite subject), he offered to drill the holes and set the pilings for $10 each. I seized the opportunity at once and began the grueling labor of cleaning out six-foot deep holes by day and slinging hash at the cafe at night.

By this time I was acquiring some major muscle, and I needed every fiber. There was no shade. Crow's feet turned into eagle claws, hands into lobster claws. I kept whispering to myself, "Only $290—only one week's wages" (for the foundation holes). I once read that you get rich by spending yourself. I was filthy, sweaty rich! My sister said I was becoming the man I wanted to marry.

Soon after the piers were set, the backhoe man I hired to dig a waterline trench just happened to have a laser-beam transit in his hip pocket. He voluntarily marked all the piers level with each other. I cut them off and notched them to receive 4" x 12" rim joists for the piano studio and 6" x 12" girders for the house.

I stood back and affectionately admired my big black pilings, spaced just so, jutting out of the stark landscape like Stonehenge. The time had come to contemplate the architectural overview of both structures and draw up the final plans for county approval.

Logic told me to build within my capabilities, but aesthetics won out. "When ignorance is bliss, 'tis folly to be wise." (Shakespeare) Hence the piano studio was to be an octagon converging into a square cupola, with triangles and trapezoids dancing heel and toe on the roof. I was like a spoiled child who wanted everything on my list, except there were no elves to help and no Santa to deliver.

I wanted archways and bay windows, vaulted ceilings and skylights, wide windowsills, and a cushioned window seat for reading magazines and eating chocolates on a rainy day. But I would not employ a center post to support the roof! It would ruin the romantic notion of a nine-foot concert grand in the middle of the thirty-foot room, with Chopin bouncing off the walls. The laws of physics have a way of humbling even the most deluded ego. I scratched my head while searching my memory banks. "Eureka!" I remembered the yurt principle. A hidden cable would defy gravity.

Yes, I wanted it all, completed in this lifetime, on a shoestring. Time and energy are the basics currencies of life; lack of money is merely an inconvenience. A sense of urgency gripped me. What started out as *we* ended up as *me*. Eric and Cynthia went off to pursue their careers and meet mates. Nature had its way. Meanwhile, back at the ranch, I was fluttering about creating a nest so there'd be something to be empty. Someday the chickens might come home to roost. I imagined future music festivals—spontaneous gatherings of diverse and harmonious spirits—and rosy-cheeked grandkids giggling and dancing about the room. Goals are dreams with a deadline, so I grabbed my hammer and got busy.

For the next three years of weekends, I toiled alone to hone my skills in a self-imposed apprenticeship program. The brutality of fact quickly replaced the delusions of wishful thinking. Every act had a consequence. I learned that the limitations of the flesh must be exceeded by will. Daydreams are free and replenish the soul, but there's no way out of the work.

Building the floor was laborious but uncomplicated. Joists and subflooring were secured with screws; no creaking allowed. When I needed to rest, I'd peel logs with my trusty drawknife. I documented all progress with construction shots and self-portraits.

The library was usually my best friend, but when it came time to square off the logs, there was no book. With the optical illusions involved in staring at a gnarly tapered log, it's impossible to eyeball the cut. One can end up with a pile of firewood. After trial and error (and a little kindling), I devised a contraption that used my chainsaw as a chop-saw, and it worked beautifully.

Erecting the vertical-log walls kept me as busy as a Beethoven sonata. The general procedure was "cut 'em off, stand 'em up, spike 'em in." Predrill like a drill sergeant. To get from here to there, hug a log real tight and waddle with it. Who cares what the neighbors think? One sunny afternoon two bicyclists rode by and one yelled, "Hey, look, they put the logs the wrong way!"

When the walls were standing and the headers were in their final resting places, it was time to place the square cupola aloft. A gin pole put it there, and scaffolding held it fast. Cutting the confounded compounded angles, where three rafters met at the corners, required some finesse with the 12-inch electric chainsaw. Next, to really challenge my capabilities, each rafter's birdsmouth notch had to be individually measured with a template and custom cut.

After transferring the measurements to a 2" x 12" x 16' rafter on the floor and making all the cuts, I pushed it up a long ladder propped against the scaffolding, one step at a time. Then I pivoted it on the top railing, using leverage to lower it slowly down onto its mark on the top-plate, and fastened it to the cupola. When the birdsmouth miraculously seated in place, I sighed, "Ahhh, life doesn't get any better than this." The word "birdsmouth" still evokes a spiritual feeling in me.

The hardest job of all was going from the delicious solitude of the country to work at the cafe, where trying to get a bite to eat in eight hours was like a giraffe at a watering hole with the lions coming. At home I had the freedom of a monkey, climbing up and down the rungs of the scaffolding. My goal was two rafters a day, sixty in all. I'd work right up to the last minute, put on my war paint, fire up old Bessie, and speed to work, curling my eyelashes with one hand and steering with the other while blow-drying my hair with the windows down—all the while protected by my bumper sticker: "Caution, Driver Applying Makeup."

I glued and screwed every rafter, then drilled holes in their tails (just above the top-plate) to receive the cable and four turnbuckles. I bushed each hole with annealed nylon to reduce friction if the cable ever needed to move. The moment of truth came with tightening the turn-buckles and removing the scaffolding. Nothing creaked, croaked, or settled. The structural integrity of my design was uncompromised.

Eight of the main rafters, like spokes, are true 2" x 12"s; the rest are 2" x 10"s to provide a 2-inch recessed nailing surface for the 1" x 12" pine ceiling-boards. With age, pine mellows to a warm and wonderful patina. I helped it along with a coat of semi-gloss lacquer.

As the place took shape and tiny triumphs added up, I realized that my Outward Bound adventure was merely the tangible manifestation of my inner growth. Call it Zen, call it zeal—whatever it was, it felt good. I saw myself as the sum of my strengths.

Now and again people would happen by offering advice—armchair experts. I never had to ask for a second opinion; dozens came, unsolicited. I discovered that common sense is not so common and gullible ears will be filled with nonsense, so after pursuing a few wild geese, I became a skeptical curmudgeon. "Why don't you just?" was the quickest phrase to make me surreptitiously roll my eyes at the dog and feign snoring, then try to get back to work. In all my brief encounters, I never met a man who hadn't once lived in a teepee and built a log house—a curious phenomenon indeed.

An old friend taught me how to use clamps as a poor man's assistant. With auxiliary hands the roof plywood went on fast. I topped it off with shingles just before the first rainfall of autumn.

I furred out the inner walls with 2" x 4"s, hid the wiring and insulation, and covered it all with Sheetrock. Via the garden sprayer, everything on the outside got a dose of the old boat-builder's recipe (linseed oil, marine varnish, and turpentine) whether it needed it or not—including my hair!

I chinked the logs with 1.5-inch diameter foam pipe-insulation, which I sanded and painted brown, then glued in place. I caulked with fifty-year silicone seal (dark brown) and smoothed out each bead manually. For one month I was the self-appointed "Caulking Queen of Ashland," as evidenced by the splayed-out middle finger of my right hand.

Because the walls were a foot thick, I made wide window framing to accommodate. I used one and a half boards (one whole and one ripped lengthwise in half) of pine 2" x 10"s splined together, screwed and plugged in place. I ordered double-paned glass to fit each opening and secured the windows with my own 2" x 2" molding. Simple brass casement adjusters open some of the smaller windows for cross-ventilation. Built-in sliding windows in the cupola, and a ceiling fan whisk out hot air.

Spatial relationships reign in the palisaded palace. Windows in clusters of three—and tile work in the entrance-way, hearth, and kitchenette bay window—repeat themes for visual appeal. To me, archways are the crowning glory in a home, perhaps hearkening back to my ancestry in a cave. I built them out of 2" x 10" splined-pine by cutting the curves on a band saw, then laminating them to the right thickness. I glued and screwed and clamped the pine boards together butcher-block style and sanded the attractive end-grain until smooth. The stout arches lend support in spanning the doorways. I covered the 1-inch subfloor with ¾-inch particle board and cozied it all over with carpet.

When the nine-foot concert grand piano was rolled into its final resting place in the octagonal sanctuary, I sighed an audible "Ahhhh!" Mission accomplished.

I tallied my expenditures. The cost of the piano studio came to $15,000—the sum total of tips I had earned and spent on it daily. I was debt free.

Three years had whizzed by, and I was putting the finishing touches on my baby. I sat down on the deck to rub sawdust out of my bloodshot eyes and pet the dog when Eric appeared like an apparition! After piano-tuning school and a three-month hike on the Pacific Crest Trail with his girlfriend to "round out" his education, he came back to visit Mom and his piano. I cleared the sawdust out of my ears and asked him to play. When I heard beautiful Mozartian trills wafting out the Dutch door and across the sunlit hills, it was all worthwhile—a labor of love.

CHAPTER 2

THE WINK

Quick-fix suspenders

Octogenarian John McCormick was a frequent customer at the Copper Skillet, where I worked as a waitress. About the time he started coming in, I was in the process of building a vertical-log piano studio and worked on it every day until my 2:00 to 10:00 p.m. shift began. John always sat in the comfortable dining area, but evidently he could hear me babbling about my daily progress to the regular coffee-break customers who sat at the counter.

One day he hobbled up to the cash register to pay and quietly said, "If you ever need any help on your construction project—any help at all—please call me." He slipped me his phone number and limped out the door.

I thought, "*E-gads*! He can barely walk; how could he *possibly* help me build anything?" I shrugged it off, but it seemed odd, so I wondered about it.

Soon after that, I was having trouble figuring what size cable and turnbuckles to use in my unique roof design and I remembered John's offer. I called him on a whim, and sure enough he rushed right over and proceeded to solve my problem with a mind that worked at lightning speed. He made some sketches and calculations and spit out the answer like a computer. I was in awe.

It turned out he was a retired civil engineer, an inventor, a brilliant mathematician, an experienced builder in his younger days, and a member of SCORE (volunteer consultants to help people starting out in small business). He had also raised a family.

Our friendship blossomed. He was a fascinating man who was still in touch with his *inner child* and had an intense curiosity about anything related to science and mechanics. To top it all off, he had a fun and playful sense of humor hidden behind his somber demeanor.

This was quite evident one day when he was helping me wire an overhead kitchen light. I didn't have a short ladder, so he bravely climbed onto a rickety barstool to reach the light fixture. Being a tall and gangly man (not to mention *old*), he teetered precariously before finding his balance. Then he reached both arms way up high to fiddle with the wiring.

That's when his pants fell down! All the way down to his ankles, revealing long black silk socks connected to boxer shorts with garters. It was beyond ridiculous, like something you'd see in an *Esquire* cartoon! We were both laughing so hard I could barely manage to hoist his pants back up so he could step down before he fell down. I then fixed *his* problem with a rope.

I learned a lot from John. He taught me how to use clamps as extra hands when working alone. He taught me how to do the wiring in the studio and coached me every step of the way. He was patient enough to simply take a deep breath and exhale a long sigh when I kept wrapping a wire splice until *all* the electrical tape was gone. I was insufferable; it must have been terribly frustrating for him, but he always came back for more.

When almost everyone else was discouraging me from taking on such a complicated design (eight-sided roof structure converging into a four-sided cupola) for my *first* building project, he encouraged me and helped me. He became my best friend.

I was a young and vibrant forty-five and had a big, strong boyfriend named Kirt, who was going to college and had very little time to lend a hand. I wanted the challenge of building the studio myself anyway and called for help only when I was desperate.

One day I *was* desperate. I was working on the interior of the studio and had just finished tiling the hearth where the wood stove would go. The 300-pound *Franklin Fireplace* wood stove was sitting on one side of the room, and the hearth was on the other. I didn't have a hand truck nor the money to buy one.

John was visiting that day, and I turned to him and said, "How in the heck am I going to get this stove over onto the hearth?" His answer surprised me. This perfect gentleman, who had never displayed any sign of impropriety before, said defiantly, "Let *muscle-man* do it!" I was shocked! It dawned on me that John was sweet on me. How could I have been so naive?

The secret was out. There was a long, uncomfortable

silence before I said, "I have to run to the hardware store, but I'll be right back. Do you want to go?" For some strange reason, he said he'd stay and wait.

The store was twenty minutes away, but I hurried so I wouldn't keep my good friend—turned "would-be jealous lover"—waiting too long. When I got back and burst through the doorway I saw him sitting in the unframed window-seat opening, nonchalantly sipping a glass of water. The woodstove that had been right there beside him was gone.

I quickly looked across the room, and there it was—centered on the hearth—exactly where I wanted it. With eyes wide and mouth agape, I looked back at John. He winked.

It was the sexiest moment in building history! With that wink, worth a thousand words, John at eighty-eight was as charming and ageless as a man can get. It made my heart skip a beat and brought a blush to my cheeks.

But not only that, he proved that brains and experience can compete with brawn and youth—and sometimes win. (He had ingeniously used some scraps of iron pipe to roll it over.)

Sadly, John died a year later, but I feel very lucky to have known such an intelligent, generous, wise, and wonderful man. Because of John, I learned *never* to prejudge anyone (only a fool would judge a knight by his chinked and rusty armor) and *never* to underestimate the knowledge and abilities of *seasoned citizens*. And I learned one more thing: no matter what the age, a man is a man is a man, and that's appealing in itself. He was a most unforgettable character.

CHAPTER 3

EXCESSIVE OVERHANG

"The only time I ever 'got loaded and tied one on,' I got caught"

I'm a short, rather top-heavy brunette, building a stout vertical-log cabin, solo, on a waitress's earnings. Being an economically challenged opportunist, I scrounge and recycle materials whenever I can.

Bessie, my ancient Ford pickup, is my best friend even though I've abused her unmercifully over the years. We've careened home down the mountain, front-end floating, with a total of 480 10-inch diameter, 8-foot logs, twelve at a time, for my various vertical-log structures. (In the nineties, you could get a USFS permit to cut and carry lodgepole pine for 3 cents a lineal foot.) We've been through a lot together, Bessie and I, without incident, until *the incident*.

A friend gave me fifty 16-foot pallets, just to take them away and clean out his shed. They were built with beautiful straight 2" x 4"s I could use for my inner wall furring and roof grid (to hold rigid foam insulation on top of the exposed-beam ceiling). I was drooling with greed.

I proceeded to haul a couple of loads of pallets a day in the standard-bed pickup, sneaking by the troll (log-truck weigh master) at the bottom of the road. He seemed too busy to notice the naturally camouflaged rust and oxidized-green truck. And of course my red flag was dancing in the breeze, well—dragging an inch off the road.

On my last load, almost home free, I was turning at the dreaded intersection, nervously humming "The Rock Island Line"—"I fooled you, I fooled you, I've got pig iron, pig iron"—when Billy Goat Gruff let out a bellow that made even half-ton Bessie tuck her exhaust pipe between her wheels!

He waved me over. I groaned to a stop and hopped out to meet him halfway, all smiley and bouncy—and guilty. It was a scorching summer day; I was casually underdressed in my work clothes—a tiny stretch top and faded blue jeans. He was short, rotund, and uniformed in bright orange like a giant pumpkin with a badge.

To avoid eye contact and remain professionally aloof, he ludicrously focused right on my chest and barked, "Ma'am, you have excessive overhang! I've never seen such excessive overhang!" I thought, "Yeah, and your waistline looks like the equator," but I attempted levity: "Only at high noon, sir. It's an optical illusion!"

That did it! He wrote me up with the expressionless eyes of a coroner.

So much for saving a buck on lumber, and so much for using my feminine wiles to wheedle my way.

CHAPTER 4

DOROTHY'S MOTIVATION

Son, Eric, 17, at the piano and daughter, Cynthia, 16

Introduction by Dave Duffy, editor of *Backwoods Home* magazine:

In the 1994 May/June Issue #27 of *Backwoods Home* magazine, we published an article by Dorothy Ainsworth that we titled: "Determined Woman Builds Distinctive Vertical-Log Studio," in which Dorothy detailed how she built a beautiful 1,000-square-foot piano studio. The article and photos were so captivating that many people wrote to thank us for printing it. Some readers, however, were skeptical. "Could a woman really do that?" they questioned. So I asked Dorothy to write the following article not only to answer the doubters, but to give the rest of us a glimpse into the determined woman behind the original article.

Dorothy's reply

Dear Dave,

The enclosed answer to the *doubting Thomasinas* had to be a personality and character study, not just a how-to article. The mind behind the motion produces the fuel that drives the machine, and that's what this article is about.

So many women have come up to me (after reading the piano studio article) and said, "Oh, I couldn't do that!" I say, "Why not? I'm just a 125-pound weakling with a little stronger-than-average will and a fair dose of common sense."

If you choose to print my article, please do so in its entirety, or important psychological ingredients may be left out. I hope it will be an inspirational human-interest story that may help men and women alike throw off the shackles of convention and forge ahead with their own dreams of affordable alternative lifestyles. Your willingness to print an article like this may be just the boost they need.

Thanks for the opportunity to share my experience with others and to teach them by example to say, "I can!" instead of "I can't."

Dorothy's Biographical and Philosophical Treatise

I grew up in the middle of a colorful, eccentric family— eight of us crowded into a one-bedroom house not far from the ocean. Six beds lined the walls of the living room, early-pioneer style. My parents were lively and creative and philosophical. Although we were poor, they made each of us feel special and unafraid to be different. Poverty was dignified by laughter, but the work ethic was *law*.

We all had a passion for classical music and science and were constantly busy with projects. The boys built telescopes; the girls took ballet. Dad, a mechanic, built boats as a hobby and painted oil landscapes. Mom was forever hanging clothes on the line and singing opera at the top of her lungs while our daily beans simmered on the stove. Oranges and tomatoes were abundant and free. It was southern California, 1952.

In the midst of all this *ordered chaos*, I fiercely wanted a *room of my own* and verbally fantasized about going underground like a mole. My father nonchalantly handed me some tools and went inside. Secretly everyone watched and giggled as the serious red-faced girl flailed movable objects against impenetrable forces. After digging only an inch in one hour, I accepted defeat and ran off to the beach where I drew floor plans in the sand with driftwood and *played house*.

Twenty-eight years later, after two kids, ten years of single parenthood, and twenty years of waitressing for a living, that driving force resurfaced like a baleen whale coming up for air and landed on a hilltop in southern Oregon.

With a farm loan, I bought ten unimproved acres that nobody else wanted on the hot, dry side of Ashland, Oregon, and began *Operation Petticoat* from the corset up. Poison oak and rattlesnakes initiated me into the world of property development. I stocked up on calamine lotion and kept my eyes on the ground. To be prepared for a surprise visit by Yul Brynner out of *Westworld*, I bought a gun.

That first summer I camped out in a big army tent, cooked on a hot plate at the power pole, and showered at the fitness center. After an eight-hour swing shift at the cafe, I'd crawl into my dark cocoon and let the sounds of hooting owls and pulsating crickets lull me to sleep. Gypsy, my faithful blue heeler, stood guard.

Romanticizing in the light of day, I envisioned giraffes traversing the rolling hills and lions crouched in the wild oats. An old windmill made haunting sounds like a trumpeting elephant.

There was stark beauty in the great panorama of bleached-blond hills and blue skies. With a splash of Walt Disney's watercolor brush, I visualized an oasis in the middle of this safari country.

Imagination was intoxicating, enthusiasm was exhilarating, but hard work sobered me right up. *Carving out* a place in the country was literally that: pick, shovel, and axe. Delusions of grandeur gave way to gut-busting discomfort. Reality reared its ugly head in the form of a black thumbnail, festering splinters, and bruised shins. Calluses and chapped lips went with the territory. Comfort was a wet rag on the forehead.

Though not pleasant, progress was meaningful and fulfilling. After securing the basics (water, electricity, and a septic system), I painstakingly acquired carpentry skills by constructing the well's pump-house from Sunset's *Basic Carpentry Illustrated*. Featuring just me and my shadow, along with a supporting cast of an Estwing hammer and Sandvik saw, my building *debut* entertained an attentive audience of one: the dog. It was a huge success, according to Gypsy, who wagged her tail and panted in approval whenever I strained and grunted and spewed forth mild expletives.

With newly found confidence, I graduated to remodeling two outbuildings on the property into usable structures. My son Eric, a pianist and composer, had been evicted from his apartment in town for playing Beethoven at midnight (terrible teenage crime), and we needed a place for his grand piano.

Deep in the convolutions of my brain, I had a plan. Always a mother first, I wanted to provide a family homestead—a safe refuge where communal living could be harmonious if times got tough. Being a survivalist, I wanted a future of independence and self-sufficiency. But my greatest desire was to create, through self-expression and perseverance, an aesthetically pleasing atmosphere to nurture talent and to foster growth in us all.

At thirty-eight, I asked myself, "If not now, when? If not me, who?" Eric and my daughter, Cynthia, had gone off to pursue performing-arts careers on their own, working full time. There had never been any child support, no rich relatives, and no government handouts (against my principles), but we had our fair share of a more precious commodity: drive.

My priorities were written in stone. First there would be a music studio, replete with the nine-foot grand piano and an array of electronic equipment for entire orchestral compositions. In today's high-tech world, a composer needs special tools to be competitive. (In 1795 Mozart could get by with jotting down masterpieces on napkins.) The studio would be an inspiring opportunity for Eric, and my heartfelt contribution to a life force that's full of ideas, full of hope, and full of purpose. The passion and sincerity of youth shouldn't wait.

Economically challenged, I was in a dilemma: how to satisfy my gourmet taste on a fast-food budget ($12,000 a year in 1981). Having a penchant for substantially overbuilt structures, I wanted at least meat and potatoes. After doggedly researching my options, I had to compromise. Although Ted Benson's timber-frame book was my bible, the USFS turned out to be my salvation.

I obtained a lodgepole pine permit to cut and carry short logs right out of the forest for a nominal fee. Instead of drooling over smooth oak timbers at $1 an inch, I'd sweat over rough logs at 3 cents a foot. Rather than using the traditional horizontal method of construction, I'd stand them up vertically. I drew plans for the 1,000-square-foot octagonal studio, built a model of it, and got a permit.

During Eric's summer vacation, he helped me stockpile 180 logs for $43 and the "Waitress Builds Fortress" saga began.

A famous quote became my motto:

"He who would do some great thing in this short life must apply himself to work with such a concentration of his forces as, to idle spectators, who live only to amuse themselves, look like *insanity*."

—*Francis Parkman, 1823*

And evidently it *did*. Boyfriends came and went. Would-be suitors, feigning interest for a possible roll in the star thistle, left permanent skid marks peeling out of the driveway.

Well-meaning friends, contemplating the enormity of my undertaking, all droned the same advice: "Why don't you just move a little trailer up here while you build a stud-framed rectangle and be done with it? You're doing everything the hard way." I argued, "There's more to life than basic shelter. Why not call a hat a roof over your head and be done with it?" They just didn't get it. To a bird like me, with a strong nesting instinct, a home is a soul investment.

Considering the time element involved in pay-as-you-go construction, the *hard way* was the only feasible way for me. The basic skeleton could be erected now and fleshed out later, as I earned the money. I'd have no worries about the weather on logs standing as they naturally grow. On the other hand, studs, unmercifully exposed to the elements, turn into pretzels, nails rust and crawl out, and walls *rack* (lean). One would have to get a loan for about $40,000 to complete that little box with a roof in one season or end up with a pile of firewood. My land payment alone took 50 percent of my monthly income.

Sometimes when I felt tired and overwhelmed, the demons of self-doubt would creep in. Through tears, I'd vow to avoid negativity and to hang onto my dreams with cat claws! I concluded that the nice thing about living in the country was the people I *didn't* meet. When I needed advice, I'd go to the library and check out how-to books. My only *support system* was my bra straps.

Daily jaunts were limited to working at the cafe, rushing my little bag of tips to the bank, doing a hundred sit-ups at the fitness center, and jogging for twenty minutes. An occasional *hippity-hop to the hardware shop* and lumberyard rounded out my small world of travels.

Tunnel vision was imperative. I stuck to *the plan* and finished the piano studio in three years, for $15,000. Building it was like having a baby—the end result was worth it, and I soon forgot the pain.

During that three-year working frenzy, I planted an orchard; landscaped with trees, shrubs, and flowers; and built a split-rail fence. From lack of attention, my garden was inadvertently *donated* to deer and insects.

When I'm busy building, a typical day is not an exciting whirlwind of activity performed by a crew of skilled craftsmen. It's just methodical me, trudging up the hill every morning, eating oatmeal and skim milk out of a kettle, as I put one foot in front of the other. Arriving at the building site, I focus on the task at hand, mustering up the gumption to get started, then clunk into low gear and begin measuring, cutting, chiseling, gluing, screwing, sanding, and staining. As the day wears on, I pick up speed like a runaway freight train and find it difficult to stop. After years of jogging, energy and endurance are not a problem.

I've never claimed to be the consummate craftsperson but by necessity have become a Jill-of-All-Trades. I'm slow and deliberate and almost always prefer working alone. To avoid distractions and annoyances, I seldom ask for help and only then as a last resort. Given enough time and common sense, I can solve most problems, odd as they frequently are.

I've learned that nothing worthwhile is easy to achieve, and you must go for it when you're hot; procrastination puts out the fire. Steady progress in tiny increments, like a clock ticking in a thunderstorm, ensures that the goal that seemed impossible becomes inevitable.

Life is tough and complicated for everyone—full of joy and full of grief. Although at times it feels like one is being buffeted by the winds of circumstance, there is a veritable cafeteria of choices (to not decide is to decide). I monitor what goes into my mind and try to twist reality in a positive direction. I marvel at beauty and seek out intellectual stimulation. I strive to remain unjaded, with a girl's heart and a woman's head. I believe humility is a virtue; I'm not ashamed to blush or cry. A smile and a wink from a kindred spirit makes my day.

Ordinary pleasures thrill me: a litter of *army cats* (calico-camouflaged) behind the barn, the cacophony of coyotes at night, a resident frog in the outdoor shower, a tough little roadside weed earning its living in the gravel. Any Bach prelude sends me to heaven; his D Minor Concerto puts me to work.

Thoreau said, "Simplify, simplify!" I drive an $800 pickup, eat like a peasant, buy clothes at Goodwill, and seldom watch TV. Creature comforts are a hot shower, a warm bed, and the wood stove a-cracklin'. Designer nails mean *ring-shank* building nails, not bright-red talons studded with diamonds. Give me my morning coffee, and I'm happy.

With my vanity years behind me, I'll do most anything for a laugh. I measure life in strong heartbeats, daily accomplishments, and peace of mind. Happiness is having my own approval.

I'll get all the sleep I need after I die, so when my body isn't moving, my eyes are. I love to read and keep up on the latest in science, medicine, and technology. Photography is my passion and my hobby. Beauty—in any form—feeds my soul.

Closing Thoughts

People frequently question whether I've really developed the property and built the structures myself. Depending on a woman's cultural persuasion, that could be taken as an insult *or* a compliment. Gender *should* be irrelevant, but I stick to the facts and simply hold out my hands to reveal the evidence. These gnarly prehensile monstrosities were a small price to pay for *a room of my own.*

CHAPTER 5

BUILD A 6,500-GALLON WATER TANK FOR $1,500

Building the concrete water tank

When I bought ten dry, barren, *affordable* acres back in 1981, I got what I paid for: no electricity, no septic system, no well, and no water. What I *did* get was a long, narrow rectangle, carpeted with star thistle and poison oak, situated on the southern face of a hill (500' x 1,320'). Buying bare land was a big gamble, but I wanted my own piece of dirt so badly I could taste it—if only I had some water to wash it down with. Thanks to the local well driller and good ol' Mother Nature, I got that drink of water. I lucked out and struck it rich with a 50-GPM well at a depth of 150 feet—for $3,000.

The next steps were basic. I procured the appropriate permits, built a pump house around the well casing, set a power pole, wired in an electrical box and meter, and called the inspector.

When all my lifelines were hooked up, I installed a submersible pump from Sears by following the do-it-yourself instructions. To my amazement, when I turned on the control box, water spewed right up out of the pipe! Now I could get serious about improving the property. I'd start with a water storage tank because I believe you are only as secure as your water supply.

To take advantage of gravity for water on demand, the logical place to put a holding tank was at the top of the hill, although the well was at the bottom. I called a backhoe man to dig a 3-foot-deep trench a quarter mile long and level a spot at the top end for a 12' x 12' x 6' concrete tank (6,500-gallon capacity).

The 2-hp submerged pump in the well would fill the tank via a 1½" PVC pipe buried in the trench. When the tank was full, I'd use the same pipe to gravity-feed water to supply all my household and irrigation needs. Every 60 feet down the line I would put a 1-inch PVC riser sticking up out of the main pipe and cap it with a non-siphoning valve for irrigation. I would later put in 1-inch PVC pipes underground off that main line as needed to supply my various structures as I built them.

With a holding tank, I would have the security of a week's or month's supply of water at a time (depending on the season) if the electricity went off for any reason. A stored supply would also save the pump motor from having to cycle on and off whenever a faucet was turned on. My storage tank would fill up in about three hours;

then the pump would rest, and the well would replenish itself. It sounded like a good plan, so I got busy hauling gravel. I would need tons of it!

I found a source for cheap crushed gravel (¾ minus, meaning no rocks bigger than ¾"), but, again you get what you pay for—I had to load it myself. I hauled a yard or two a day in my pickup until I stockpiled enough to build the tank. I had it down to a science: each load took 300 shovels full. When the tires were flattened *just so*, I knew that that amount of too much was just enough. I'd creep home, front end floating, turn into my driveway and step on it full throttle to get a run at the hill, fishtailing all the way to the top. (I had no roads yet.) Poor old Bessie, my 1971 half-ton Ford pickup, has endured cruel and unusual punishment for twenty years, hauling a hundred 1-ton loads of gravel for roads and 780 logs for houses, but she's still going strong.

It took two weeks of shoveling rock to have enough for the job, but loading and unloading the truck twenty times was just the half of it! Each of those 6,000 shovels full of gravel would have to be lifted *again*—either thrown on the ground to level the pad or heaved into a cement mixer with sand and cement and water, then dumped and tamped into forms. I looked forward to the day when the *cruel gruel* would be entombed forever in the shape of a tank.

The Floor

I had no electricity on top of the hill, so I borrowed a cement mixer and a gas-powered generator from a neighbor. He was a Bill-of-All-Trades who *also* did everything the hard way to save money. I paid him what I could to help me with the general layout of the tank site, which consisted of setting up batter boards and making sure everything was plumb, level, and square.

I covered the large pad where the tank would sit with about 8 inches of gravel as a base. Then we built the forms out of 2" x 8" lumber, set the 2-inch diameter PVC drainpipe in place, and poured the 8-inch-thick floor in two grueling days (32 mixers full = 4 cubic yards).

We used a garden rake and a shovel to evenly distribute the mix around and work it into every corner. Together we dragged a 2" x 6" on edge across the surface of the wet concrete floor, using the tops of the forms as guides—a procedure called *screeding*. Bill advised me to use no rebar in the slab because it would be filled with water inside and sitting on wet ground outside and the rebar would eventually rust, leaving voids that would weaken the concrete. Right or wrong, I had no experience to question him, so that's how we did it.

Before the floor set up as hard as a rock, we roughed up the sides of the slab and a 2-inch wide strip around the top perimeter to serve as a keyway (an overhanging lip) to help tie the vertical walls to the floor. We used ⅝" plywood nailed to 2" x 4" frames for the 8-inch-thick walls. I sprayed the sheets of plywood with a petroleum-based oil (using a garden sprayer) so they wouldn't stick to the concrete when it was time for removing and repositioning them.

We secured vertical rebar at 2-foot intervals inside the wall cavities. Bill helped me with the floor, but then he had to go to another job, so I carried on solo. All I was physically capable of shoveling, pouring, distributing, and tamping in twelve hours was 1½ cubic yards of concrete. I let each daily pour set up, then moved the forms up, and raised the cement mixer platform and piles of ingredients to the new level. Bill stopped by on his way home from work each day to help me lift the heavy stuff.

Dorothy Ainsworth

A series of separate pours meant *cold joints*—the lines of demarcation between pours. If the preceding surface is roughed up while the concrete is still *green* (firm but fresh), the next layer bonds just fine. It's not as ideal as a monolithic pour, but it was the only doable method for me.

The Recipe

There are three basic mixtures that are commonly used for concrete construction, from strongest to strong enough. They differ in the ratio of the three basic ingredients: cement, sand, and stone. How they are proportioned makes a huge difference in strength and durability. The more cement, the stronger (richer) the mix, with 1:2:4 being a happy medium for most projects. The less water you can use in relation to the dry ingredients and still maintain a workable consistency, the stronger the mix. A runny mix is weak.

The consistency of freshly mixed concrete should feel like oatmeal cookie batter—but don't lick your fingers! The trick is not to touch the mix at all with bare hands. For a novice, that's easier said than done because it's tempting to catch the drips and smear them around.

Because Portland cement has abrasive silica and caustic lime in it, I ended up with no fingerprints at all until the *tread* grew back. It would have been a good time to take up a life of crime, but I stayed on the straight and narrow—and plumb!

When you make a batch of concrete, the sum of the ingredients mixed together will result in a much smaller volume than the separate components—kind of like what happens to that mountain of flour when you make a loaf of bread, or when you can't believe you just used half a gallon of ice cream to make only two decent-sized milkshakes!

Bill advised me to use a 1:3:5 mix: 1 heaping shovel of cement to 3 of sand and 5 of gravel. For me, that mixture would be economical for my budget and yet strong enough for my particular application: a heavy foundation and thick retaining walls. Because the tank would be sitting on impenetrable hard rock, I knew it would have to be back-filled to bury it partially underground, which would also help equalize the pressure on the walls. (Water weight pushes out; wall of dirt pushes in.) Backfilling would also keep the water cool in the summer and prevent freezing in the winter.

Calculating What You Need

Using simple math, I estimated the walls would require 8 cubic yards. Here's how: Multiply length (12') x height (6') x thickness (¾' = 0.75) x 4 walls and divide by 27 because there are 27 cubic feet in one cubic yard.

The Walls

The growling, gyrating cement mixer held about ⅛ of a cubic yard (approximately 3.5 cubic feet) at a time, gobbling up 2 shovels of cement, 6 shovels of sand, 10 shovels of gravel. I worked as fast as I could slinging them in, counting and alternating the ingredients very carefully, while constantly adding water with a measuring bucket—about 4 gallons. (Water was available from the pipe in the trench.)

When the batter was just right I shut off the motor, swung the cement mixer around on its axis, and dumped the load into the forms. Then I tamped, tamped, and tamped with the business end of a short shovel. I also tapped the sides of the forms with a hammer to vibrate the concrete into every nook and cranny. On the fifth and final pour, I set a pipe through the wall near the top to make an overflow hole. I would later run a 1½" polypipe through that hole and out to my pond.

Each daily pour amounted to 12 mixers full, which totaled 24 shovels of cement, 72 shovels of sand, 120 shovels of gravel, and 48 gallons of water. I guzzled another 10 gallons of water and dumped even more on my head. It took a week of working from daybreak to backbreak to complete the walls. The whole project had to be a marathon because concrete sets up fast in extreme heat and time was running out on my *vacation* from waitressing.

Needless to say, I put my fitness center membership on hold for a while. "Sixteen Tons" by Tennessee Ernie Ford was my theme song for the week, although the tank ended up weighing 24 tons. Blistered hands on Monday had turned into lobster claws by Friday.

The Roof

On top of the last pour I dragged a short 2" x 6" on edge across the 8-inch-wide wet surfaces to smooth them out. I then set four 2" x 4" pressure-treated sill-plates in the concrete and leveled them with a long level while tamping and wiggling them into place around the outside perimeter, making sure the corners were squared. I would later drill a few holes down through the sill-plates and into the *green* concrete and install anchor bolts (½" x 6") to secure the plates to the walls. (The bolts should have been set first but it was impossible for me to do it alone.)

The sill-plates would be an integral part of the roof construction, providing a wood surface to build a short stem wall on. The *pony wall* would be screened for cross-ventilation rather than covered with plywood. I built a gabled roof on the tank, with the rafter tails secured to the top-plate of the stem wall.

When the job was done (floor *and* walls), I had used approximately 55 sacks of Portland cement, 6 cubic yards of sand, 10 cubic yards of gravel, and about 400 gallons of water. Not exactly like building Hoover Dam, but it felt like it!

I kept the concrete slab and walls wet while they were curing by spraying everything down with a hose, including myself, as often as possible. Water was handy from a hose I had temporarily hooked up to the inlet/outlet pipe in the floor of the empty tank.

Note: When working in hot weather, this spraying procedure should go on for at least a week.

Sealing the Tank

I think the reason my tank has held up so well for twenty-three years now, in spite of the 1:3:5 *poor man's mix* I used, is that I coated the inside of the tank with *Thoroseal,* a cohesive sealer.

Thoroseal is a Portland-cement-based coating that, when mixed with a milky-looking catalyst called "Acryl 60," fills and seal's voids and waterproofs the concrete. It prevents water from seeping into fissures, where it might freeze, expand, and crack the concrete. It also resists hydrostatic pressures (water pushing out) and is nontoxic in potable water tanks. It can be brushed on, but Bill advised me to trowel it on about ¼" thick for an impenetrable bond. It took a lot of elbow grease to apply it in smooth swipes on the entire inside surface of the tank, but it covered up all those rough cold-joint seams and made it look as smooth and beautiful as a baby-elephant's butt.

I don't claim to be an expert on the subject of concrete

tank-building. We built the tank during possibly the hottest July in history, so my memory of the details may be a little off due to sunstroke. All I know is that I built it under Bill's tutelage, and it has stood the test of time.

When I look up the hill and see the water-level flag sticking out of the tank's roof and dancing in the breeze, it helps to quench my thirst for security and self-sufficiency.

Back in the summer of 1983, the finished tank with its shingled roof cost me a total of $750 to build, including the lumber and plywood used for the forms.

Note: You can buy construction-grade sand and gravel already mixed in the ratio you want at any large rental equipment yard or your local sand and gravel supplier for a 10-cubic-yard dump truck full, delivered to your site. That sure beats the way I did it. Having the raw ingredients delivered would have been heaven, instead of that *other place!*

Roof: I recommend composition roofing (cheap) or metal roofing (fireproof). I used cedar shingles back then, but now I would choose metal roofing and divert the annual rainfall via rain gutters into the tank, to supplement the supply, or into a cistern.

The same tank today would cost about $1,500 for materials—still not bad for a permanent 6,500-gallon water tank. I say *permanent*, but now I have my doubts after overhearing an old-timer at the hardware store drawling to another old-timer, "There are two kinds of concrete—concrete that's cracked, and concrete that's gonna crack." Then he slapped his thigh and they both cackled and wheezed.

Closing Thoughts

Any able-bodied person can mix and pour concrete.

Building the forms to contain and shape it is easy and elementary carpentry. Even though *my* cavewoman ordeal with concrete might sound difficult, don't be intimidated by *the stuff*. It's malleable and infallible. My style is to overbuild everything; it needn't be yours. If you have a little extra cash and aren't in a big hurry, working creatively with small batches of concrete mixed in a wheelbarrow can be downright *fun*!

Conservation Facts

When you live on well water and have to pump every drop, here are some astonishing figures to consider:

- A running faucet uses 3 to 5 gallons a minute.
- A running faucet while you brush your teeth can use 5 gallons.
- A running faucet while you do dishes can use 30 gallons.
- Washing machines use 30 to 60 gallons for each cycle. Wait until you have a full load of clothes before doing the laundry.
- A long shower can use 50 gallons if you don't use a flow restrictor. You'll know it was too long when you run out of hot water. You'll know it was way too long when you run out of cold water!

CHAPTER 6

THE ZEN OF WASH DAY

"An excuse to play in the water"

There's something about washing clothes in an old wringer washer that feels good for the soul. The organic process of transforming a pile of dirty laundry on the floor into a sun-kissed bouquet gathered off the line is more deeply satisfying than should be expected from a mundane task.

I bought my shiny white Maytag in a secondhand store for forty bucks, brushed off the spiderwebs, and took her out of retirement. We've worked together for fifteen years now, outside on the deck—partners in grime. We're the same age, vintage 1942, both short and stout, built for longevity, and still going strong.

Old Girtie seems to have a life of her own—breathing, sighing, and groaning as the wringer heaves open and closed, while her rhythmic heartbeat goes thunk, thunk, thunk, swishing the clothes back and forth in her belly full of soapy soup.

I meditate as I play in the water, feeding cleansed clothes through the hungry wringer, watching suds squeeze out on one side while they flatten and dive into ice cold water on the other.

The alpha waves flow. It's my way of taking time out without taking time off. I go through the motions—oceans of motions.

I splash around, lifting and plunging the colorful collection in clean rinse water, then reverse the wringer and run them back through. This time I take care to *iron* each item nice and flat before hanging it on the line. Blackbirds, dive-bombing my nose, add excitement to my *fairy tale version* of life in the country.

For country folks just getting started, a wringer washer is a simple and practical way to go. All you need is electricity, water, and a set-tub. You can do the whole laundry on one filling of the washtub. Just add more biodegradable, cold-temperature detergent to each load to *gobble up* the new dirt. Start with whites, then add colors, and end with jeans. Or if you're a guy and want to advertise that you're single, throw everything in together and end up with homogenized duds—all grouchy gray. It's the *bachelor look.*

You alone determine the length of the wash cycle: five minutes for lacy unmentionables, twenty minutes for ring-around-the-collar, and thirty minutes for filthy overalls. Let a pair of stiff new Levis thrash around for a couple of hours and they'll be as good as old.

It's important to change the rinse water a few times as soap accumulates. Drain the gray water off onto thirsty trees and bushes. They'll appreciate it, but the plumbing inspector won't! If he catches you in the act, cry, "Drought!"

Make sure the machine is grounded and stand on a dry spot as you work.

Wash day can be *loads* of fun! I've never met a kid who didn't beg to help do the laundry. It must be the *lure of the wringer.*

The only drawback is washing outdoors in the dead of winter. Water freezes, and wringer washers hibernate. Compromise. Wear the same outfit for a month or go to the laundromat on a Saturday night *out,* have a beer, and watch the dryers go 'round. Come spring, you're back in business.

CHAPTER 7

WINDMILLS AND WATER SYSTEMS: A Primer

Windmill and holding tank with water-level flag

Standing tall like a giant sunflower in a sea of undulating prairie grasses—or in *any* rural setting—a windmill is a thing of beauty. Not only are windmills a joy to watch but they are incredibly useful. Powered only by wind, they work perpetually, like quietly purring non-polluting creatures, to keep our storage tanks overflowing with fresh water. They operate effortlessly, efficiently, reliably—and *free!*

History of the Windmill

Windmills have been around for a thousand years (since the Middle Ages). The first recorded evidence of windmills being used for pumping water and grinding grain were in 7 a.d. in Persia. Then China got hold of the idea and it spread to Asia, Africa, and the Mediterranean. Because its design is so different, the European mill appears to have developed independently from the others. The predecessor to our modern windmill dates back to France in 1105 and England in 1180. In the fourteenth century, the Dutch took windmills to a whole new level with their *tower* mills that used canvas sails stretched across four wooden lattice frames (like a big X). Their objective was to move enormous amounts of water into higher basins and canals. By the end of the sixteenth century, thousands of windmills were *pumping and grinding* in western Europe. By the late nineteenth century, the count was 30,000; yet, miraculously, there was still enough wind to go around!

The American Windmill

The American multi-bladed windmill bears little resemblance to its European counterpart. Unlike the Dutch *scoop mills* that could move 16,000 gallons an hour but lift it only 16 feet, the new *Yankee* design could lift water from hundreds of feet below the surface. It was invented in Connecticut in 1854 by a young mechanic named Daniel Halladay. Its wheel, made from *sails,* could be transported in sections and assembled on location.

He ingeniously designed the wheel to automatically turn its face into the wind by wind pressure on the vertical tail behind it. If it got to spinning too fast, a weighted mechanism came into play that turned the wheel partially out of the wind to slow it down.

Halladay sold thousands of his machines, and before long there were 300 competing manufacturers producing similar wooden-bladed beauties. Then in 1886, Thomas Perry designed the more aerodynamic steel-bladed windmill with curved blades (to catch more wind), and that design is still used today.

In the late 1880s and early 1900s, windmills were sprinkled all over the American landscape. They were indispensable to the latecomers, who were forced to move farther west to the sun-parched, remote plains after all the more desirable spots near rivers and streams had been taken. In the Great Plains and the vast territory known as the Great American Desert, water was more precious than gold.

Windmills were also indispensable during the construction of the railroads to provide drinking water for the crews and boiler water for the steam locomotives. Workers erected a windmill and an adjacent storage tank every three miles along the tracks. Some of the biggest railroad mills were 30 feet or more in diameter.

That entire chapter of history is written in the wind— the wind that powered those windmills. There would have been no life, hence no progress, without water.

Windmills were once status symbols. In 1910, a farmer or rancher who could afford the best Sears & Roebuck "Kenwood Back-Geared Galvanized Steel Pumping Model" with red-painted tips on the vanes and tail ($25) had something to crow about. Poorer homesteaders had to make their own mill heads and towers out of wood.

The windmill, barbed wire, and the six-shooter were the *big three* technological advances in those days.

The great windmill boom lasted for over fifty years. Between 1880 and 1935 more than six million windmills were sold by about twenty manufacturers. But, sadly, the big spinning wheels came to a screeching halt in the early thirties with the advent of federally subsidized power to remote farms and homesteads. The REA (Rural Electrification Administration) made it possible for people to use electric pumps delivering 20 to 30 gallons of water a minute, and that drowned out the windmill era. By 1970, only three companies in the US produced windmills: Aermotor, Dempster, and Baker Monitor. They are still in business today.

Windmills in rural America were once as plentiful as barns and silos. Some of their skeletons are still standing as nostalgic monuments to a bygone era that could be called "Gone with the Wind." (Hey, that would make a good movie!)

How a Windmill Works

The windmill's wheel (fan) has fifteen to forty galvanized-steel blades that spin around on a shaft. The shaft drives a geared mechanism that converts rotary motion to an up-and-down motion like a piston in a car engine. That motion drives a long pump-rod (aka sucker-rod) up and down inside a pipe in the well. Attached to the submerged end of the pipe is a cylinder with a sealed plunger going up and down in it. (The seals are called *leathers*.) Each up-stroke pulls water into the cylinder, but on the down-stroke a check valve (aka foot valve) in the bottom won't let it be pushed out, so the water has nowhere to go but *up* (with the next stroke). It's a simple, efficient design that has remained virtually unchanged for more than a hundred years.

An average windmill (6- to 8-foot-diameter wheel) spinning in a brisk breeze (15 to 20 mph) will pump about 3 gallons a minute whenever the winds blows, which is about 35 percent of the time in many areas. That adds up to about 1,500 gallons a day. Another example of output could be calculated by using a 10- to 12-foot wheel pumping against a theoretical 100 feet of *head* (the column of water lifted from the static water level in the well to the tank). This larger windmill will pump an annual average of 4,500 gallons per day, or 1.64 million gallons of water a year. This figure is based on moderate winds (8 to 12 mph) blowing part of the time, running the mill at half its rated capacity, and brisk winds (15 to 25 mph) blowing about 30 percent of the time and running the pump at maximum capacity.

Wind speed has an important effect on pumping capacity. Below certain speeds, the mill can't *get going*. Above 25 to 35 mph (depending on the model), the windmill's over-speed controls limit the output by turning (*furling*) the direct face of the wheel out of the main wind direction. This design feature protects the windmill mechanism, but it also limits the pumping rate no matter how fast the wind blows.

There is an optimum wind speed for every windmill size and model. The number of vanes (sails) in the wheel increases its sensitivity to low wind speeds (to get started), but other factors, such as fan diameter, the depth of the static water level in the well, and cylinder size all play a part in output capacity.

Note: The *static* water level is the measurement from the top of the well casing to the water surface down in the well—*not* the depth the pump is set.

Dorothy Ainsworth

Uses for a Windmill

The most common practical uses for a windmill are to irrigate pastures and gardens, water livestock, and supply and aerate ponds. Anything more than that requires a holding tank on stilts or a water tower, to provide enough pressure for water to be on tap for household use. I placed my water system on top of a hill so the water is gravity-fed for all my needs on the property. (More about my system later.) I love the idea that if the power fails, I'll still have fresh water—lots of fresh water. To me, that's self-sufficiency and a nice sense of security. Evidently a lot of country folks feel that way because windmills are making a comeback.

Aermotor claims that sales of windmills are increasing worldwide, and more windmills are pumping water today than at the turn of the century. Because of the varied needs of diverse populations, there will always be a demand for alternative energy. OPEC is mighty powerful, but it can't control the sun or the wind!

Is a Windmill for You?

If you are contemplating putting up a windmill on your property, the first consideration is to determine whether your site and your budget can accommodate one. Then scout out the best location for it. A basic rule of thumb is to place your windmill a minimum of 25 feet above any obstructions (such as trees) within a 150-foot radius of the mill.

Next, set up an anemometer or wind odometer to measure wind speed, volume, and direction over a period of time (a year is good). You can buy or rent a wind odometer that will measure the number of miles of wind that runs past your site. Divide that figure by the total hours it ran and you will get your average wind speed for the site. You can also call the local airport and weather station for comprehensive wind data in your area.

Having a Well Drilled

First you'll need to obtain a permit from the local county offices.

Next, call a good, reputable well driller (from the Yellow Pages under *wells and pumps*, or by word of mouth) and see what he can do for you. If he predicts the water is somewhere else on your property other than the site you picked, you'll have to do some compromising.

The going rate to have a well drilled is about $15 per foot here in southern Oregon (surprisingly the *same* cost as back in 1981 when I had my two wells drilled). That figure includes the steel well casing installed in 10- to 50-foot lengths (depending on your soil) and possibly a well liner all the way down (4- to 6-inch diameter PVC pipe). Some soil stratification *requires* a well liner to keep the fractured strata from caving in on the well.

Chances are you'll hit a good water table between 100 and 400 feet, the average depth being 250 feet. Figure a well will cost you somewhere between $1,500 and $6,000. Of course, there are no guarantees. These are just average ballpark figures I gleaned from well drillers around this dry and spotty valley.

The good news is that you won't have to drill to China in search of huge volumes of water because a windmill can only pump a few gallons a minute. You can tell your well driller in advance to stop drilling when he reaches a depth that fulfills your limited requirement.

Even a 5-gallon-per-minute well would be sufficient

for a small windmill. Because the refreshment rate would be greater than the pump rate, there would be very little, if any, *drawdown*. Drawdown is the measurement of the static water level going down, down, down, as water is being used out of the well. A well with a windmill on it is constantly being replenished (static water level going up, up, up) when the wind is not blowing.

There are two distinctly different methods of drilling a well: One is the rotary method, where a big auger on a boom truck drills a deep, clean hole—not unlike a drill bit in a hand drill—and hits water when it gets to a water-bearing layer (aka water table).

The other method is called *cable drilling* and basically *hammers* a hole through rock and other strata, fracturing everything in its path, and causing each layer it goes through to release its water (if it has any). Proponents of this method claim they get more water all the way down than the conventional rotary method delivers. The geological debate can get downright steamy on this dry subject!

Finding, Installing, and Maintaining a Windmill

After your well is drilled, cased, and capped with a well seal—and the water is tested to make sure it's safe—it's time to size the windmill that will fit your well and your needs. If you want a *new* windmill, contact the three major manufacturers (mentioned previously) and ask for brochures and price lists and installation fees. If your budget decides that you must buy *used*, there are sources on the Internet and ads in farm journals, etc., to help you find one. Thousands of good used ones are available all over the United States. Do your research, and it will pay off.

Keep in mind, though, that most used windmills will need some rebuilding work. Parts are available for most models, and there is *no* problem getting parts for Aermotor, Dempster, and Baker Monitor windmills.

Here in the Rogue Valley (southern Oregon) there is a guy I call the Windmill Man (for obvious reasons). He is passionate about windmills and knows pert'near *everything* about every model ever made. He not only sells, installs, and repairs used windmills, but he also has a huge collection in his own yard.

He's the *real deal*—an authentic craftsman who is trustworthy, knowledgeable, and skilled. If a windmill has a broken part that can't be found, he makes it. If a windmill system needs customizing or improvising, he *does* it. For years he has done the maintenance work on my 1942 *David Bradley*—an old Sears model I bought in 1982 for $450, and it's still going strong.

If you can't find an eccentric, eclectic windmill aficionado in your area (they're a rare breed), contact John Cox at jcwindmills@centurylink.net.

Windmill Maintenance

Maintenance on a windmill is minimal: Change the 10-weight oil or ATF (automatic transmission fluid) in the gears every year, put a little grease in the bearings in the *turn-table* (between the gearbox and the top of the tower) at the same time, and replace the *leathers* (cupped seals that ride up and down in the pump-cylinder) every two to ten years (depending on how much sand you have in your water). Longer-lasting neoprene instead of leather is used in most cylinders today.

The *stuffing box* (usually brass) has to be repacked and the nut tightened occasionally. This curious-sounding component is a simple design and an easy-to-understand concept if you *see* it working but hard to explain on paper.

Dorothy Ainsworth

It's what caps off the *top* of the well pipe (the cylinder pump caps off the *bottom* of the well pipe).

The pump-rod goes up and down through a hole in the stuffing box (which is *stuffed* with graphite rope). This stuffing (aka packing) allows only enough water to leak out around the hole to lubricate the up-and-down action of the rod.

When the packing gets old and compressed, it allows too much water to squirt out. Then it's time to unscrew the nut on the unit, put some more packing in, and tighten the nut down *gootintite*. Without the stuffing box, there would be metal rubbing on metal, wearing the rod away in no time. (The same thing would happen without seals on the cylinder plunger.)

A stuffing box is needed on a windmill only if you have to pump water *uphill* to a tank, but *not* needed if your water will flow *downhill* to a storage tank or horizontally into a watering trough or pond. That just about sums up the maintenance on a windmill.

A Cheap Irrigation System and Water Tank Flag

My property is a hilly piece with the well down below and the water storage tank up above. There's a quarter mile of pipe and 165 feet of head (vertical rise) between the two. The well driller confidently predicted that my *big water* was at the bottom of the hill, so after the well was in, I had to dig a long trench to bury the water line all the way to the tank at the top of the hill. That gut-busting labor turned out to be a blessing in disguise because now gravity works in my favor.

I built a 6,500-gallon water storage tank out of concrete (12' x 12' x 6'), put a roof on it, and, for ventilation, screened the space between the tank and the rafters.

Then, so I could check my water level at a glance from anywhere on the property, I put a brightly colored flag on a pole that goes up and down through a hole in the roof. The wooden pole and its PVC guide (sleeve) are set into a 5-gallon bucket of air with a gasketed lid on it. The bucket floats on the water level. The pole *could* be calibrated, but that would require getting the binoculars out to read it, so just plain *high* and *low* are good enough for me. When the flag is dancing in the breeze three feet above the roof, the water tank is full—and I'm happy.

I built the holding tank to eliminate the need for a captive-air tank in the pump house (small steel water tank with an *air bladder* inside). The tank works on a pressure-gauge system that turns the submersible pump on and off constantly as the bladder compresses or expands (when the tank fills and empties). This action eventually wears out the pump's starting capacitor. With ten thirsty acres to irrigate, the pump would have had to cycle on and off every few minutes all summer long.

My stored water supply is gravity-distributed for irrigation and household use upon demand, via a maze of pipelines and on/off valves (non-siphoning type) that staggers even *my* imagination, and I'm the one who did it! As I developed the property over the years, I crisscrossed the land with thousands of feet of additional water lines as needed. I used inexpensive ¾" utility polypipe (about 7 cents a foot) for landscape irrigation and poked a hole or two with an ice pick wherever I planted a bush or tree. It's the poor man's answer to drip irrigation.

This gravity-feed system and flagpole alert has worked great for twenty years now. I'm so glad I bought a *hill* to live on! Gravity is free and gives me 70 pounds of water pressure down below and 40 pounds at the house (the halfway point on the hill), which is plenty. (Figure every 100

Dorothy Ainsworth

feet of head = 43 pounds per square inch [PSI] pressure). Because I use a drip irrigation system, even low pressure up near the tank works fine.

Wind is free too, and I just happen to love windmills—the water-pumping kind. These giant *pinwheels* are as beautiful to watch as they are practical, useful, and affordable. For long-range self-sufficiency and in case the power goes off, I put in a second well (low capacity) adjacent to the holding tank and put a small windmill on it (6-foot-diameter wheel). Whenever the wind blows, which is often, it pumps 2 GPM into the tank and supplements the water supply. An overflow pipe exiting the top of the tank feeds a small pond that nature has generously stocked with frogs and mosquitos. The county vector control supplies free *mosquito fish*—hardy little critters that vacuum up mosquito larvae faster than they can hatch, so everything balances out.

I planted hybrid poplars around the pond, and they grew huge in no time, so now I have a shady oasis to hide in from the summer sun while the dogs jump in the pond and cool off. Life *on the hill* is good; the windmill purrs and the frogs croak.

Years ago I almost let a fast-talking salesman sucker me into buying an elaborate and expensive water-level gauge system of brass and copper ball-cocks and levers floating in the tank (like a toilet-flushing mechanism) that would turn my pump on and off automatically when the water went above or below a certain level—"While you sit in your easy chair eating chocolates," he said. It sounded like a good idea (the chocolate part), but it would have required a quarter mile of buried electrical cable and a complicated hook-up system.

My water is high in calcium and other minerals, so every part would have already corroded beyond recognition and jammed up. Being economically challenged, I came up with a cheap solution and sent *Mr. Bells and Whistles* on his way. Instead of eating candy, I run down to turn the pump on and stay slim!

My advice to new landowners is to think long and hard before buying gadgets that will eventually need repairs or replacement. Think *long-range*, think *simplicity*, think *self-sufficiency*. That's what the *Backwoods Home* philosophy is all about.

CHAPTER 8

WAITRESS BUILDS FORTRESS

Building house #1

New dreams beckoned. Having served my trial-
and-error apprenticeship on the piano studio, and
with the foundation pilings already in place, I felt
ready to get started on the main house. I was still limited

by the harsh arithmetic of a $12,000/year income, a rudimentary level of craftsmanship, and mostly hand tools, but that didn't discourage me. Brimming with enthusiasm and confidence, I forged ahead with tunnel vision.

Back to the drawing board, in and out of the forest, and back 'n' forth to work I went. Like a squirrel, preoccupied with survival and security, I was oblivious to anything but *acorns*. Until I met *Him*, with a capital "H." Somewhere between doing sit-ups at the fitness center and serving two eggs over-greasy at the restaurant, Cupid got me. I fell in love.

He was quiet and good-natured and had the most magnificent shoulders I'd ever seen—not to mention arms like legs and legs like tree trunks. Hercules! Blond curls, blue eyes, sparkling teeth, and a dimple in his chin (excuse me while I faint). Never mind he was half my age. We adored each other, and time stood still.

The year we met was spent giggling like children at recess while stockpiling 300 logs from the forest. We were madly in love and feeling no pain. Every date for three summer months was a romantic rendezvous in the woods, where togetherness meant one of us on each end of a log. We *bonded* like construction adhesive. When I couldn't lift my end, Paul Bunyan carried the whole 300-pound log on his shoulder! I swooned and snapped photographs.

On our first Christmas, visions of sugar *pines* danced in our heads to the *strains* of the Nutcracker *Sweat*. A conventional courtship it was not. Gossipers called us Jock and Jill. I called us lucky. If this rough-hewn figure in a flannel shirt and Levi's wasn't the marryin' man, he was certainly the carryin' man!

Kirt was wise beyond his years, and authentic. He respected my wishes and nurtured my dreams. Equality was a given. We both knew how to make work seem like play. Our similarities far outweighed our differences. There was no gap. Contemplating that, it seemed too good to be true. I asked him, "Where have you been all my life?" He answered with a wink, "Sorry, honey, for the first half I wasn't born yet." Still going to college, he was pursuing his own goals but was unobtrusively there if I needed him. We truly lived and let live.

I designed the house—structure, form, and content. First of all, it wouldn't be too *precious* to live in and live-it-up in, with dogs and cats frolicking about. It would be spacious and well lit and functional. Simplicity and naturalness would prevail, with plenty of room to get *artsy* in the finishing touches. Commensurate with my level of craftsmanship, I needed a straightforward hilltop design, like a Panama hat, to direct the winds up and over. I opted for the unpretentious grace of a lofty gabled barn with sweeping shed *wings*. (When a tornado hits, this Dorothy will see you in Kansas!)

From years of forethought and soul-searching, I knew exactly what I wanted, but *how* was a bothersome technicality. With tips from the cafe, I'd *pay as I go* and go 'til I dropped. Labor was *time*, and energy was a renewable resource. Judging from the cost of the piano studio, I predicted the house would also be $15 a square foot. Except for big-ticket items such as appliances, fixtures, and a wood-burning stove, I would make everything from scratch, including deep windowsills and wood frames for the glass (no aluminum or vinyl allowed).

Planning ahead was essential. I drew my own blueprints and built a scale model to manifest the joinery inherent in my design: mortise and tenon joints, connecting girts and knee braces (all out of logs). I would use timbers as ridge-beams, top-plates, and cantilevered deck supports.

The model allowed me to *play house* and get the feel of the floor plan. Inside, ambient light would stream through a bank of large south-facing windows up high. At eye level, the spectacular view of snow-capped mountains by day—and city lights at night, like jewels on black velvet—would be given its proper status. I would settle for nothing less than a round portrait window to gaze out of for visual refreshment, never to be taken for granted. French doors would open onto a huge front deck with steps leading down to a wood-fired hot tub.

On the north side of the house, I pretended to be up in the loft with its *naughty pine* walls, an acre of bed, and a river rock shower. My imagination slid down the fireman's pole into the den below. Every home needs a hermetically sealed enclave where one can escape the capricious distractions of everyday life. My *cave*, with its porthole window and hobbit door, would be the place to run away without leaving home. I would cherish my time-out moments to read, listen to music, and watch the Discovery Channel on TV. (No hysteria, canned laughter, or police sirens for me, thank you.)

An easterly kitchen would be the bright spot in the morning where the first rays of sunrise would meet me for coffee in the breakfast nook. I would sit on my tuffet in the cushioned window seat. For me, one of life's most profoundly simple pleasures is to sip and think and contemplate the universe.

When I designed the house, I gave myself permission to satisfy, not deny, my eccentricities. So what if the building inspector raises one eyebrow when he signs off the checklist—as long as I'm legal. (And I *was*; my blueprints passed code without a change or correction.)

I wanted low-maintenance housekeeping. *Let* moss grow on the river rocks in the shower; lichen and mushrooms are charming!

The bathroom would have a beautician's sink, with a place for the neck, where lovers could wash each other's hair to Rossini's *Barber of Seville*.

I love to cook, but not within the confines of a traditional cramped kitchen. I also like to bake, but not if the pie dough drapes over the sides of a tiny cutting board. The kitchen is where my personality takes up a lot of space. Give me a massive butcher block and a cleaver, and I'll get serious about dinner. Fresh vegetables are a must, and so is a big set-tub for washing them in. I want to throw spinach in the built-in *pond* and let the silt fall several feet to the bottom. Floating fruit would make canning season a breeze.

When it comes time for the main course, only an industrial-strength stove will support *the vat*. To save on power, a good refrigerator door seal should crop the cat's tail, not just kink it! Hide and seek is not my game; open shelving all around would ensure easy access and low frustration.

The dining room table is the most popular place in any home. Everything happens at the dining room table. Mine would be colossal (4' x 8') and built with planks thick enough to support a feeding frenzy of hungry relatives.

I love to sew. After dinner, when I clear the decks, I want to be able to roll out a bolt of 60-inch canvas on the table and make huge awnings for the house.

Doors are symbolic. As a shelter defines our living space and controls the atmosphere, a door determines who enters that private realm of being. I wanted a front door that would break Hitler's toe if he tried to kick it in. Massive and medieval, it must creak with hand-forged hinges and black hardware, and provide a peephole to say, "Who goes there? Advance and be recognized!"

Each kind of door has its own character. The quaint Dutch door in the country kitchen will cool an apple pie on its mantle, wafting aroma out the top half. A cute little cat door in the bottom will let "Foo-Foo" bring a mouse *in*.

Sophisticated French doors make a woman feel like a princess in gossamer, even when clad in blue jeans and a T-shirt. There's something about a large view divided up into little pieces that makes it easier to take in. Smaller French doors in the loft would open onto a cantilevered deck, for sipping mint juleps in the cool north light on a hot summer day.

Mandatory for decoration, mirrors are like magic. They're a poor man's way to double the square footage and keep an eye on things. They repeat architectural patterns for visual appeal and keep you company when no one's home.

I won't be without my ballet bar—the last remnant of my childhood fantasy of becoming a great dancer. It will be something to hang onto when I have one too many at our housewarming party!

Yes, my humble abode will be my castle, and I reserve the right to keep the IRS out with a moat and drawbridge if necessary, or let the whole Mormon Tabernacle Choir in if I so desire. (I don't!)

"I was giddy; expectation whirled me round!" (Shakespeare). It was time to roll up my sleeves, flex my little biceps, and grab the drawknife. I peeled and stained 150 logs. My sister from Santa Barbara made the mistake of coming up for a week. She peeled and stained another 150 logs and escaped by plane when her *vacation* was over.

The next step was squaring off the 600 log ends. Kirt and I worked together using a Rube Goldberg contraption I devised to ensure a straight cut.

I built the floor in three months in my spare time. It

was supported by a pier and girder foundation, connected together by 2" x 12" floor joists on 16-inch centers. It would support a house full of hippos.

Unlike the piano studio, with its eight sides and giant circular cable holding the roof intact, this 2,000-square-foot design incorporated mortise-and-tenon joints to tie it together. The log-dominated *timber frame* consisted of four bents (each bent being two uprights and a horizontal) creating three bays (space between bents), joined together by connecting girts (also logs) and reinforced with knee braces.

Yikes! Mortise-and-tenon joints! The words were scary and the concept subliminal. There lay eight 400-pound 14-footers and four 500-pound 20-footers on the subfloor. And there stood I with a hammer and chisel. It was my moment of truth. Whispering my own motto for courage, "Dissect, demystify, and conquer," I started in.

I laid out each bent as it would appear standing up, flatted the surfaces where the tenons would plug in, and cut the mortises (slots) just so, using an electric chainsaw, ship's auger, and chisel. I cut a tenon on each end of the horizontal log after taking great care to ensure a 90-degree junction when the big *H* was reassembled upright. Everything had to be kept square with the imaginary centerline of each log. That was achieved by shimming up the smaller tapered end so the measurement from floor to center of log was the same on both ends. Being a compulsive photographer, I recorded every step on film.

All went well. Kirt helped me erect the framing members one at a time, fastening the vertical logs to the floor and down into the foundation beams with 12-inch pole-barn spikes. Then we raised the 20-foot horizontals in place with a manual *Genie-Lift* (rented), slid the tenons into their respective mortises, and drove the pegs home.

Squealing with delight, we ran off for pizza and beer. It was Halloween and the skeleton of our house was standing eerily in the light of the moon.

I rented scaffolding and donned my imaginary oxygen mask for the stratosphere. For the next few days Kirt manned the Genie-Lift way down below, and I hammered in rebar way up above (20 feet up). The 9" x 9" ridge-beams and top-plate beams, perched atop their upright log supports, swayed in the breeze. Until each half-lap joint was secured with spikes, we didn't feel safe; when we raised a beam, it raised our hair. Tension was high. Affectionate bickering now and then revealed a little cayenne pepper in our salad of love!

We eagerly stabilized the structure with ten pairs of 4" x 10" rafters on 4-foot centers. They were joined together at a 6-in-12 pitch *over* the ridgepole and gusseted into place. At the overhang end, I predrilled and drove rebar into each rafter, down through the top-plate and into a log, eliminating the need for a birdsmouth cut. We scoffed at earthquakes and ran off for pizza again.

Now I was on my own and welcomed the challenge. Kirt was busy with college and his own career. I wanted to tackle this new project myself, so after he helped me with the logistics of raising the frame we agreed he would come running only if he heard a blood-curdling scream.

For the next three months I worked on the roofs...all four of them. Because 2" x 6" T&G (tongue and groove) pine was installed on top of the rafters to create the vaulted ceilings, I had to build a grid on top of that roof to receive insulation, plywood, tarpaper, and metal roofing.

Every day was spent aardvarking around on my hands and knees, or limping back and forth with one foot higher than the other. Like a drunken sailor, even on solid ground I favored a gimp in my hind leg on the starboard side.

Sometimes, to avoid the sun, I would work at night with a flashlight strapped to my forehead, like a firefly from hell.

When I purchased the 2,200 square feet of barn-red steel roofing panels, 4,000 gasketed screws, and all the trimmings, the salesman remarked, "This is definitely a two-man job." I thought to myself...gulp...*how about one woman?*

It *was* a little scary, flirting with the undertaker 20 feet up on a slanted (6-in-12) pitch—but affordable. After spending all summer on the roof, I came to the conclusion that roofers, who are mercilessly exposed to the elements, like human weather vanes, are the unsung heroes in the construction world.

By autumn I was working inside the house—with a Mona Lisa smile on my lips—so glad to be on level ground again!

I methodically put up the walls, one log at a time, and spiked them in place. To save my wrists for waitressing, I gripped the hammer with both hands and wailed away. I swapped the log ends alternately (big end up, big end down) to even out the taper and keep the walls plumb, and set each log two inches over the edge of the bottom-plate, for a drip edge.

Next came the thirty-six windows and nine doors to button the place up. I built doors from T&G pine and window frames from Douglas fir 2" x 4"s. Limited by only hand tools and a band saw to work with, I had to call on my eighty-year-old master-craftsmen friends, Merle and Ivan, to make the fancy cuts (rabbet joints). Casement hardware opened rows of windows awning-style (to shed rain) on the east and west sides of the house for cross-ventilation.

To save money, I picked up the huge double-paned glass order in my old Ford truck (four trips) and summoned Kirt to help unload and lift the heavy windows into place. While he pressed the fixed panes (some of them 6' x 3') against my prepared *stops*, I secured them all around with 2" x 2"s. No cracks, no shards, and no gaping wounds; that was reason enough to go out for Chinese dinner!

The inner walls of the house remained rustic (visible logs), but the outer walls had to be insulated. I furred them out with 2" x 4"s to receive fiberglass batts and Sheetrock, then chinked between the logs on the outside.

I hired an electrician to do the extensive wiring but painstakingly did the plumbing myself and passed inspection (a miracle).

"Let there be light!" But not just any old light. I suspended chandeliers from ceiling fans (*they* said it couldn't be done) and marveled at my handiwork.

To help support the 12-inch diameter, 20-foot horizontal log that spanned the middle of the living room, I fashioned two *hanging knee braces* out of black chains and turnbuckles—a trick I hadn't seen used before. I was thrilled with my handsome invention and snapped more photos.

Time consumption seemed to be my modus operandi. The roof took all summer. The plumbing job ate my fall vacation. Window installation consumed the winter, and chinking gobbled up the spring. Repairs and maintenance were endless. I was able to do everything myself but complex electrical wiring—and for superhuman lifting, I called Kirt.

Six years had passed since I started this project. I rented scaffolding again, but this time for the outside, to caulk every crack and apply a beautiful protective stain to the entire house. Night and day, up and down the rungs and ladders I climbed, buttering the logs with my linseed oil concoction until they glowed like a sunset. I wiped the

Dorothy Ainsworth

baseboards with a tiny cotton T-shirt and laid it out to dry.

It was a blistering hot June 28th, and I sighed with relief thinking back on the 6,000 hours of labor it had taken to build the house, and now it was almost ready to move into. When Kirt came home from work I playfully attempted to carry *him* over the threshold. Our hysterical laughter was short-lived. On June 29th—the very next day—that *dry* little rag spontaneously combusted and burned the house down in two hours. We put the fire out with tears.

End of story…back to log one.

CHAPTER 9

OUT OF THE ASHES

Kirt 'Bunyan' Meyer and 500 lb. log

I got the dreadful call from my son, Eric, an hour after I'd gone to work at 2:00 p.m. on a hot June 29th. "Your house is on fire, Mom! I'm afraid it's a goner. I was in the piano studio. It happened so fast, all I could do was call the fire department." His voice broke...

I ran out of the cafe, sped three miles home in my old pickup, and rounded the bend just in time to witness the most horribly spectacular sight of my life. The entire black skeleton of timbers and logs, engulfed by fluorescent flames, stood out in bold relief against a backdrop of bright blue sky. The metal roof panels were rising and falling as if waving goodbye. The image seared into my brain like a branding iron.

As I stood there in disbelief, watching my castle burn to the ground—the log home I had painstakingly hand-crafted for six years—it never entered my mind that anything good could possibly come out of this tragedy. *Nature is a hanging judge,* I thought to myself. *One strike and you're out!* A tiny linseed oil rag had transformed 6,000 hours of hard labor into a huge pile of charcoal briquettes in just two hours.

Although I was surrounded by firefighters and news reporters, I felt all alone in my grief. Memories harkened back to the financial insecurity and heavy responsibility I had experienced years ago when I was virtually abandoned with two young children to raise. I had learned to trust no one but myself.

I sighed in silent resignation at the facts of reality and wondered if I would be able to muster up the enthusiasm and money to start over. (My insurance was nominal.)

Feeling like Scarlett O'Hara in *Gone with the Wind*, I sat down to contemplate the ruins of Tara and pet the dogs. "I must rebuild, yes, I *will* rebuild. But I'll think about it tomorrow," I whispered to Gypsy, Dottie, and Joe. They wagged their tails in unison.

That was to be my darkest hour. Unbeknownst to me, the dawn would come soon and bring sunny surprises. I had a lot to learn about the benevolent nature of my fellow man and the humble art of accepting help.

First thing, Kirt (my devoted boyfriend) was truly there for me. He came home from work to the shock of no house on the hill and was devastated. He shed real tears, and we comforted each other. Even though the house had been *my* coveted project, together we had carried each of those 300 logs out of the forest six years ago.

That tragic evening, while standing together in the black rubble and holding onto each other for dear life, Kirt stated in no uncertain terms, "Honey, I want to bring your house back for you. It was your life's dream. I'll do all the major work this time. You can bring home the bacon, be the director, and do the finish work. Okay?" Still in a state of shock, I shuffled around in the charcoal and nodded meekly.

Then, before the coals had even cooled, editor Dave Duffy sent a representative from *Backwoods Home* magazine to check on my welfare and asked permission to tell *BWH* readers of my fate. He hoped the notice would generate positive responses from all over the United States. (And it did!)

The day after the fire, help started pouring in, and our spirits were buoyed up by waves of moral support in a sea of positive people.

Out of the blue, I got a call from the nicest stranger I've ever met: Christina Johnson, a young woman from Medford, who said she and her husband wanted to help by organizing a clean-up crew and a music benefit on my behalf. She said the Lutheran Brotherhood Church pledged to double whatever money was raised by the concert.

Next, my employer at the cafe where I waitressed called to tell me he had opened a donation account for me at a local bank. The *Ashland Daily Tidings*, the *Sneak Preview* of Ashland, and the *Medford Mail Tribune* all printed sympathetic stories about the disaster and mentioned the donation fund. Each local TV station, in turn, interviewed me and informed people who to contact if they wanted to help. District 5 Fire Department said they'd clean up the mess and offered skilled help in rebuilding. Copeland Lumber and Ashland Hardware volunteered special discounts on all rebuilding materials and supplies.

Cleanup day was a huge success. Everyone showed up nice and clean and left hours later nice and dirty. Ashland Sanitary donated a huge Dumpster for the *party* and hauled away my whole former house in one fell swoop. Several businesses around town sent food.

The "Out of the Ashes" music benefit was a magical evening filled with the spirit of love and empathy. Local musicians played and sang their hearts out. Son Eric wound up the program with some impromptu humor followed by a magnificent classical performance on the piano. My daughter, Cynthia, flew up from Hollywood to hold my hand and wipe my tears.

The spirit of helping one's fellow man was alive and well, here and everywhere. Offers of help and gifts flooded in. Donations added up. Letters filled with encouragement and contributions arrived daily for about three months. Several prison inmates responded, egging me on to rebuild so they could keep their own hopes up for a new start. Even people at poverty level put $5 in an envelope and humbly apologized that it couldn't be more. My heart was touched forever by the kindness and generosity that is out there.

Ashland should be called "The little town that could— and did!" Locals donated about $6,000 to my rebuilding fund. *Backwoods Home* readers generously contributed over $3,000 to the cause. I've joyfully written more than 200 thank you notes and now correspond with several new pen pals.

With donations alone, I was able to put in a new concrete foundation, build the floor, buy the supporting timbers I needed, and secure all the logs. Although I had neglected to update my construction insurance policy since completing the floor, at least I had *some* coverage, including tool replacement. With that settlement, plus donations and my perpetual waitressing job, I was back in business by September.

The owner of Grizzly Log Homes of Jacksonville, Oregon, pledged to sell me all the logs for the new house at his cost, and said he would deliver—just like pizza! Kirt and I jumped for joy and danced a little jig at the prospect of being able to build the same house without the gut-busting labor of carrying logs out of the forest again. It sounded too good to be true and it ultimately was, but we enjoyed four months of ignorant bliss. When it turned cold and the skies looked ominous, Mr. Grizzly called with *grizzly* news that, due to unexpected log shortages, he would be unable to keep his promise. We groaned when we had to eat our words of *never again* logging the hard way.

Desperate to duplicate the original house—or have to go through the entire permit process again—I was highly motivated to find a source nearby for lodgepole pine. (The Forest Service had closed most of the public cutting areas.) After a zealous search I found a man who owned 600 acres of timberland twenty-five miles away and told him my story. He kindly agreed to let us take all the logs we needed for the house off his land, provided we burn the slash piles and thin trees along the irrigation canal.

Once again we jumped for joy and danced a little jig— in spite of ourselves!

Kirt "Bunyan" Meyer, the human forklift, single-handedly felled a hundred trees, limbed them, bucked them to length, and carried them to the truck on his *not* genetically average shoulders. This time around the 12- to 16-inch-diameter logs were green and three times the weight of dry ones (300 to 500 pounds). Even though I'm an industrial-strength woman, I was unable to lift my end of a single decent-sized log, so I happily demoted myself to truck driver and cheerleader. Witnessing Kirt's Herculean feats of sheer power and strength was one of the most awe-inspiring and profound experiences of my life! I stood by, taking photos and worrying aloud about his lower back and adjacent giblets.

My job was maneuvering the old Ford half-ton pickup loaded with one and a half tons of logs downhill all the way home without burning up the brakes. It took twenty-five loads to get what we needed!

Without a scratch or a bruise, Kirt managed to stock-pile 300 logs in just three weeks, finishing the job only minutes before the first snowfall of the season. What a guy! I felt like the luckiest unlucky woman in the world!

Note: You can see a video of Kirt lifting a 500-pound log at www.dorothyainsworth.com.

CHAPTER 10

REBUILDING AFTER THE FIRE

Rebuilt house after the fire

The first thing we had to do was level the burn site with a tractor and blade. Kirt's father, Ron Meyer, trailered the equipment over from his pear-orchard business (Meyer Orchards in Talent, Oregon) and was kind enough to do that big job for us.

The original house had been on huge creosoted piers that burned off, so this time we poured concrete sono-tube piers on below-grade footings. Kirt connected them with a grid of 10" x 10" DF (Douglas fir) girders, with shouldered half-lap joints anchor-bolted down over each pier.

The T&G subfloor (⅞" oriented strand board, or OSB)

was supported by 2" x 12" BCI joists on 16-inch centers and fastened with screws. The 44' x 48' subfloor was finished and ready to receive the logs, so I got busy peeling them with a drawknife and squaring off the ends to specific lengths.

Due to the unconventional nature of timber-frame construction using logs instead of timbers, I was unable to use the services of any of the enthusiastic volunteers after the fire, with one exception: Vadim Agakhanov—Russian immigrant, contractor, engineer, workaholic, and great friend. He tirelessly donated his exceptional craftsman skills to the project whenever he had a spare moment.

Just as we had done on the first house, the framing began with the most critical job inherent in the design— shouldered mortise-and-tenon joints.

As a team, Kirt and Vadim prepared the joints, then erected the post and beam members one at a time, fastening them to the floor structure with 12-inch pole-barn spikes in predrilled holes. They raised the horizontal monsters (logs) with a manual Genie-Lift and slid the tenons into their respective mortises, drilled holes through the joint, and drove the pegs home.

Next all four bents were joined together by connecting-girts lag-bolted to the posts.

With the basic rectangular frame now secured, there was only one way to go—up. Way up. Short vertical logs would support the ridgepole, rafter ties, and top-plates. The log lengths were calculated to create a 6-in-12 roof pitch.

Just as we had done on the first house, Kirt hoisted these shorter logs onto an 8-foot roll-around scaffold, precariously stood them up in the middle of each horizontal span (on pre-flattened spots), and spiked them in place.

He then climbed back down to solid ground (the floor)

to operate the Genie-Lift. With the concentration and finesse of a mortal man who has great respect for Newton's laws, he skillfully placed the 9" x 9" top-plates and ridge-beam sections on top of the short uprights he had just secured.

Vadim had arrived for this big event and was perched twenty feet up on another scaffold, waiting with sledge in hand, to do the dastardly deed: pound rebar down through each joint and into a log. (Better him than me this time!) I could hear an imaginary drum roll as they repeated this balancing act until all twelve roof-framing beams were installed. We sighed with relief and jokingly scoffed at earthquakes.

Then Kirt and Vadim set the rafters and proceeded to cover the framework with T&G plywood. After the roofing was on and the floor was protected from sun and rain, Kirt put up the walls one log at a time, hammering three 12-inch spikes, equally spaced, around each log-base. He used a small sledge with one hand and ten whacks to bury the heads, whereas before, it had taken me both hands and forty whacks to do the same job. I could see that with manpower, this house was going to go up fast!

The inner walls remained rustic (visible logs), but the outer walls had to be insulated. We furred them out with 2" x 4"s to receive fiberglass batts and Sheetrock, then I chinked between the logs on the outside with foam pipe insulation and caulking.

Just as I had done on the first house, Kirt built thirty-six window frames from small-knot pine and set the glass with molding and brass brads. Friction-operated "WhitCo" hinges opened rows of awning-style windows on opposite sides of the house. Kirt and Vadim donned their protective grommet-studded sleeves to handle the huge and heavy glass panes for the picture windows. (I was happy to get out of that dangerous job this time!)

I built the nine doors again from T&G 2" x 6" pine boards held together with battens and big black bolts and hung them with the same old barn hinges (sandblasted and painted black again).

Another one of my self-assigned jobs was to precisely cut and fit the curved knee-braces (45-degree angle braces at every 90-degree junction) and bolt them in place. Knee braces are critical components of a timber-frame; they help keep the structure from racking from wind and other forces over time. I used small curved logs for aesthetic appeal.

I fashioned a more elaborate king-post "tree" in the loft this time around and attached the "branches" to the trunk with rebar and to the rafters with large screws.

The only items I was able to salvage from the wreckage were the door hinges, the hanging knee-braces (chains and turnbuckles), and the nautical porthole (cast iron) in the front door. After sandblasting and painting them black, I used them as before.

I hired an electrician to do the extensive industrial-type wiring (same guy again!), but Kirt and Vadim did the plumbing (as I had done on House #1). I installed the sinks, toilets, and appliances as I acquired them over time and continued to do the rest of the finish work for the next three years, paying as I went along.

I documented the project with photos and videos and kept track of every cent spent on materials. House #2 cost the same as House #1: $15 per square foot, for a total of $30,000.

Closing Thoughts

On the day of the fire, bleary-eyed with tears, Kirt

made a noble promise, and as clear-eyed as a superhero, he kept it. Only two years later my knight in natural armor (steely muscles and a T-shirt) carried ME over the threshold this time!

I've come to the conclusion that it's better to have built and rebuilt than never to have built at all.

CHAPTER 11

THE BEAUTY OF BUILDING WITH LOGS

Rebuilt house, living room

Five years after the fire I finally had my house back. Artistically speaking, I liked it even better than the first one. This time around we were able to find *curved* logs for the knee braces, stair rails, and king-post tree.

Lodgepole pine usually grows straight and narrow, but two lone trees drowning on the edge of a wet and soggy meadow were *beautifully deformed*. We took all those dramatically arched and gnarled branches and ended up using them as the most prominent supports and handsome finishing touches on the house.

That's the charm of building a log home. There is an inherent beauty and uniqueness in every log. You simply relocate and rearrange Mother Nature's handiwork. Natural elements, with all their flaws and character traits, transform even a modest shelter into a stunning work of art.

You don't need a degree in architecture to design your log home. Do some soul searching, use your imagination, and make a list of everything you've always wanted in a home. Then sit down at the drawing board and incorporate those features into a floor plan and exterior design you like. Build a scale model out of balsa wood and ¼" dowels (logs) to test-drive your layout. From your model you can determine how many and what size logs you need.

The vertical-log method of building is extremely versatile. The logs stand on their own, have incredible strength, and don't shrink in length. Put up a wall anywhere you want as long as you have a sturdy foundation under it. Create archways and round windows, a curved wall, or—what the heck—an entire round house! Stand the logs up and spike them in; the possibilities are endless.

There are books galore to help you calculate foundation loads and roof requirements. Draw up your plans and submit them to the local building department. The experts there will work with you if changes or corrections are necessary. Chances are, they'll tell you, like they told me, "It's overbuilt," and that's it. As soon as your plans are approved, you can get on to your next step, which is the gut-busting work of gathering and stockpiling your logs. Now is the time to muster up some real pioneer spirit.

I celebrate a certain degree of poverty; it's the mother of ambition. Because I had a lot more drive and energy than money, I had to resort to the self-serve, cut 'n' carry mode of logging. Although it wasn't easy, it turned out to be one of the most satisfying and rewarding experiences in my life—thrice! I highly recommend it.

Tromping around in the forest is more than a breath of fresh air; it's an awakening of all the primeval senses and it inspires a startling appreciation of the huge and the awesome. Then, to top it all off, you get to run around with your USFS permit in one hand and a chainsaw in the other while selecting the trees that will actually become your home. The dialogue can get downright emotional: "Oooh, there's a beauty." "Hey, I want that one right in the middle of the living room!" "Let's cut it here to preserve this chipmunk hole." "Look at this big protruding knot— you could hang your coat on it."

There's no substitute for the exhilaration and exhaustion you feel after hours of extreme labor and artistic choices, except maybe winning a marathon. As you drive the old pickup home with another load of perfectly imperfect logs, you know you've just spent a day actually living your dream. You can't rush the process—you are only human—but with each trip in and out of the woods, you are a little closer to your goal, and that is profoundly satisfying.

Kirt and I tried our best to be compassionate, environmentally responsible tree surgeons and thinned out only the trees in grossly overpopulated areas. We had a 600-acre shopping mall of timber to choose 300 short logs from and did so judiciously. Several logs came from storm-damaged and root-sprung trees, and many tall trees provided four or five logs each. I even hugged a few logs real tight, but only to facilitate carrying them as I waddled along, grunting and panting, to the truck.

After you have all the logs you need, the next

aerobically enjoyable and artistically satisfying step is peeling them. It's Zen-like. You and your drawknife become one—slicing off the bark in rhythmic strokes, creating a hand-carved design of dark and light swaths. You can alternately cut long and short, deep and shallow, and straight and squiggly—to achieve any pattern you like. It's easy, and it's fun. The only problem: it's addictive. Even after you stop for the day, you continue to feel the urge to chamfer (bevel cut) the edges off everything! I've peeled 780 logs for three structures and the drawknife remains my favorite tool.

While each log was still on the peeling stand, I splashed it with a concoction of linseed oil, turpentine, and maple-colored stain. I couldn't wait to see the knots and grain and swirls and whorls come alive in Technicolor. That visual inspiration kept me going, and the stain protected the logs from fading in the sun.

With the preparation stage over, you now have a massive stockpile of well-groomed logs—all spruced up with a haircut, shave, and a tan—ready to stand proudly at attention in their permanent places to protect you from the elements.

The rest of the story is just carpentry: hammering, sawing, drilling, gluing, and screwing. Every little accomplishment is its own reward in a long and arduous process. By the time your house begins to take shape, so will you. Your building skills and physical prowess (strong muscles) will grow right along with your confidence and self-esteem. Don't be surprised to discover that the journey itself is so fulfilling that moving into the finished house is almost anticlimactic.

After you celebrate the completion of your masterpiece, you can wallow in the luxury of decorating it. This is the fun part. There's an old saying I adhere to: "Never have anything in your home that you don't believe to be useful or beautiful." Stick to that, be true to yourself, and you can't go wrong.

But you might ask, "What goes with logs?" I would answer, "Almost everything." My rule is no rule. A combination of rustic motifs can go together with logs and each other. Wood goes with leather, metal, stone, mirrors, and plants, just to name a few compatibilities.

Personally I am fond of wood, iron, copper, brass, and terra cotta pottery. Anything nautical is beautiful to me: portholes, brass lanterns, masts and nets, and wainscoting. If I hadn't built a log house, I would have built a wooden boat with a big, cozy cabin and a galley. In fact, I once entertained the idea of building a huge ark if I was unable to get a building permit for a house. To foil the inspectors, I would pretend to be a religious zealot preparing for the next flood. Alas, it was just a fantasy! But I did fashion a *widow's watch* at the top of my stair landing. And along that same theme, I built two large, round windows for visual appeal and lined the deep frames with narrow T&G fir and brass nails.

I also like the Western influence: saddles and ropes and leather and hats; my daughter's saddle and chaps are on display in the living room. The horse tack fits right in, as does my son's nine-foot grand piano. The log interior compliments both. And, I might add, the acoustics are sensational!

The stair banister, kitchen-pot hangers, and closet rods are all black iron pipe attached with black flanges and brass screws. The house wiring is visible in black electrical conduit, for an industrial look. The front door has a black iron porthole with brass wing nuts. All the doors are T&G pine with massive black hinges and wrought-iron hardware.

I used huge laminated beams—recycled free from the ridge beam in an old store—for my countertops and dining room table. I built a solid butcher block out of hard-rock maple for my kitchen. It's 3 feet square and a foot thick. Needless to say, it stays put.

There's a river-rock shower in the loft bathroom. I painted the stones warm, earthy tones to go with the rest of the decor.

Some of the exterior log walls had to be Sheetrocked on the inside for insulation purposes (code requirement), but it turned out to be a good thing. The delicately textured white walls contrast nicely with the rough, amber-colored log walls and provide a flat surface for hanging shelves, mirrors, and artwork. A mix of rusticity and refinement, like leather and lace, is pleasing to the eye.

For all the windows I sewed cotton-duck drapes and curtains, installed brass grommets and black shower-curtain rings to hang them with, and used black electrical conduit for the rods. (Fabric was $3 a yard, rings twelve for $1, conduit 10 cents a foot.) On hot summer days, diffused light filters beautifully through the curtains and is sufficient for all the plants to flourish.

For the beds I made diamond-patterned Levi quilts from recycled jeans. I built a log crib, early pioneer style, for my grandson, Zane, and made him his own little Levi quilt to match the others.

Just as low-budget decorating is a necessity, low-maintenance housekeeping is a must and dictates most of my decorating decisions. I chose low-nap, heavy-traffic carpet so dogs and cats and kids can run wild through the house and nobody cares. Rustic materials weather well and don't show the dust. Nicks and spills are camouflaged in textures and colors that grow richer and richer with age.

Being a minimalist, I resist accumulating stuff that

requires a lot of time and energy to take care of. For me, life is too short to starch and iron doilies, no matter how pretty they are. I'm a wash-and-wear kinda gal. I'd rather build a house than clean one!

CHAPTER 12

CURIOUS GUY AND OFFENDED WOMAN:
A Philosophical Treatise and Rebuttal

Dorothy, 52, after the fire

The March/April 2004 issue of *Backwoods Home* magazine came out with me on the cover and my house-building story inside. I was happy to have the opportunity to share my story and inspire other people to build their own houses, and I was thrilled that it was the cover story!

Dorothy Ainsworth

The Curious Guy

Then the first email came in. It was from a man who asked, "Are they real?" (referring to certain female physical anomalies). Editor Dave at *BWH* asked whether I wanted to answer it or ignore it. Because I always look for the humor in any situation, my first reaction was to banter. I immediately thought of a few lighthearted retorts and fired them off to Dave to choose from, a not-so-funny one being just the word *genetics*.

The guy's tactless question didn't really bother me. I'm basically good-natured, I love being a woman, and I give people the benefit of the doubt. I assumed this *curious guy* was just trying to be funny with his one-liner, and he let his biology override good taste. Maybe he's had a lot of disappointments in his life over things not being what they seem (who hasn't?), and he's cynical. Who knows? We could speculate all day.

I'm not excusing him, but in spite of all the cultural pressures to be politically correct these days, sometimes a man is a man is a man, and even a nice guy can forget his manners. I was a waitress for forty years. I learned to laugh off almost everything and to give people enough rope to hang themselves, which they always *did*.

But later on, and being the philosophical type, I got to thinking a little deeper about it: What if this guy had busted *his* behind developing a piece of property over a twenty-two-year period, had built a house the hard way and then it burned down, and *his* smiling photo was on the cover of a magazine—all happy because he now had his new logs to start rebuilding with—and the *only* question I had for him (after zeroing in on the bulge in his pants) was: "Is that real, or do you have a penile implant?" (Sorry to have to get graphic here to make my analogy.)

No one should be reduced to two mammary glands or a *penie winkle*, even in humor, so I decided not to honor his question with an answer.

I emailed Dave with this new perspective, and he encouraged me to come up with (quote): "An insightful answer to address the guy's question that, in its simplicity, reveals the way many men perceive women, no matter what their accomplishments are." He went on to say: "This guy may represent a dismissive attitude some men hold about women." He continued: "I'll bet there are a lot of women out there who need a woman like you to tell them, 'You can do it too!' So what if you're feminine, so what if you need a little help from a man's brute strength? It's *your* will, brains, guidance, determination, and whatever else you bring to bear that ultimately determines what does or does not get accomplished." (Yay, Dave!)

So now I was inspired to elaborate on this very important social, cultural, and philosophical subject, but not in a man-bashing way.

I have a son. I have brothers. I love men, and I really believe they have a hard time proving themselves in this society. I have great compassion, especially for men who struggle with their egos to the point of having to put women down to feel better about themselves. It's very sad.

Nobody (man or woman) should have to stay stuck in his or her *place*. Life is all about growth and change and evolving over time. The best relationships are solid friendships where both partners are acknowledged, accepted, and encouraged to develop to their fullest potential, and applaud each other every step of the way.

Unfortunately, too many relationships are not balanced, and both parties lose. One person tries to control the other, and it doesn't last. Givers and takers attract each other like magnets, but that doesn't last. The best combination is two givers trying to out-give each other.

My point is that two people working together in an atmosphere of mutual admiration, respect, and cooperation can work miracles. It's the only way to have a healthy relationship. I found that out the hard way myself.

I was raised in the 1950s generation that did not regard women as equals, and I was conditioned by my upbringing to dutifully accept my subservient role as wife, mother, and also full-time waitress—for ten years of a one-sided marriage.

I finally broke free and started the new life that I actually wanted. It was no accident that I was attracted to an enlightened younger man (Kirt) who automatically believed women were equals. It helped that his parents were good examples of equality too. Our age difference did not define our relationship; our common values did. We *both* blossomed.

In summary, a guy who has reached the level of maturity to see the whole woman, not just her body parts, is in for a friend, a partner, and a helpmate for life. Why not have it all?

I would advise the *curious guy* not to judge a magazine by its cover!

Woman Offended

Just when was I finished dealing with the *curious guy*, an email came in that gave me the shock of my life! I learned that a woman representing the feminist movement was actually offended by the cover photo! She contended that it was a blatant example of sexual exploitation used to sell magazines, and how could I have allowed that photo to be used? She implied that using that photo set the feminist movement back a few notches.

My first and immediate response was emotional and defensive: "Hey, gals, that's just *me*—in my work clothes! It's summer; I'm sweltering hot, and I'm in a T-shirt. So what? Everybody wears T-shirts, or less, in hundred-degree heat!"

Then I got to thinking again (a dangerous pastime). I came to the conclusion that, if I were flat-chested, I'm absolutely positive that not a word would have been said about the cover photo.

This woman (or these women) obviously needed a lesson in Logic 101, so here is the deductive reasoning:

The photo would have been okay if I were flat-chested, so *size alone* is the issue here.

Because size is the only issue, I'm being discriminated against for a physical characteristic, so *I* should be the one offended!

Women who take offense at something as illogical as this are the very ones setting the feminist movement back to chest-binding or to wearing burkas! *They* are the repressors and oppressors.

Dave had seized the opportunity to run this inspirational story about a woman who is a combination of femininity and competence, and he chose the cover photo to celebrate a woman, not exploit a woman. He thought that, if anything, the article would portray a step forward for women. He is a wonderful example of the *new-man* era and sincerely acknowledges the tremendous contributions that women make right alongside men (sometimes hand in hand). Dave and his wife Ilene are shining examples of that kind of partnership.

When somebody protests too much, a red flag goes up. I ask, "What are they afraid of? Why are they threatened?" Something is wrong with this picture, and I don't mean *my* photo. The person on the cover and the person in the story are one and the same—and they are both authentic. It's not a model on the cover, misrepresenting the contents inside.

I challenge these women, with their not-so-hidden agenda, to be honest about where their outrage is coming from. It's time to check their premises, because they're not making sense.

There's a big credibility gap here—*and* a double standard (the very thing they've been fighting against for years). These same women who scream at their boyfriends "I want you to see the *real* me—the *inside*—not just my body" are just looking at *my* body and protesting! They couldn't get past being offended long enough to read the story inside! If they don't see this discrepancy, it's laughable.

As hard as they try, they'll never be able to overpower biology and make everyone blind to outward appearances. That would surely result in *de-evolution*. Nature and the perpetuation of the species count on our making choices, and some of those choices are visual.

Would I have to *chaw tobaccy* and strut around with my hands on my hips with an attitude like Aileen Wuornos in *Monster* to be an accepted image on the cover?

I'm not a tough chick at all, but I managed to build a house, so the cover photo is accurate. I giggle, I cry, I whimper, and I whine, just like any girl (and some guys). It hasn't been an easy life, but I don't have a chip on my shoulder, and the only axe I grind is the one I sharpen so I can split wood for my fireplace.

I've never been the type of woman who premeditates exploiting what she can get from a man by using her feminine wiles. I don't believe in getting something for nothing. I *want* to pay my own way or trade value for value. I couldn't bear to feel beholden to anyone.

I also don't expect somebody else to *make* me happy. I wouldn't put that impossible responsibility on a man. I have earned my *own* approval by actually achieving some of my goals, and I have no desire to flaunt myself. I have so many great hobbies, I could almost be a hermit.

I've tried to pass on to my kids the universal values I've learned: embrace the work ethic, earn your self-esteem by accomplishing good things, create your own reality by being true to yourself, love and nurture with all your heart and it will come back to you many fold, but *never* cast your pearls before swine! Amen.

I took the time out to address the *offended women* because I hate injustice. I don't usually waste precious energy on people who have an agenda to unload onto somebody else—in this case a person who has been minding her own business and getting things done, and who was attempting to share the experience with others for inspirational purposes.

I refuse to be ashamed of my photo on the cover of *Backwoods Home* magazine—for better or for worse, it's me!

CHAPTER 13

Start a Post-Construction
Cleaning Business for $1,800

Perfectionist Eric doing my windows

Wherever construction is going on, there will be a big mess left in its wake that somebody has to clean up. That somebody can be *you*, and you can make excellent money doing it! Cleaning only one sizable house a week can gross you $2,000 per month.

If you're the energetic type, in good physical shape, and a fussbudget about detail work, you're "da man" (or da woman) for the job. You should be comfortable with ladders and heights, be willing to work long hours on short notice, and maintain a positive attitude and cheerful disposition. But most importantly, you must be dependable, even if you're a grouch.

Contractors are almost always in a pinch to meet deadlines (open-house showings, escrow closings, etc.) and will be calling you at the last minute to clean a house. You'll have two or three days max to complete the job, no matter how large the place, and with subcontractors still underfoot making messes. (That's where the cheerful disposition comes in.)

To build a great reputation, you have to just *do it*, no whining allowed. You and you alone will be responsible for making the house presentable to sell, or if it's presold, making it turnkey ready for the new owner to move in— maybe Martha Stewart herself. It has to sparkle!

Getting Started

Check out some good books at the library on cleaning and read up. The experts have a lot to offer in tips and advice that will help you look and feel like a pro, even on your first job.

Think up an original name for your business. Beware of borrowing anyone else's idea. You will need a name (DBA: doing business as) to apply for a license.

The next step is to get licensed, bonded, and insured. This is the part none of us likes, but there's no way out unless you want to risk a fine if you get caught. (The contractor who hires you can also be fined.)

A city license is nominal. Here in Oregon you also have to have a contractor's license to do post construction cleaning. Call the *Construction Contractor's Board* under the state listings in your phone book for specific info in your area. Regulations are always changing. The CCB will send you an application packet. Simply follow the steps.

Bonding and insurance for one year cost us $500 (2002), but it depends on the amount of coverage you need (accident and liability), and is available through the CCB or privately. They have a chart to determine your needs. Look under *Business Insurance* in the phone book and call around for the best rates.

This may all sound complicated, but it isn't. Just pick up the phone and get started. Professional people are exceedingly helpful. They will guide you through the process; they do paperwork for a living. All you have to do is sign on the dotted line and give them a check. There's no mystery involved. They *want* your business.

Now it's time to sit down with your *partner-in-grime* (if you have one) and dream up a business logo for your business cards and ads. Keep it simple; keep it cheap. It can be a simple sketch of a squeegee or a broom. You don't have to hire a graphic artist unless you have money to spare. Print shops, such as Kinkos, or online printers such as VistaPrint.com, have catalogs of sample illustrations and lettering styles to choose from. They'll even help you design your card.

While you're at it, have them print up some flyers announcing that you are ready for business. Then look through the Yellow Pages under *Contractors* and send a flyer to each one. It'll add up to spending about $0.50 (envelope, stamp, flyer) per potential $500 client. It's well worth the effort and expense.

You can also go around to construction sites, locate the general contractors, and personally hand them a flyer and a business card. Introducing yourself, along with a handshake, is great PR, especially if you have a Jim Carey or Julia Roberts smile! Keep in mind that they will be taking a chance on you the first time around, so you might offer *satisfaction guaranteed* or something to inspire their confidence in you. No good businessman likes to take a giant leap of faith without some convincing.

Equipment and Supplies

You're almost ready to start swabbing the decks—but you need a mop! Actually, you need a lot of things, starting with a pickup truck or van or any vehicle that can carry a ladder. (I wouldn't recommend a motorcycle, although that might be a cute logo.)

If you spent all your cash getting licensed, go down to the hardware store or janitorial supply house, open an account, and yell, "Charge!" like Teddy Roosevelt. Or use a credit card. Or borrow money from the proverbial brother-in-law. With the profit from your first two jobs, you'll be able to pay off all your equipment and supplies. The rest of the year will be gravy.

Note: You can buy the specialized window tools you need from a janitorial supply or order them from a catalog. There is also a huge list of supply houses on the Internet.

The total of the above list is about $850 (2002). Now you're ready to roll.

The Bid and the Contract (2002)

Here in southern Oregon the going rate for post construction cleaning is from $0.18 to $0.20 a square foot (referring to living space, not the garage). The higher end of the range is based on difficulty in cleaning, such as huge or high picture windows, hard-to-reach skylights, the number of windows, complicated fenestration, extensive high ladder work (steep hillsides, etc.), and other architectural details that require extraordinary work.

In addition to the rate based on square footage alone, you may charge extra for anything that is unusually time consuming, beyond the normal procedures, such as excessive glue on floor seams.

To simplify the paperwork, your contract and bid can all be on one page, with a provision stating that when the bid is actually signed by both parties, it then becomes binding.

If you are a glutton for punishment, you could offer to clean up the outside premises too, which may include dump runs. There is always a lot of scrap lumber to be salvaged if you want it for your wood stove or whatever. When in doubt, *ask*, but the contractor probably won't care; he just wants the place cleaned up.

The time to secure this extra work is when you make your initial contact with the head honcho. Ask to be called well in advance of the interior cleaning job, so you can schedule in enough time for the exterior job. Before you write up your bid, also ask if he (or she) wants the garage floor included in the estimate. (The garage windows are automatically included.)

Perfectly cleaned windows are a priority for a successful business. You will be a great asset to the contractor if you can do it *all* when you give him a bid. It simplifies his life and saves him time and money by not having to call in another specialist. Contractors love that!

The following advice is from a professional window cleaner:

To avoid liability, examine all windows carefully in advance and report any scratches to the general contractor. Almost without exception double-paned window glass comes from the factory with a few blemishes, scratches, or anomalies—some even between the panes. They must be noted ahead of time. It will be hard to go back later and say, "I didn't do it!" His furrowed brow and red face will reveal his skepticism.

Proper blade technique is critical because if you scratch a window, it will have to be replaced. Even label removal can be risky with improper razoring. You and your reputation are at stake here. Practice on your own windows first. Cleaning windows is an acquired skill that requires enough practice to make it look like an art. Needless to say, do not use an inexperienced worker to help with the windows.

This same expert informed me that it's a misnomer to use the term window *washing* in the industry. It's called window *cleaning*. He said if you want to get really pretentious, you might call yourself a *vertical-silicon-surface engineer* who specializes in architectural fenestration. Back to reality...

The Procedure

1. Spray labels liberally with window-cleaning solution to soak and loosen them. Spray the tracks (window-sliding grooves) at the same time and let them soak while you're doing the window.
2. With a new razor, remove labels and other debris by using the scraper in one direction only. Dragging a razor backward does not remove anything, but it can trap grit under the blade and scratch the window.

Dorothy Ainsworth

3. Spray the window again, wash it with a special window mop, then squeegee down or across in broad, overlapping strokes, blotting the squeegee edge on a lint-free rag occasionally as needed.
4. Closely inspect your handiwork when finished. If you find any stubborn specks the squeegee didn't get, scrub them off with #0000 steel wool. (Use only the finest gauge.) Spray and squeegee again if necessary.
5. Wipe tracks until perfectly clean. Use a toothbrush and/or skewer stick to get into the corners. Cleaning the tracks can sometimes be the most time-consuming job in the house.

There are several techniques and tricks-of-the-trade used by professionals. This article just *scratches the surface.*

Standard House-Cleaning List

1. Don your rubber gloves and carry a dust mask and earplugs with you.
2. Remove all window labels.
3. Vacuum window tracks.
4. Clean window tracks first, or as you clean the windows.
5. Clean windows inside and out, wiping errant drips off the tracks, frames, and sills as you go.
6. Vacuum all cupboards and drawers in the entire house. Remove bottom drawers and vacuum beneath. There will be sawdust in every corner— be methodical so you don't miss any.
7. With a bucket of cleaning solution and lots of soft, clean rags, wipe, wipe, wipe every surface of every cupboard, drawer, closet shelf, bookshelf, door,

baseboard, and windowsill in the house. Be sure to get the tops of doors and the molding and trim throughout the house. Again, be methodical so no surface is skipped. Rinse rags often so you're not just spreading dust around to dry into fine powder. Remember, Martha Stewart may be checking it with her white glove.

8. Clean showers, tubs, basins, and toilets with a soft scrub brush and cleaning solution. If label removal is a problem, use acetone (first choice) and a plastic putty knife. For very stubborn label-adhesive residue, you may have to experiment with *Goof-Off*, lacquer thinner, methyl alcohol, or as a last resort, toluol (a serious solvent).

9. Rinse all porcelain surfaces and polish them with a soft, dry cotton towel. Polish all chrome fixtures until they gleam. Clean mirrors with your special window solution and squeegee. (Use this opportunity to look in the mirror and comb your hair; you're probably a mess by now.)

10. Mop bathroom floors and dry with a towel to a lustrous sheen, whether tile or linoleum.

11. Wipe and polish kitchen and utility-room appliances and all countertops. Use stainless-steel spray cleaner on stainless. Ammonia products (like *Windex*) streak stainless steel and are a definite no-no on marble. (When in doubt, always read labels.) Scrub and polish the kitchen sink and fixtures.

12. Vacuum out all heating/cooling ducts by snaking the vacuum hose far down the ducts to suck up all the debris you can reach. This job is very important because when the system is turned on, it can spew clouds of fine Sheetrock dust all over the

house. And smoke will come out of the contractor's ears!

13. Vacuum all carpet in the entire house, using the hose attachment along wall edges and baseboard ledges.

14. Wipe the tops of all electrical outlet covers. Micro-dust settles on everything. This special attention to detail will not go unnoticed by Martha's eagle eye.

15. Gently wipe chandeliers and light fixtures or dust them with a lamb's-wool duster. Vacuum the insides of sconce-type lights.

16. Clean all thresholds.

17. Damp-mop the kitchen floor. If the kitchen and dining area is hardwood, save this job for last and mop as you back out of the room so the floor will remain unscuffed. Use a few drops of lemon oil in the mop water and wring the mop almost dry. This trick of the trade leaves the floor with a flawless sheen.

18. Sweep and/or vacuum the garage if it was included in your estimate. Wipe off the water heater and any other dusty surfaces.

19. As a finishing touch—like Tinkerbell and her wand—leave a little vase filled with a bouquet of flowers (supermarket priced) on the kitchen counter with your business card and a congrat-ulatory note, along with a "thank you for your business." This gesture is well worth the $10 cost for the goodwill it spreads around. You'll soon earn a reputation for being the best, and you'll have all the referrals you can handle, including repeat business for maintaining clean windows for the new homeowners.

Hiring Help

If you need to hire help, I recommend you do it through a temporary-labor service agency, such as *Labor-Ready*. You pay them directly for the hours an employee works and they act as a surrogate employer, handling the payroll for you (federal and state taxes, insurance, workman's comp.). Of course, they charge a fee and a one-time security deposit, but it's worth it.

When you are first starting out it's the easiest route to go because it's responsibility-free for you. The agency will provide you with the manpower you need, satisfaction guaranteed. If you aren't happy with who they send out, they'll immediately send a replacement.

If you choose to pick your own help, the agency requires your prospective employees to register with them in advance and possibly be screened by undergoing a drug test and background check—which is understandable because *they* are insuring them.

The agency issues you a timecard to fill out and send in upon completion of the job. Then they promptly send the employee a paycheck and bill you at the same time. At the end of the year they issue W-2s and spare you that grief too.

On average you can expect to pay from $10 to $15 an hour for help (2002). After a trial period, if an employee proves to be an excellent worker, it would be wise to give him or her a raise. Good help is such an asset to your business and so hard to find (in any business) that it's just common sense to pay people what they're worth and keep their morale high.

Keep in mind you'll have to train your employees on the job to do the work exactly the way you want it done— fast and efficient, as well as methodical and meticulous.

Dorothy Ainsworth

You can't just turn 'em loose on the house and expect a miracle. It's imperative to type up a checklist so nothing gets overlooked. After the first house, you'll know how long each chore should take, so make a note of that on your list too. From experience I've found that the average 2,000-square-foot house takes a minimum of twenty hours to complete.

Someday, when your business grows to the point that you have crews of employees, you may want to incorporate and become the big-shot employer yourself. At that juncture you can drive around from site to site overseeing the worker bees, take coffee breaks, and hire a bookkeeper and an accountant. But for now, your partnership with a friend, or your husband-and-wife team, or just little ol' you working your glutes off, is the starting point.

If you are a conscientious person and a hard worker, there is no doubt you'll make it in this business.

Seize the opportunity! Good luck!

CHAPTER 14

ALTERNATIVE LIFESTYLE
"Better Gnomes and Gardens"

Illustration by Dorothy

My brother Leonard was a devoted but comically unconventional single father with two teenaged sons. He worked as a consultant for city and private water departments as a chemical engineer on call, and he traveled a lot.

On one such three-month assignment, his supervisor encouraged him to stay on the premises of the huge stockyard where he worked as a water-quality inspector by day and a watchman at night. The grounds had an office with bathroom facilities and a shower.

Since it was summer, and the kids were out of school, Leonard thought of a brilliant idea for the housing situation and acted on it without hesitation.

He bought three little sixteen-foot self-contained travel trailers cheaply ($300 apiece in *The Nickel* want ads), towed them one by one into a shady corner of the yard, and set them up *pow-wow* style...in a circle with all the doors facing the *campfire*. Each brave had his own private realm of being, but the chief could keep an eye on things.

It worked unbelievably well. Leonard's son, Tim, seventeen, decorated his *bachelor pad* with rock star posters and practiced his guitar constantly. His other son, Dwain, thirteen, was into *Star Wars* and played handheld video games that went *bleep bleep* incessantly. Now Dad could finally rest in peace in his own quiet capsule after a hard day's work.

Because they each had their own space, the boys didn't feel a need to compete or rebel. If they had a temporary grievance with Dad or a spontaneous outburst with each other, they could take great pleasure in slamming their doors shut and locking themselves inside. Being able to run away without leaving home was the perfect solution for disgruntled teenagers.

When they were in the mood to socialize, which was often, they'd all prop their doors open, sit on their makeshift steps, and contemplate the universe—or affectionately banter and tease each other. When it came to the wit and humor department, though, the boys were hard-pressed to get the best of their old man, who was a combination of Dave Barry, Gary Larson, and Einstein. I've never known a funnier man.

Almost every evening Leonard would bring out his acoustic guitar, and, together with Tim on electric guitar and Dwain on harmonica, they'd enjoy a laughable jam session trading licks from Elvis to Aerosmith.

No matter what the mood of the day was, one sure

way to coax the boys out of their holes was by their noses. Leonard would cook up some aromatically enticing concoction, like hamburger and onions and fried potatoes, and pretty soon he'd hear two doors pop open. Then *sniff sniff, knock knock.* "Hey, Dad, we're hungry. What's for dinner?" Right on cue.

Leonard saved a lot of money that summer. Before going on to the next job, he sold the trailers, got his investment back, and moved to the big city—this time to a permanent position as superintendent of a water department in southern California. He rented a conventional house and tried to live a conventional life (Studebaker collection notwithstanding), but nothing ever quite compared to the fun, freedom, and camaraderie of those good ol' campout days. (Sadly, we lost Leonard in a plane crash in 1999.)

When I visited the *Tin Men* that summer and saw their communal arrangement firsthand, I was impressed and amused by such a creative idea and have since concluded that it would work in a variety of circumstances.

Instead of burying your teenagers between the ages of thirteen and seventeen and digging them up later (as the saying goes), just lovingly set them up in travel trailers in the backyard or carport. Ideally, they could work and save enough money to buy their own trailers, thus earning their precious privacy and valuing their real estate purchases to the max.

There are other practical applications for *disposable* trailers. If you are developing a piece of land and building a house, you could buy two or three or more camp trailers and enjoy temporary modular living for the fun and novelty of it, while saving money on rent. Search the want ads or Craigslist for retro *Sputnik-era* trailers—they're a dime a dozen, and you can always recycle them.

Involving the whole family in the building process is

an enlightening and bonding experience. Mom and Dad could set up the main (larger) trailer or RV, add a communal electrical hook-up and plumbing connected to the septic system, then stake out the kids here and there in the outpost camp trailers. After working together all day, each party would retire to their own cubbyhole to R&R.

If they'd listen carefully they would probably hear an audible sigh of relief coming from Mom and Dad's trailer too.

Another use for a travel trailer is to convert it to a bathroom on wheels. Gut it out, build a painted-plywood shower, install a toilet and wash basin, hang a mirror, and you're all set until the house is built. Of course, you'll need electricity for the water heater (installed next to the shower stall), a water line, and a septic hook-up, but that's it.

I know because I did just that while I was building my own house, which took *years*. When I was through using my *humble commode* I advertised it in *The Nickel* want ads for $500 and got so many calls I could have sold twenty of them. Mobile is the way to go. You can get rid of anything that has wheels and a trailer hitch!

CHAPTER 15

BUILD A LOG CRIB

Zane's log crib

Baby Zane is probably the only newborn in Hollywood sleeping in a log crib made by his grandmother in Oregon, but it was inevitable. He inherited a chainsaw-wielding grandma who builds log houses and a horse-loving mom who dreams of having a ranch someday. Their California apartment is decorated Western-style, right down to his diaper bag hanging on a saddle horn, so the crib fits right in.

After hearing the exciting news from LA that a grandson was on the way, I was all a-twitter with ideas for homemade gifts and turned to what I know best—logs.

I designed a crib that could be assembled and disassembled in minutes, so it could be moved into an upstairs apartment. Then I ventured back into the forest with only a handsaw this time, but in the same old Ford pickup that has carried 800 logs for three houses.

If anyone out there wants to tackle this fun but time-consuming project, here's how to do it with a small electric chainsaw, an orbital sander, and a ½" electric drill. (If you have a lathe and drill press, it's all the better.)

You can obtain a firewood or pole permit from the USFS or BLM. There are designated cutting areas, and the fee is nominal.

My plan called for four posts, eight rails, and forty-four rungs. I gathered plenty of extra footage without cutting anything that was rooted in. The forest has downed trees and fallen limbs everywhere. After a few minutes of tromping around, you get an eagle eye for spotting the perfectly sized logs.

Carefully pick straight logs with very little taper (preferably lodgepole pine). Choose the longest logs and branches you can find and cut them to length later. You never know what's under the bark until you peel it. When you're back home, you may find a knot or crack in just the wrong spot, and you'll have to move up or down with your measurements.

Build a rudimentary peeling stand out of 2" x 4"s with two braced Xs about 5 feet apart. The Vs will hold your logs and branches securely and allow you to turn them as you peel with a drawknife. Drawknives are available at most hardware stores for about $35.

Peel your stock, sand the attractive knots, and smooth down anything rough.

Cut all posts and rails to length and lay them out on the floor, arranging them the way you'd like them to show in the finished crib. Number and mark them with masking tape. Each log will have its own character, and you may have aesthetic preferences in pairing them up.

Do not precut your rungs to exact lengths yet. Cut them all 2 inches too long.

Now you're going to make eight giant rolling pins. Find the imaginary centerline of each rail by eyeballing it as best you can and draw a 2-inch circle on each end to mark the tenon size. Measure up 7¼ inches from each end and draw a circle around the log to mark tenon length.

Grab your chainsaw and lightly go back and forth along the length of the tenon, rat-a-tat-tat, moving the saw like a machine gun. As the chips fly, turn the log frequently until you shave it down to a 2-inch diameter cylinder the full length of the tenon. Sand it smooth. Do this sixteen times.

You might want to practice on a scrap log first until you get the technique down.

You're now ready to drill sixteen holes in the four posts so you can plug the tenons in and erect the frame.

Use a 2⅛" diameter self-feed bit for clean, accurate holes and fast boring. To mark your hole centers, measure up 14 inches and 38 inches respectively from the bottom of each post. Then turn the posts exactly 90 degrees and measure up 10½ inches and 41½ inches to mark the second set of hole centers.

Secure the post any way you can and drill the holes. (I clamped it in the peeling stand.)

Now for the moment of truth. Put the entire frame together to see how square it is. If your holes are a little *off*, you can make adjustments by shaving the tenons to fit then using a plastic or white rubber mallet to *coax* them into submission.

When you get to this point, buy a standard crib mattress (52" x 27") and make sure it fits into the rectangle you've created. If not, chisel and sand, chisel and sand. Mattresses are about $40 to $80 at Sears and Wal-Mart.

Next step is to determine the rung lengths. Take your three-dimensional crib apart and lay the four separate sections down on the floor and square them up nicely (no parallelograms, please). Place your slightly over-length rungs 3¼ inches apart O.C. (on center) on top of the rails, to form a grid.

You'll be gluing the rungs into holes drilled in the top and bottom rails, so run two horizontal strips of masking tape (exactly parallel to each other) at the depth you want the bottom of each row of holes and mark a line. If your log is tapered, holes will be deep on one end and shallow on the other.

Still using the tape as your guide, mark the rungs at the length where they will bottom out in the holes, but not a micron longer. Too long won't work, but too short can be fixed with extra glue in the hole.

Now number the rungs in their correct order and lay them aside. Remove tape and turn the rail 90 degrees, snap a chalk line for your row of holes, and mark them 3½ inches apart (on center). This measurement is critical because there is a safety law to protect babies; the actual space between rungs cannot exceed 2⅜ inches.

Drill the holes to your depth line with a 1¼-inch drill bit. Whittle or sand the tenons—on both ends of all the rungs—down to 1¼" diameter so they'll plug into the holes. A stationary table-top belt sander would come in handy here.

With Elmer's or Titebond, glue the rungs into the holes one row at a time. Make gravity your friend when it comes to thin glue!

When all the rungs are set and the glue is completely

dry, put the crib together. Use a little *friendly persuasion* again with your mallet, and make sure all members fit tightly together and are plumb, level, and square.

It's now time to drill a peg hole down through the top of each tenon.

Place a short dowel on the tenon where you want the hole, vertically, as close to the post as you can get, and draw around it with a pencil. To ensure the pegs will pull the frame together when they're *drifted* in, you may need to chisel grooves in the posts above where the pegs enter, so you can slide them into the holes. Gnarly logs always require custom fitting. Drill the holes with a long ⅝-inch bit.

Make sixteen pegs 6 inches long out of ⅝-inch dowels. Whittle or sand each one to a slight taper and then drive 'em home. This is the fun part.

Finish the crib with a nontoxic water-based polyurethane stain, and you're ready to *hang* the spring to receive the mattress. You can buy a standard-sized flat crib spring at almost any used baby-clothing store, Goodwill, or Salvation Army, for $5 to $10. Plywood is also an option. Put hooks or brackets at two separate levels so you can adjust the mattress height as the baby grows. I set my hooks at 17 inches and 25 inches (up from the bottom of the posts). Install the spring and mattress.

You're finished! Make the bed with a mattress pad, a new sheet, a padded crib liner, and a soft homemade quilt, and it's ready for baby—maybe even generations of babies.

CHAPTER 16

MAKE A LEVI QUILT

King-sized Levi quilt

ack in the 1980s I worked as a waitress in a busy little cafe where our mandatory uniform was a pair of Levi's and a T-shirt. The only variation on the rule was that the dinner-shift waitresses had to wear the more *formal* Levi *skirt* and a T-shirt. That was as regimented as it got.

In the age of Denny's pink-and-orange polyester stripes, starched blouses with name tags, and panty-hosed legs stuffed into clodhoppers, who would protest the Levi's dress code? Certainly not us—nor our male customers. It was heaven! We loved our benevolent boss, who understood freedom.

I cheerfully worked away at that job for twelve years, smiling and comfortable in my blue jeans, cotton T-shirt, and tennies.

The place sold in 1992, and of course the new owners changed the uniform to a straight jacket with arm and leg holes, bound by an apron, so I quit and went elsewhere. Instead of taking all those beautifully faded duds to Goodwill, I decided to cut them up into little pieces and turn them into a quilt. Not only do I love to sew and to indulge in compulsive fabric collecting, but I also have a nostalgic passion for homemade quilts.

I vowed to put into practice an old World War II slogan about conservation my parents used to bark at us: "Use it up, wear it out, make it do, or do without." What could be more all-American than a Levi quilt, symbolizing capitalism (Levi Strauss & Co.), the work ethic (blue-collar clothes), and the recycling trend? My quilt would be an historical document written in cloth, manifesting my belief in the free-enterprise system of earning one's way through life.

Every pair of my Levi's had walked the walk and talked the talk. Each piece in the quilt would represent 1,000 miles and 1,000 words ("May I take your order puleeze?").

There were other considerations. Levi material is tough and durable and doesn't show the dirt. A Levi quilt is practical and versatile. Drag it to the beach and the sand brushes right off. Have a picnic on it and the mustard washes right off. Throw it on the floor for the kids to romp on and it's heavy enough to stay put. Carry it in the car for any occasion: an impromptu stop in the park, putting on chains in the snow, or keeping warm at a drive-in theatre if they ever come back in vogue. One thing is for certain—your Levi quilt will always be in style.

Levi quilts make great gifts; they are handsome, unique, and useful. College kids love 'em—think Levi and plaid for a guy or Levi and flowers for a gal. They're also perfect for baby showers and are quick and easy to make: Use the softest blue-jean fabric you can find and alternate small six-inch squares with pink or blue calico. Back the quilt with cotton or flannel and tie it out with tiny tufts. Levi material is ideal for babies to crawl on because it doesn't *bunch up.*

There will never be a shortage of old jeans, and the variety is endless. In any given family you can find a motley assortment: Grandpa's *Can't Bust 'Ems,* Dad's Wranglers, Mom's designer jeans, the boy's *Baggies,* and the girl's hip-huggers—all discarded for some reason or another.

Start collecting; it won't be long before you stockpile enough jeans to make a quilt. If you come up short on the home front, ask your neighbors for their castaways or pick up the free rejects from a used Levi outlet store. While you are sorting through the stacks, conjure up some creative ideas about what you want your quilt to look like. Let your imagination go wild, but make sure your design is compatible with your ability to sew it.

I personally envisioned a diamond pattern of faded blues and dark blues and maybe just enough army-green corduroy and white or pinstriped denim to make it interesting. I wanted to create a symphony of muted blues and subtle hues, accented by Levi's signature gold stitching to emulate the *brass section in the orchestra.* A few labels placed here and there and a tufted yarn tie in the center of each diamond would complete my "Rhapsody in Blue." I couldn't wait to get started.

The first step was to make a cardboard diamond-shaped template. Each diamond would be 9" x 12" with an added

½-inch seam allowance on all four sides. I drew a vertical 13-inch line on a piece of cardboard and halfway down crossed it with a 10-inch horizontal line. I made sure the lines intersected exactly at their midpoints and at 90 degrees. Then, with a ruler, I connected the tips of the cross to form a diamond and cut it out with an X-ACTO knife. (A template cut out of a flat plastic lid would work nicely too.)

Next I put the huge pile of Levi's on my dining room table and, like a bad surgeon in a hurry, slashed open the inseams of all the legs and pressed them into flat pieces to trace the pattern on. I was careful to place the template on the straight grain of the denim, either vertically or horizontally, and drew around it with a black fine-point *Sharpie* (permanent-ink marker). From past sewing experience, I knew that if I cut pieces on the *bias* (45 degrees to the grain), they might *pull funny* or pucker later—especially when washed.

I purposely included gold-stitched seams as a design element crisscrossing many of the diamonds and threw in a few pockets for visual appeal.

While cutting out the diamonds with pinking shears (very important so the edges don't fray), I kept visualizing the finished quilt for inspiration. In this daydream stage, I decided I would use my little name-brand tag collection to decorate the plain blue diamonds. (For years I had cut the neck-scratching tags off my clothes and saved all the creative, artsy ones.) It would be a touch of whimsy and also date the quilt for future generations (clothing companies come and go, and it's fun to look back).

I had planned a larger-than-king-sized quilt, with my (then) *Oregon-grown* Bunyanesque boyfriend in mind, so I had to cut, cut, and cut diamonds until I was (Levi) blue in the face. It turned out that cutting was the easy part!

Squares are more straightforward to work with than diamonds, but to the eye they're not as pleasing in large quilts (kinda *blocky*). However, squares are quite attractive in small quilts—using *small* squares. When you sew diamonds together, you end up with diagonal strips. This takes a little head-scratching geometry to lay out so that you will end up with a large rectangle.

The best place to mark out your quilt dimensions is on the floor—with masking tape. First, make your longest strip of diamonds, which will span from the upper-left corner of the quilt to the lower-right corner. Now you can determine in advance how much shorter to make each row on either side of that middle strip. At both ends of each strip will be a half diamond, which is a triangle. A row of these triangles *square off* the quilt all around the perimeter.

After you finish sewing the separate strips (of all different lengths) to fit into the rectangular perimeter you have laid out on the floor, you sew the strips together. This sewing can get a little tricky, so pin the seams as you go. It's easy to get lost *swimming in diamonds*—like Zsa Zsa Gabor.

By the time you have sewn several strips together, things start to get a little *heavy*, especially your breathing. You may need some help wrestling the quilt around while you smoothly control the flow of fabric, which is moving in a nice, straight ½" seam-line under the sewing machine needle.

Assuming all goes well, it's now time to turn the quilt *wrong side up* on the floor and press the seams flat with a steam iron. You don't want lumps and bumps between the layers when you put the batting and backing on.

Because the quilt was so big and heavy, I used thin flannel sheets for the batting (two sewn together for enough width but then trimmed to exactly the size of the quilt-top). For a more standard-sized quilt you won't have to worry about the weight, so you can buy conventional batting that comes in a variety of thicknesses (starting with ½"), depending on how *fluffy* you want your quilt to be.

For backing, I found some lightweight dark-blue denim on sale at a fabric outlet store and bought the whole bolt for $2 per yard. You can choose anything you like for the reverse side of your quilt, but I suggest it be a fabric that wears well and is dirt resistant.

It's important to prewash the yardage to preshrink and soften it because cotton shrinks. I cut my 12 yards of backing into three equal lengths (each about a foot longer than the longest dimension of the quilt) so the washing machine could handle the load. Again, I used the pinking shears so I wouldn't end up with balls of tangled threads to trim off. The dryer finished the shrinking job; then I ironed the fabric flat.

I sewed the three pieces together lengthwise along the *selvages* (factory-bound edges), pressed the seams open, and laid the backing *right-side down* on the floor. I placed the diamond quilt-top over the backing and then trimmed the backing (with pinking shears) 4 inches bigger than the quilt-top all the way around. I removed the quilt-top just long enough to sandwich the batting in and heaved the quilt-top back on. Whew! That left me with 4 inches of backing to overlap the face of the quilt all the way around. I pinned it in place for now but would sew it down later after I got the quilt *tied out* to keep the layers from separating.

I chose yarn that would not be too heavily gauged to pull through Levi material. I bought a yarning needle (big-eyed) and thimble and went to work on my hands and knees tying a tuft with a square-knot in the center of each diamond to hold the three layers of the quilt securely together. While I was already *down there,* I sprinkled my little labels all around the quilt in a pleasing arrangement and sewed them on by hand.

I then hefted up the giant quilt and, beginning at one corner, sewed the overlap down, force-feeding the entire perimeter of the blanket inch by inch under the sewing machine needle. It was slow going, but doable, even on my 1929 Singer! It took 153 diamonds to create this last vestige of the old *Copper Skillet* days. My *brilliant career* as a waitress inadvertently spanned forty years. (Nobody actually *plans* on being a waitress for life.) I donned my uniform 12,000 times, walked 100,000 miles in circles, and talked myself silly.

Now as I lie around on my king-sized quilt with my two dogs and two cats, I call my long-awaited and much-deserved leisure time "hemmed-in happiness."

CHAPTER 17

BUILD A CHICKEN COOP

Happy family: Mattie Sue, Splatty Goo, and Fu-Man Chu

Y ou can buy a dozen eggs at the supermarket for 99 cents, or you can go out to the chicken coop you built and fetch a warm egg out of the soft pinewood shavings in the nesting box—and that's priceless.

Every day I gently carry my three brown eggs into the house, marveling all the way to the refrigerator. Maybe I'm a hopeless romantic, but I love my three old hens: Mattie Sue, Splatty-Goo, and Fu-Man-Chu.

Chickens are delightful characters. They're colorful and animated and a constant source of entertainment. They peck and scratch and strut around kinda jerky, like in an old-time silent movie. But it's their cackling I enjoy the most. My favorite sound resembles the long, drawn-out inhaling effort of old Aunt Ruby when she choked on cake crumbs at the family reunion.

While one hen is laying, the other two hover around like midwives *egging her on.* Then they all join in the celebration by clucking and hiccupping and *doing the Aunt Ruby.* After the deed is done, they ruffle their feathers, take a dust bath, dig a crater in the cool dirt for an afternoon snooze, eat a few worms, and go to bed early. It's the good life.

One of the best reasons for keeping your own chickens, and feeding them a varied diet that includes table scraps, is the quality of the eggs. The dark-gold yolks and firm whites are so fresh they squawk when you fry 'em!

Chickens are low-maintenance pets, inexpensive to feed, and they give back that little prize every day. All they ask for in return is a light and airy shelter, kept clean, dry, and safe. They like a little shade in the summer and warmth in the winter, just like the rest of us.

Build this sturdy, attractive coop designed for three or four fine-feathered fowl, and you too can enjoy what a country dweller calls the good life.

List of Materials

- One 4" x 4" x 8' (pressure treated)
- Four 4" x 4" x 12' (pressure treated)
- Six 2" x 4" x 8' (to make five 8-footers & two 4-footers)
- Four 2" x 4" x 10' (to make eight 5-footers)
- Ten 2" x 4" x 12' (to make twenty 6-footers)
- Six 1" x 4" x 12' (utility grade is fine)
- Two 2" x 6" x 12' T&G Douglas fir or small-knot-

pine (to make four 6-footers)

- Fifty 1" x 6" x 6' cedar fencing (pecky cedar is cheap)
- One 4' x 8' sheet of ⅝" plywood (CDX is fine)
- One 4' x 50' roll 1" chicken wire or hardware cloth
- Tar paper & shingles to cover 40 sq. ft of roof
- Four or five hinges and latches (for two doors)
- Sheetrock screws or galvanized nails (3" for framing, 2" for siding)
- One quart of stain/sealer

Materials cost me $250 total, but you can improvise to fit your budget. Save money every step of the way by scrounging scrap lumber, using painted plywood for siding and doors, and 1" x 4"s to frame the *chicken-run* (space to run around in adjacent to the coop).

Start by picking a spot with wind protection, some shade, and good drainage. Level an 8' x 14' pad as best you can. Lay the 4" x 4"s down in troughs filled with gravel, to form a 6' x 12' rectangle divided at 4 feet for the house and at 8 feet for the run. Build up the low ends with flat rocks or scraps of concrete, and, of course, level the parallel beams with each other (use a long level). Toenail all the 4" x 4"s to each other at 90-degree angles, remembering the golden rule of carpentry: "Plumb, level, and square."

Frame the henhouse walls one section at a time on the ground, then stand them up and screw them into the foundation beams (the 4" x 4"s).

The rear wall consists of five 5-foot vertical studs at 18-inch centers, capped by 6-foot top and bottom plates. The front wall consists of four 6-foot studs at 18-inch centers, also capped by 6-foot plates but without the middle stud for now. That 36-inch gap will be spanned by a horizontal 2" x 4" installed as the windowsill, 15 inches down from the top-plate.

Support underneath the sill, in the middle, with a vertical 2" x 4" cut to fit (about 55½"). Now frame in the little 12-inch-square hen door by fastening a horizontal 2" x 4" between two studs to create the passageway from coop to run.

Plumb and brace the two parallel walls with temporary diagonal braces and install the four rafters (with precut birdsmouths) at 2-foot centers. Allow a 14-inch overhang at the front and a 4-inch overhang at the back.

Frame the sides with studs cut to the roof angle, leaving a 20-inch door opening. To stiffen the structure and support the roosts, screw two 7-foot-long 2" x 4" diagonals onto the front and rear walls inside the coop. Notch them out at 12-inch centers to hold three 2-inch-diameter branches or dowels that will step up to the top roost (their favorite). The roosts must be *round,* but a little textured, for feet to grasp and breasts to rest on.

Roof the coop with plywood, tarpaper, and shingles. Install all the cedar siding, the outside corner trim, and the fascia boards to cover the rafter tails.

Frame the run with three upright 4" x 4" x 40-inchers in the front, toe-nailed in from every angle, and horizontal 2" x 4"s for the top.

Line the run and the henhouse subfloors (dirt) with chicken wire, attaching it to the insides of the 4" x 4"s with staples. This important step will foil any attempts of predatory critters from digging under the foundation in hopes of a juicy chicken dinner. Now fill the coop and run with nice earthy soil to the tops of the 4" x 4"s.

Screen the 15" x 36" window opening with chicken wire and frame around it with trim. Cover the sides and top of the run with chicken wire and staple it all securely with hammer-in chicken-wire staples. (Don't use little staple-gun staples that the chickens might eat!)

Build-in-place an 18-inch-square nesting box by the door—about 6 inches off the dirt floor. Trim the front with a 2-inch lip so the eggs won't roll out. Three or four hens will share one nesting box.

Build the main door out of 2" x 6" T&G using clamps to squeeze the four boards tightly together until you get the paired-up battens bolted through on both sides of the door.

Measure the door opening for the run (between two upright 4" x 4"s) and make the door out of two identical 1" x 4" frames *sandwiched* together using glue as the *mayo* with chicken wire in between. Screw together every few inches all around.

Hang the doors and install the latches. If you use a gate latch on the main door, attach a shoestring to the catch lever and thread it through a hole drilled to the inside of the coop—before you lock yourself in. (I learned the hard way!)

Now for the fun part. Go to the Grange and buy a galvanized chicken feeder and water dispenser, a big bag of layer-feed, a bag of scratch (cracked corn and grain), grit for their gizzards, and some oyster shell bits for calcium. You'll also need straw or pinewood shavings to spread around everywhere to facilitate cleaning the pen every month or so.

You'll have no trouble finding mature hens for sale cheap or free. (See ads at the Grange and on Craigslist.)

Your happy hens will love their new *mansion.*

If you're anything like me, you'll take great pleasure in imitating chicken sounds every time you go out to the coop. Don't be shy—unless, of course, somebody is listening.

Dorothy Ainsworth

CHAPTER 18

BUILD A RIVER ROCK SHOWER

River-rock shower

I had always wanted a river rock shower. Who knows why—we all have our idiosyncrasies. Maybe it just sounded like a beautiful idea. Maybe it conjured up images of two lovers washing each other's hair to

Rossini's *Barber of Seville*, surrounded by walls of a thousand stones, and the shampoo sitting on its own little rock ledge. But whatever the reason, I knew I was a hopeless romantic and would still want one even when I got to the age where I should be wearing a helmet in the shower!

I finally got my chance to go for it while finishing up the rebuilding of my log house after the first one burned in 1995. It would have been much easier and cheaper to use tile, but I knew that if I built what I really wanted, I'd cry only once. So I started in, not quite knowing where to begin.

Over the years I had collected a pile of small, smooth, flat river rocks, but cumulatively they were extremely heavy. Since this shower was in the loft bathroom, and even though the floor was supported by 4" x 10" beams, I'd have to consider weight.

I had heard of cultured stone (pumice and Portland cement) cast from molds made from river rocks but only half the weight. I looked in the yellow pages and found the local distributor for *cultured stone* products. They showed me samples, and I was delighted to see that each stone looked exactly like a real river rock but was flat on one side for ease in installation. They also gave me a leaflet of how-to instructions but warned me that they had no data on showers, so their thirty-year warranty would not apply. I didn't care—I'd take the chance. Their stonework holds up outside in the rain; what's the difference?

I had already built the shower walls out of ⅝" plywood attached to 2" x 4" studs put around a 3' x 5' shower pan, so I measured the square footage and ordered nine boxes of their smallest stones, called *skimmers* (each one about the size of my clenched fist). Each box, called a *handipak*, equaled 8 square feet and weighed about 90 pounds. The total cost was $600.

Following the instructions, I installed a vapor barrier over the plywood. I chose roofer's *Stormshield*—tarpaper with a sticky backing—but regular tarpaper or heavy gauge (6-mil.) plastic sheeting can be used instead.

Then I covered the plywood with cement board (*Wonderboard*) and caulked the seams and screws, then fastened sheets of metal lath (2.5-pound galvanized diamond mesh) to the cement board with small washers and screws. The mesh creates a textured surface to *grab* the mortar.

I was advised by the *Cultured-Stone* tech line to apply a *scratch coat* of mortar ½" to ¾" thick on all three walls of the shower first, texture it with a ¼" notched trowel, and let it cure for at least forty-eight hours before laying up any river rocks. Using that method, I could take my time installing a few rows of rocks whenever I felt like it, by mixing up a small batch of mortar for each session to *butter* the rocks and press them against the scratch coat. Sounded good to me.

I bought six 94-pound bags of the Cultured Stone company's recommended *Type-S* mortar and mixed up half a bag at a time to the consistency of peanut butter, dyed it a terra cotta color with iron oxide powder, and troweled it on with a tremendous expenditure of energy but no real skill. A lot of it fell off and made a huge mess that included permanently staining my shoes to look like *feet of clay*.

Because cement starts to harden within one hour, there was no time to lollygag. I quickly developed my own technique for forcing it into the metal mesh. Using rubber gloves, of course, I scooped up *balls of mortar* and threw them as hard as I could at the mesh: *splat, splat, splat*. After splatting on a row or two, I troweled it nice and smooth to about ⅝" thick, then *raked* it horizontally with the notched end of the trowel. Thank goodness no one saw me in action, but the end result was great!

Every night for a month, I worked a couple of hours on the shower. It became a late-night ritual to mix up my bucket of *mud* and lay up a few rows of stones while listening to Fox News and the possible whereabouts of Osama bin Laden (2002). The first 2½ feet of the stone wall, starting from the bottom, required squatting on one's haunches, and the last 2½ feet required perching on a step stool. There was only about 2½ feet of *comfort zone* in the whole process. I felt like a strange bird in a grotto with red droppings all around. Setting 1,000 rocks used up another five 94-pound bags of mortar and 25 pounds of iron oxide powder.

Before I ever began the actual stonework part of the project, I had laid out all the river rocks in a *mock shower* on the floor. I thought it would be a good idea to choose and arrange the rocks in each row in advance and then transfer them to the shower. As it turned out, that time-consuming step was not necessary. One can do just as well picking rocks out of the box as one goes, laying each row out on the floor to make sure the width corresponds to the shower-wall measurement before cementing the rocks onto the wall.

It's aesthetically pleasing to alternate the big and small, fat and skinny, and flat and bulbous stones throughout the entire structure—to achieve a balanced look.

Because my log house is dominated by warm, earthy colors (even my carpet is a deep red-orange), I did not want anything gray. Not only did I dye the mortar, but I painted the rocks with colors I mixed from acrylic craft paint (from Walmart). Since I wanted a natural look and not the bright jelly-bean look, I mixed all the colors with lots of white to create a more realistic *dusty* look to the rocks. When they were all painted to my satisfaction, I sealed the walls (rocks and mortar) with a multipurpose, water-based sealer for concrete, tile, and masonry. The brand I chose came only in medium gloss (I wanted flat) so the rocks appear perpetually wet, but it's a nice look after all.

Note: The Cultured Stone people recommended *water*-based sealer. It didn't sound logical to me for a *shower* but I took their advice, and they were right—it is durable, non-toxic, and has no odor.

I'm happy with my 2,000-pound, $800 river rock shower, and I'm so glad I didn't take the easy way out. My dream is now written in stone.

CHAPTER 19

DOORTHY'S DOORS

Illustration by Dorothy

We expect a lot from a door. It must protect us from the elements, ensure our safety, give us privacy, swing back and forth with ease, and accommodate our moods and situations. When we're mad, we slam it; when we're happy, we swing on it; when our arms are full, we shove it open and kick it shut; and when we're sneaky, we don't want its hinges to creak. If that isn't enough, we want our door to look beautiful and to present a warm welcome to our guests. Indeed, a good or not-so-good impression on a visitor can literally hinge on the front door.

The bathroom door and the refrigerator door are usually the busiest servants in a house, but the front door is the symbolic butler who stands guard and determines who enters our private realm of being.

Naturally, the type of front door one chooses has to fit the architecture of the house. Its style and character gives a hint about who lives or lurks within. I like solid security when I'm indoors, so I gravitated toward a medieval door design (see illustration). I chose the board and batt look, also known as a "batten door," because it met all the criteria on my list for a hand-made door on a hand-to-mouth budget:

1. The door is beautifully rustic.
2. It is strong and sturdy.
3. You can build one for less than $100.
4. It uses common lumber and standard nuts and bolts.
5. You need only a few hand tools or electric tools to build it (saw, drill, clamps, wrench).
6. It can be built to any size and shape and can accommodate a window of any size and shape.
7. The versatile design can be easily converted into a Dutch door.
8. One can go hog wild with decorative hinges: cast iron, hand forged, old barn strap-hinges, or whatever.
9. The ancient design has been proven to weather well under extreme use and abuse.
10. The design can be adapted to many different styles, such as early pioneer, gothic, ranch style, nautical (wooden sailboat doors), and even mixed in with high-tech decor for a contrasting look.

The construction was within my capability, and it complemented the style of my log and timber-frame house, so I stuck with the motif. To date I've made *fifteen* batten doors for various and sundry buildings on my property. I might add that *five* of them have dog doors—and for good reason. The late poet Ogden Nash said it best: "A door is what a dog is perpetually on the wrong side of"...and he was right. The dogs and cats keep the door flaps flappin'.

Where to Begin

The first step is to measure your door opening width to figure out how many 2" x 6" T&G boards you'll need to go across. Fitted together tightly, each board will measure 5 inches wide. Keep in mind that on the last board on either side, you will be trimming off the tongue on one side (ouch!) and the groove on the other side (½" each) *plus* any additional trimming your measurement requires. For instance, if your door opening is 42 inches, it will take nine boards across (45 inches), so you will have to trim off a total of 3.5 inches (1¾ inches off each side). That extra ½ inch you trim will allow a ¼-inch clearance on each side so the door will fit in the opening and there will be room to install the door hardware. Not only that, wood moves. Batten doors tend to expand and contract with the weather, so extra clearance is necessary.

Standard doors are 80 inches tall, but if you are building your own house and you don't care about standards (maybe you're a hobbit), you can make your door opening any height you want. Measure from the threshold up and subtract ½ inch (¼ inch top and ¼ inch bottom) for clearance again. Professional homebuilders allow only ⅛- to ³⁄₁₆-inch clearance all around a door, but when you build a rustic or nonconventional house, the door opening could be just ever so slightly out of square. I allow ¼-inch clearance all around just in case I end up trying to fit a perfect rectangle into an unintentional parallelogram. You can cover up a multitude of sins later with ¾-inch doorstops and weather stripping.

Choosing Your Lumber

The secret to a good door is to pick out nice, straight boards to begin with. You might want a drink *with a twist,* but never a board! One crooked board can tweak your door out of alignment. Sight down each one at the lumberyard to make sure it doesn't have a major crown, bow, cup, or twist. Even though you will be able to force the tongue in the groove by cranking down on the bar clamp, a naughty board will exert its bad behavior on the others, just like peer pressure.

I recommend 8-footers because shorter boards tend to be straighter. But if your door height is 80 inches to 84 inches, go ahead and buy 14-footers to cut in half, and you will have very little waste, if any. You can make that decision at the lumberyard by checking out the quality of the boards in each length.

Most lumberyards carry a good supply of small-knot pine or Douglas fir in their T&G department. Pine is softer and light colored; Doug fir is harder and darker. Take your pick—they are *both* beautiful.

A Variation

If you have a table saw or router and want to make your own *spline and groove* (S&G) lumber so you can use wider boards or some other type of wood besides T&G pine or fir, the technique is quite simple. To cut the groove the same width as the plywood spline you'll be fitting in, run your boards lengthwise *on edge* through the table saw blade (or double blades). Be sure to center the cut! I used this S&G method on a door I built out of 2" x 8" DF boards and ½" splines.

Building the Door

Now you can get right to it. Saw each board to length as accurately as possible. Before cutting with a circular saw or jigsaw, run masking tape along the marked cut-line to prevent the blade from splintering the wood. Lay down the number of boards you need (side by side) across two sawhorses that are about 6 feet apart. If the tops of the sawhorses are too short to handle all your boards, screw a longer, flat 2" x 4" temporarily on the top of each horse.

Line up the tongues and grooves and press all the boards together by hand. Place three bar clamps across the door (one on each end and one in the middle) and squeeze the boards together evenly by tightening each clamp a little at a time alternately until all the seams are tight. But just before that final squeeze, take a carpenter's square and make sure the corners are square (no parallelograms allowed!) and the top and bottom of the door boards are perfectly lined up. If not, take a hammer and *gently* tap any errant board back into line. Note: Never use glue on a batten door; it needs to be able expand and contract, as previously mentioned.

Installing the Battens

Now you have a door that's ready to be secured with battens. You will need eight pine or fir 1" x 6"s for the batts. Cut the batts 2 inches shorter than the width of the door to allow a 1-inch setback on each side.

Ideally, for the *outside* of the front door, each batt should receive a 30-degree beveled cut along the top edge, to shed rain. This can be done easily with a table saw or any power saw with an adjustable blade, or with a hand plane. I made several doors *without* the slanted cut on the batts and I regret it. The doors are fine, but that ¾" ledge tends to gather water and dirt. If there's an optimum way to *do batts*, it's to bevel them.

Placement of the batts is important for the strength and stability of the door. I generally put them 4 inches down from the top and 4 inches up from the bottom of the door. I divide the rest of the space evenly, creating three *bays*—the spaces between the batts where the three hinges will be mounted.

Secure each pair of batts with C-clamps so they precisely oppose each other on the front and back of the door. (Note: Pad the clamp with a shim or spacer so it won't mar the wood when tightened.) Now that the door is barred, shackled, and clamped every which way but loose, put two 1⅝" drywall screws (or nice-looking screws of your choice) close to the ends of the batts—¾ of an inch *in* from the edges. This extra step will keep the batts exactly lined up in case a clamp slips or gets bumped.

Drilling the Holes

The next step is to drill the holes that will receive the bolts, nuts, and washers. Space the bolt holes evenly about 5 inches apart after the first one is marked 1 inch from the edge of the batt. The drilling technique is critical. You must drill the holes straight up and down at 90 degrees to the door, or when you put the bolts through, they'll be cattywampus (yes, it's in the dictionary). As you are drilling, keep stopping and checking in both directions (12:00 and 3:00) to make sure you are holding the tool perpendicular to the door and the bit is going in as plumb as possible.

Stop drilling just before you break through the backside, then crawl under the door (between the sawhorses) and finish the cut from the bottom. This technique will avoid splintering that occurs when you blast right through. To ensure you don't go too far and break through by accident, measure the thickness of the door plus both batts and mark your drill bit on the shank with a black Sharpie or a piece of tape. (Using common-dimensional lumber, the distance will be 3 inches total, so make your mark at 2¾".)

Installing the Nuts and Bolts

Sometime during the door-making process you will buy the nuts, bolts, and washers, and prepare them for painting. I use standard-thread 4½" galvanized bolts and ½" flat washers, lock washers, and nuts that go with them—common items at the hardware store. The door and batts add up to 3 inches of thickness, so 3¾- or 4-inch bolts work out perfectly because the washers and nuts also take up space on the bolt. For a sizable door (e.g., 44" x 80"), the nuts and bolts will total 12 to 13 pounds! Before painting them with metal spray paint (I recommend *Rustoleum*), I soak them for a minute in Jasco metal-etching solution so the paint will stick better. It's cheap and available at most paint stores. Some people use vinegar, but I've found that it's not very effective in preventing paint from peeling off over time. But using vinegar would be better than nothing for cleaning and etching your galvanized assortment. Note: Don't use non-galvanized hardware; it will eventually rust and run, even if painted.

When all the holes are drilled, the fun begins! It's very satisfying to put the bolts through the holes, with a large washer on each side and a lock washer on the nut side, and then tighten the nuts down. I use a ratchet and a deep socket on the nut side while I hold a wrench or socket on the other side. I thoroughly enjoy the smoothness and expediency and even the *sound* of the process, which must be repeated about forty times. (I need to get a life!) Tighten the nuts snugly so the washers sink slightly into the wood.

Staining the Door

You've just built a door! Your next step will be to enhance its inherent beauty with a coat of finish. Now's the time to sand off any rough edges, imperfections, dirty spots, or pencil marks on the wood.

I use a random-orbital sander (lightly) with an 80-grit sanding disk for this touch-up work, but if you are careful not to sand "zones" in your wood, any kind of sander will do the job. I also *dress* the sharp edges by running the sander all around the perimeter of the door to slightly round them.

While the door is still horizontal, seal it with a clear or tinted sealer, whichever you desire. I use a combination of a quarter-pint of Ace Hardware's golden oak and Ace's quarter-pint colonial maple oil-based wood stain, mixed into a quart of Ace's *light-oak glossy stain and polyurethane in one easy step* (that's what it says on the can). I love the color, protection, and sheen this combo affords. On some of my doors I have used Behr's cedar gloss finish, with beautiful results, but it dries slowly and catches bugs if you have to work outside.

One cabinetmaker I know stains his wood creations with whatever color he likes, then rubs and polishes them with Johnson's paste wax. He swears there is no better preservative and waterproofing than paste wax, and he uses it on *everything*! It might be worth a try.

Hanging the Door

Now it's time to hang your door. Cinch up your corset; this baby's heavy!

A large, solid T&G door weighs about 125 to 135 pounds. Two people can easily carry it, but it's cumbersome for one. A padded hand truck would be one way to wield it around solo, but to prevent scratches, it would be best to get help moving it *and* placing it in the door opening. You'll be able to take it from there.

I fastened three 1" x 2" x 12" temporary *stops* around the doorjamb—one on each side and one on the top, recessed 1.5 inches. That way, when the door was pressed into the opening, it didn't fall in, and it also ended up flush with the outside wall and ready for the hinges. With a hammer I tapped in shims all around the door, leaving an even ¼-inch gap left, right, top, and bottom. The shims held the door tightly in place, but for extra security, I screwed a flat stick to the outside wall (with one screw) and twirled it around to hold the door. This allowed me to install the hinges without *incident*.

Note: Small packages of carpenter's shims are sold at lumberyards and hardware stores. I can't build anything without them!

Once the hinges and door hardware are mounted, I close the door and trace a pencil mark all around the door *on the jamb*, then open the door and make another mark spaced ¼" inside the first one. I then screw the 1" x 4" door stop molding all around the doorjamb on that second mark.

That gap between the two marks will be filled by

¼"-thick weather-stripping that self-sticks to the edge of the molding. This foam strip will keep the weather out and will cushion the door from rattling in the wind.

Hinges

Handsome hinges can make your door look regal enough for a castle. You can find old hinges in many predictable places if you actively look for them...antique stores, flea markets, dismantlers, Internet, restoration-hardware catalogs, estate sales, auctions, and even garage sales. You can also buy sizable heavy-duty hinges at the hardware store.

I lucked out by knowing an old farmer who was tearing down his huge, dilapidated barn. He told me I could have all thirty of the rusty cast-iron hinges if I wanted to handsaw them off the gray splintered barn-wood (no electricity was available). I jumped at the opportunity and put in a hard day's work, but those hinges happily ended up on all my doors in the house. I had them sandblasted, then spray-painted 'em black. When finished, they looked as good as old.

For the front-door entrance handle, I mortgaged the farm and hired the local blacksmith to make two large, curvy, respectable door pulls for $100 each, but they were worth every penny. If you prefer the warmth of wood, I've seen wooden hinges and door handles carved or fashioned from hardwood, and they were sensational!

Installing the Door Hardware

Door-entry sets, deadbolts, and all the trimmings are available for reasonable prices and in a wide variety of colors and styles at every hardware store and at all the big do-it-yourself outlets such as Home Depot and Lowe's. Just follow the directions in the package. You'll need two hole-saw sizes, one for the door face where the doorknob goes (usually 2⅛-inch diameter) and one for the door edge where the latch goes (usually 1-inch diameter).

The instructions come with a template to mark exactly where to drill the holes. You should use a jig (guide) that clamps on the door to ensure that you drill perfectly straight (plumb) holes. (Buy or borrow a *door lock installation kit*.) The hole-saw will have a *pilot* drill-bit sticking out of the center of it about ½" beyond the hole-saw itself, and that bit will break through the door first. When you feel the point coming through, stop drilling! Then go to the other side and drill a clean hole back the other way. This important step will avoid any splintering that your doorknob might not cover up.

Installing the door hardware may seem a little intimidating at first, but it's actually quite easy if you make sure each step is done as accurately as possible (particularly the template markings and the 90-degree hole-cuts). If you don't have electricity, a brace-and-bit takes Popeye forearms to operate, but cuts very nice holes and can give you the opportunity to impress Olive Oyl. But if you *are* Olive Oyl, better call Popeye!

After the door is hung and latched, I sometimes install two water-deflector metal strips—one screwed on the building at the top of the door, and one on the bottom face of the door. They are common items at the hardware store. They deflect the driving rain, as the name implies.

Dutch Doors and Other Variations

When it comes to batten doors, there are unlimited variations you can adapt the design to, to suit *your* architectural preferences and your creativity. You might want to build an interior door using 2" x 4" (instead of 2" x 6") T&G boards and *narrow* battens. You could paint the door white or any color you like and attach fancy brass hinges and door handles. Maybe you like the boards horizontal instead of vertical? No problem. Let your imagination and your personality be your guide. Don't be afraid to think out of the rectangle.

If you want to get *violently creative* and prematurely age your door, there's a process called *distressing* the wood. This time-worn look is achieved by beating up the wood here and there with various tools to dent, nick, and even char it. It sounds terrible but can result in quite an authentic antiqued effect.

Dutch Doors

I transformed one batten door into a Dutch door for the piano studio I built. The top half could be opened for ventilation—and for the music to waft out—and the lower half could be latched. I put in a bolt-latch to fasten the lower half to the upper half and installed regular doorknob hardware on the lower half.

Dutch doors are ideal for kitchens. You can open the upper half to air out the smoke after you burn the beans, or you can use its mantle to cool a pie or a batch of cookies. The lower half will slow down the stampede when the kids playing outside get a whiff of the aroma.

Dutch doors are used a lot in horse stalls and barns. For those locations it's a good idea to put *cross* battens on the doors for extra strength. To keep the door from sagging, a cross batten should slant from the lower hinge side to the upper latch side (like the hypotenuse of a right triangle).

Another Quick and Easy Door Design

In addition to my batten doors (and for special applications) I've made a few other easy-to-build doors out of 1" x 4"s in utility-grade pine and/or fir. One was a 7.5' x 8' hanging-track sliding door on a small piano-repair shop, and the second was a 4' x 7' door for a larger shop, and the third was a triangular-shaped door for a tree house. These doors were inexpensive, easy to build, and look good. The 1" x 4"s are simply screwed together in a grid, with all verticals on one side and all horizontals on the other (no glue). They are strong, and they don't warp. Hanging-track hardware is available for any width of door, such as for barns and shops. The large doors slide easily on rollers that ride in the overhead track and, when opened, stay flat against the building and out of the way.

A Business Idea

A good craftsman woodworker could *specialize* in building every conceivable variation of the batten-style door, take orders for custom sizes and styles, and probably sell them like hotcakes. I reckon it could turn into a cottage industry, backwoods home style. Batten doors are here to stay and regaining favor as more and more people are appreciating the natural rugged and rustic look, as well as the medieval look that has been popularized by Harry Potter movies and recent pirate movies.

Closing (Door) Thoughts

I don't claim to be a consummate door maker. Far from it. I'll leave fancy conventional doors to the expert woodworkers with well-equipped shops full of stationary saws, jigs, planers, routers, and sanders.

I wouldn't even attempt to build a complicated door requiring extreme accuracy in its construction, like something you'd see in *Fine Home Building* magazine, such as a door consisting of rails and stiles surrounding one or more raised panels, all put together with mortise-and-tenon joints and sporting decorative molding such as pilasters and pediments. It makes the revolving door in my head spin just contemplating such a task.

I'm perfectly happy with my batten doors. It's a good thing I find them so presentable and attractive, because that's what I know how to build.

CHAPTER 20

MAKE SHADE WHEN THE SUN SHINES

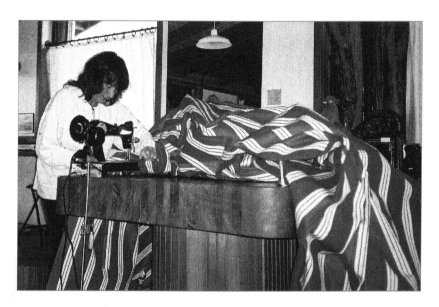

Sewing 40 yds. of awnings on 1929 Singer

While others are basking in the sun and loving it, I run for the shade. I know there would be no life at all without that huge ball of hydrogen fusion radiating down on us, but after being scorched a few times, my motto is: "Use it but diffuse it." Sunlight and heat, over time, will oxidize, vaporize, and brutalize everything it blares down on that isn't protected.

After building my vertical-log home and piano studio a few years ago, I've been watching the logs on their southern faces dry and crack and bleach out, in spite of regular restaining. Last summer I decided to protect them from the direct rays of the sun, once and for all, with nice big awnings.

Like most DIY projects, I started with a little research. I looked on the Internet for sample fabrics and custom-made awnings and their prices. I entered the dimensions and styles I wanted for the main house and optimistically clicked on the *quote* button. A total of $4,000 popped up—$1,000 in materials and $3,000 in labor. Excuse me while I gasp! I earn $8.50 an hour as a prep cook making chicken shish kebabs. I figured out I would have to make 10,000 shish kebabs to *have* the job done, or 2,500 to do it myself. Either way, it's a lot of *skewering*, but 2,500 was the number I was willing to make *for shade.*

Fortunately, I know the *awning guy* here in town, and he agreed to order the special weather-resistant awning fabric I needed (Sunbrella) at cost plus 10 percent. He has plenty of business from people who want a professional job and *can* pay for labor, so he was kind enough to help out this do-it-yourselfer. Note: You can expect to pay $12 to $20 per yard. for fabric.

I don't have a welder or a tubing bender, so I turned to what I'm familiar with for the awning frames: pipe construction. It doesn't take a lot of skill to use a couple of pipe wrenches together—that's why they call 'em *monkey* wrenches! (Well, cousins to monkey wrenches for you tool purists.) I also know how to use a sewing machine, so I was all set to tackle the project.

Here's How I Did It

I measured and measured and fussed and fussed, but in spite of mistakes, I never once cussed! It's one thing to see an awning already up on a house and say, "Oh, no biggie; that looks easy," and quite another to wave your wobbly tape measure around in thin air trying to get exact measurements—especially in a breeze.

I had drawn the basic layout on paper first, so I filled in the measurements as I took them. The math in the layout stage has to be extremely accurate—adding up the lengths of all the tees, nipples, and unions that go in between the long pipe pieces, and the elbows that go on the ends. In my case, all those fittings and pipes, when screwed tightly together, had to total exactly 19 feet. After much deliberation and preplanning, I finally completed my pipe order and took it to the hardware store, where they cut and threaded the various lengths of ½" galvanized pipe on the list. I bought the fittings at the same time and couldn't wait to get home to assemble the frame flat on the deck to make sure it ended up as a rectangle instead of a parallelogram or a trapezoid. Miraculously, it did. Note: ½" pipe costs about $0.75 a foot, and pipe fittings are amazingly cheap (2005).

A rude awakening about pipe-construction of a closed rectangle is the way it *has* to go together in the proper sequence or you end up unscrewing a pipe that you just screwed in! That's why God made *unions*. They allow you to screw *righty-tighty* without simultaneously *un*screwing *lefty-loosey*. It's not as complicated as it sounds on paper; it's completely logical *after* you unwittingly do it wrong. In fact, it's almost worth the laugh when you catch yourself saying, "What the?" But the important thing to remember here is that every rectangular or square or triangular section of the frame has to have its *own* union.

My assembled frame was a grid of rectangles made from two 19-foot pipes linked together by nine 12-foot pipes perpendicular to the 19-footers, and was now ready to receive its covering.

It was time to cut the fabric to fit the frame. Standard awning fabric is 47½ inches wide (I don't know why they don't make it 48 inches). My awning had to be 12' x 19', so some head scratching ensued (like a monkey again). There were some other considerations too. My fabric had stripes, so they would have to go in the right direction. There would be a series of long, narrow pockets (4 inches wide), sewn 24 inches apart on the underside of the awning, to hold each cross-pipe of the frame. The cross-pipes have to be close together (18 inches to 24 inches), or the awning fabric will sag in between, no matter how tightly you try to stretch it. You have to keep in mind the wind flapping, rain pooling, and snow loading your awning will have to endure over time.

I proceeded cautiously: more measuring—more scratching. I finally got brave enough to cut six 13-foot lengths off my 40-yard roll of fabric, allowing the extra footage for seams and end flaps. It's wise to think ahead before you get scissors-happy, or you'll be very *un*happy ordering more fabric! Important tip: Cut with *pinking shears* so the edges won't fray.

I sewed only two of the 13' x 47½" pieces together at a time (lengthwise), then laid them out on the frame to mark where the long pocket strips had to go. While sewing the long strips on, I took great care to provide some slack space for the pipe to fit in by bunching up the fabric as I went along to create a *tunnel* the entire length of each strip. If you sew the strips on flat, when you push the round pipe in, it'll pull and pucker everything out of shape.

I didn't sew all the 13-foot lengths together first and then sew the strips on because it would make the awning too huge and cumbersome to work with. When you are sewing an awning on a small sewing machine, the sequence of putting it together is very important. After all the pocket strips are sewed on, *then* you sew the sections together, and *then* you hem the entire perimeter of the giant rectangle. Note: It's important to use 100 percent polyester thread because it is more weather resistant than cotton.

Since I have an old 1929 Singer sewing machine that sits on top of my dining table, I clamped it securely to the table with a bar clamp so it wouldn't skate around as I guided yards and yards of fabric under the needle. Projects like this make going to the fitness center entirely unnecessary!

I gathered up the huge awning (300 square feet of fabric) and wrestled it outside to the deck to *try it on*. That required taking the frame apart (in place) and inserting each 12-foot pipe into its respective pocket (tunnel), then screwing it all tightly back together again. Tightening the fittings by straining two pipe wrenches against each other is another great workout.

Everything fit beautifully, so I danced a little jig on the deck (high on oxygen) before tackling the actual installation of the awning on the house. While the sleeping giant was still lying down, I sprayed two coats of invisible silicone water repellent on its *skin* (fabric) to make it even more weather resistant than it naturally is.

The assembly would first be raised straight up, flat against the house, then fastened along its 19-foot edge to a horizontal beam above the picture windows—16 feet off the deck. I got a couple of husky friends to lift it vertically and hold it there while I climbed up a ladder and screwed clamps around the pipe and to the beam at 2-foot intervals. The U-shaped clamps allowed the 19-foot pipe assembly to rotate in the *cradles* as we pivoted the awning out and propped it up on four supporting pipes.

The pipe-legs were screwed into tees already installed

five feet apart in the outer 19-foot pipe, 12 feet above our heads. I had used ¾" x ¾" x ½" tees so I could slip the ¾" holes onto the horizontal ½" pipe and rotate the tees at any angle I needed. Then the ½" threaded hole of each tee was used to receive a leg. I screwed a pipe flange onto the bottom of each supporting pipe-leg and fastened the flanges to the deck with hefty #12 screws.

The lengths of the vertical legs determined the pitch of the awning. I wanted a 4-foot drop in the 12-foot run—steep enough for good sun protection and rain runoff, but not too steep to block the view.

Everything went well, and my sigh of relief echoed across the canyon. The hardest part was over.

The next step was to make the triangular pieces to close in the sides of the awning. For now it was just a big wing hovering over the south-facing deck. A triangle on each side would provide more shade east and west and would help stabilize the awning.

I had planned in advance how I would attach the two triangular frames to the house and to the outer corners of the awning. I had installed 90-degree *street ells* on all four ends of both 19-foot pipe assemblies to receive the horizontal pipes of the right triangles. (Street ells have male threads on one end and female threads on the other.) The right triangle itself was formed with a 90-degree elbow connecting the two legs. The vertical leg was screwed into a tee that was *waiting for it* in the 19-foot horizontal pipe on the house.

After a test run, I took the triangular frames back down and made their respective awnings to fit, then put them back up. The dress rehearsal went well, so I attached them permanently to the house with a pipe flange on the horizontal leg, and U-clamps on the vertical leg. The hypotenuse edge of the fabric was pipe-less but had a

2-inch-wide industrial-strength Velcro strip sewed on it that mated to a flap I had presewn on the main awning.

Finishing Touches

I live on a windy hilltop, so I set about to make sure the awning would not *rack* and turn into a giant parallelogram in a strong wind, or worse yet, into a pretzel. I fastened two large Xs—made from ⅛" aircraft cable and closed-eye turnbuckles—to the underside of the awning frame (diagonally corner to corner). The two 10' x 13' X-shaped crosses, pulled taut by tightening the turnbuckles, keep the awning braced for a hurricane.

Caution: If you live in a windy area, this step is absolutely necessary.

After successfully completing the large front deck awning, I made two small box-type awnings for the side windows—also out of pipes. Then I decided to put an awning over the loft-deck on the back of the house. After finishing that one, I went completely awning-crazy, being only mildly awning-crazy to begin with. I bought fifty more yards of awning material from the *awning man* and made awnings for the piano studio deck, its south-facing windows, and its entrance way. Even my shop will eventually get the awning treatment.

The nine awnings I've made so far have cost a total of $2,000, one-fourth the cost of having them custom-made. They have increased the value of my house and studio proportionately, but what's most important is that they have increased my enjoyment and quality of everyday life.

It was well worth the 5,000 shish kebabs I ultimately had to make to pay for all nine of them.

Closing Thoughts

Dorothy Ainsworth

I don't think there's a house alive that wouldn't look better with an awning or two. Depending on the architectural style of one's home, the setting, and the type of awning, they can add a whimsical holiday look (festive and inviting), a European or Mediterranean look, a classic look, a quaint and charming look, or a distinctive modern and stylized look, just to name a few.

Awnings appear to increase the size of a home, and give it a well-groomed, cared-for attractiveness. They prevent birds from flying into picture windows and help insulate the glass from heat and cold, but best of all—they offer delicious shade.

You can go out on your deck when it's raining or snowing—or stay in. At least you have the choice when you have an awning. You can thumb your nose at Mother Nature when it starts to sprinkle during your barbecue, and not a drop of water lands on the sizzling steaks (or tofu burgers).

Another serendipitous use of an awning is for a photo shoot. The diffused and reflected light under its canopy is perfect for taking pictures of friends and relatives who come to visit. You can also temporarily close in the sides of the awning with gauzy material or bamboo curtains or whatever you like for added privacy and shade. Simply hang fabric between the vertical pipes and secure it to the legs with handy spring clamps. Your once-exposed deck could also be a nice sheltered place to camp out on a warm summer night.

Visualize *your* home with awnings. Take a photo of your house and draw awnings on it to see if you like the look. Even small, visor-type awnings over the windows dress up a home and are easy to make.

There are many ways to build awning frames, but I found that playing with pipe fittings is a whole realm of creativity unto itself. It's a world of adult tinker toys, and there seems to be no end to the possibilities of practical things one can build with pipes. They are strong and versatile, come in many sizes, and if galvanized or copper, are almost weatherproof. I recently made curtain rods for a motor home out of gleaming copper pipe and bronze fittings. They looked so beautiful that it was a shame to cover them up with curtains.

After building the frames, you can get as wild and creative as you like with fabric and trim. Your choice of awning colors and style of valances (trim) can be an extension of your personality, like choosing a bright, colorful tie or scarf to go with a conservative suit.

Making awnings is fun and requires only a few tools: two pipe wrenches, a sewing machine, pair of scissors, tape measure, screwdriver, hammer, and a grommet tool. It helps to have a high pain threshold, a little brawn, a little brain, and a little money, but that goes without saying for *any* construction project. If you have none of the above, then you need *lots* of money!

Next time you walk out onto your patio deck bathed in bright sunlight and have to scrunch your eyes into little slits like *Squint Eastwood*, do something about it. Go ahead—make your day—make an awning!

Dorothy Ainsworth

CHAPTER 21

BUILD A SPLIT-RAIL FENCE IN IMPOSSIBLE SOIL

Split-rail fence

A piece of property in the country is just a romantic notion with a mortgage attached, until you put some sweat equity into it. Then, for a do-it-yourselfer, the improvements are so gratifying, it can become your passion.

The quickest and most visual way to transform plain old land into the status of *homestead*, *farm*, or *ranch* is to put a handsome fence around it. It's like outlining a chapter before you write the book. And because we're territorial animals, fences define our boundaries and make us feel secure.

Some people like white picket fences, some prefer post and wire, but most of us back-woodsy types love natural wood when we can afford it.

A split-rail fence, whether straight or zigzagged, is inherently rural in its meandering style and retains a poetic beauty even after it's old and gray.

I had always wanted to build one, so when my neighbor offered to sell me eighty-two hand-split cedar rails (10-footers) for $4 apiece (half price), it was a deal I couldn't pass up. While visualizing the finished fence in all its rustic splendor, I bought them on the spot. Then reality hit, and I wondered how in the heck I was going to anchor my dream fence into nightmare soil.

The hard, rocky ground along the front of my property was virtually impenetrable by conventional digging, so I immediately thought of rebar posts.

Rebar has been a quick, cheap, and strong solution to a lot of my problems over the past twenty years of property development. I had fastened my log and timber house together with rebar, built a retaining wall with railroad ties and rebar, staked out trees with rebar, and, of course, used rebar in all my concrete work.

Rebar is as versatile to this lady *pink-neck* as Jeff Foxworthy says bailing wire and duct tape are to a bona fide *redneck*.

I came up with a workable idea, but it involved some help. I'd ask my boyfriend Kirt to pound several pairs of rebar posts into the ground with a sledgehammer. Then I'd wire the posts together top and bottom to keep them parallel (at 6" apart) and use the bottom wire, set 6 inches off the ground, to rest the first rail on.

I would need forty-eight 5-foot lengths of ¾" rebar

(twenty-four pairs) set at 8-foot centers, for a 184-foot fence. That length would use all my rails. With gut-busting effort and some real luck, I figured they'd go into the ground 18 inches, leaving about 3 feet for the fence height.

Like so many projects before, high-energy expenditure had to compensate for low money expenditure ($12,000/ year income). My cost for this fence would be a tenth of the going rate. There's an old saying: "You can augment your means or diminish your wants." Since I'm not willing to do either, I spend myself (a rechargeable resource) and try to have it all!

The local steel supplier had ¾" rebar in stock for 30 cents a foot and cut it to length free. I recruited Kirt and we started in, using a small-diameter post-pounder cylinder (homemade) and a big sledge. With sheer power and brute force and all the accompanying sounds, Kirt "Jackhammer" Meyer drove the rebar in like a madman on *The Gong Show*. As we moved along the staked-out line, I stabilized each post with a coward's grip and wincing face while dodging the *near misses* with every blow and making a few of my own sound effects.

If I hadn't had Kirt on hand, I would have ground a pencil point on one end of each rebar post to help it penetrate the ground. I've found that grinding metal on an electric grinding wheel is surprisingly fast and easy, and it's fun to watch the sparks fly! Also, because I'm short, I would have stood on a stepladder for better striking power with the sledge. There's almost always a way to work alone, but the task takes longer.

When Kirt's job was done, so was he—understandably. As he staggered off to take a well-earned rest, I proceeded on with the fun part.

For wire, I had chosen solid 10-gauge copper because of its warm color, ease in bending, and no-rust properties.

I bought a 200-foot roll at 10 cents a foot (2001).

I twisted all the bottom wires around and between the posts, satisfied that the rough-textured rebar gripped the wire securely. Then I laid on the courses of split-rails, alternating four, then three, then four, on down the line for a pleasing design.

I placed the final wire 4 inches down from the top so the last rail would cap off the fence, hiding the wire and the post-ends. Any rebar sticking its head up too far was decapitated with a Sawzall.

I splashed some stain on the rails, and the fence was completed in one day, for a grand total of $2.50/linear foot. That was six years ago and the fence hasn't aged a bit. I wish *I* could say the same!

CHAPTER 22

ASHLAND, OREGON

Ashland, the "Monterey of So. Oregon"

Ashland is a little green oasis that sparkles like an emerald at the base of the snowcapped Siskiyou Mountains. Mount Ashland (altitude 7,500 feet) looks down on the long, narrow corridor called the

Rogue Valley, with its meandering rivers, blossoming pear orchards, and rolling hills.

After the slow climb to the summit from the California side, impatient drivers either race down or slide down the mountain (depending on the season) to the valley floor, where they can take one of three exits into our small but linear town (one mile wide and five miles long).

Ashland (population 20,000) lies at the southernmost tip of the valley, only fifteen miles north of the California border. Go another fifteen miles north and you'll be in Medford, Oregon (population 75,000). Beyond Medford is Grants Pass, then Roseburg, Corvallis, Eugene, Salem, and Portland. That pretty much sums up the state from Interstate 5.

Somehow Ashland ended up a comfortable 300 miles from *everywhere*: 300 miles from Reno, 300 miles from San Francisco, 300 miles from Sacramento, 300 miles from Portland. That's good. We love our neighbors—just not too close. If we want to travel to where the action is, we can get on a plane at the Rogue Valley International-Medford Airport.

Klamath Falls is an hour to the east on Highway 66, a winding road with breathtaking views; the ocean beaches are an hour to the west, on the scenic Redwood Highway.

It was love at first sight when I drove into Ashland in 1980, shopping for a small cultural town, and I've been entranced ever since with its irresistible beauty and charm. *Sunset* magazine had named it one of the best small towns in the US, and I was checking it out.

At 2,000 feet above sea level, Ashland proper is spread out along a main boulevard, surrounded by wooded hills on the west and rolling hills on the east. Houses sprinkle the steep hills all around and at night look like fairy lights on a riviera.

Dorothy Ainsworth

The foothills that lead up to Grizzly Peak on the east are a sight to behold. The play of light and shadow on those hills is a year-round panoramic feast for the eyes, as colors change with the time of day and the season. In art and photography it's called *chiaroscuro*—a quality strived for by the Renaissance masters, but an everyday gorgeous view from Ashland.

There are four distinct seasons here: sunny, rainy, foggy, and snowy. The weather is fairly mild, though, with average temperatures ranging from thirty to ninety degrees. Spring brings fleecy white clouds and rainbows. Summer comes on fast, hot, and dry, making the lush fields of purple lupine and vetch disappear almost overnight.

Fall *falls* in the form of rain (20 inches a year), but the fall colors in Ashland rival the Northeast for brilliance and variety. Autumn here is spectacular. Winter is off-again-on-again cold, with very little snowfall on the valley floor—just enough to make at least one snowman with the kids. Every year there is a week or two of thick fog that settles in like an unwanted guest who stays too long.

We have a growing season of 170 days (USDA Zone 7), which is excellent for gardening and especially conducive to growing roses. Southern Oregon has always been pear country.

Downtown Ashland was actually *planned*, and designed to be people-friendly. It has a central hub, called *the plaza*, with the *hubcap* being an area to sit, chat, and taste, if you so desire, the stinky *lithium* water (a famous elixir) from the fountain. A tourist-information kiosk is nearby to make sure you are properly welcomed and don't miss seeing everything the town has to offer.

The plaza, lined with historic buildings and buzzing with quaint shops and small cafes, serves as the gateway to Lithia Park (aptly named)—a ninety-three-acre paradise of ancient trees, a sycamore grove, a Japanese garden, well-kept expanses of lawn, two ponds with ducks and swans, tennis courts, and a kiddie playground, just to list a *few* of the amenities.

Lithia Park, established in 1908, is so enchanting there is no description that can do it justice; you have to experience it firsthand to believe the palpable and emotional effect it will have on your senses.

Ashland Creek runs through the park, cascading over huge granite boulders and providing pools for kids to splash around in. You can hear a lot of squealing with delight in Lithia Park, not to mention birds tweeting and baby ducks peeping.

The creek is flanked on one side by jogging trails and on the other side by picnic tables, with every species of shrub and flower imaginable filling in the spaces. Orchid-like Rhododendron blossoms are so plentiful you might think you are in Hawaii. Handsome curved bridges straddle the babbling brook so you can leisurely stroll through the park European style. Just thinking about the setting, I can hear the mandolins serenading a kissing couple.

You can even get married in the park. There's a special elegant setting with white steps leading up to stately columns surrounding a fountain full of coins tossed in for wishes. Ashland would be a wonderful place to spend a honeymoon!

The park has a band shell for summer performances by our exceptional city band and *Ballet in the Park* (put on by the Oregon State Ballet). Locals and tourists alike sit on the beautiful grassy slopes and socialize while enjoying free entertainment in July and August. Free-spirited children dance to the music and provide a delightful distraction to the program.

For winter fun, the park has an ice-skating rink with a skate-rental office where prices are nominal.

There's a large kiddie playground surrounded by lawns to put blankets on and launch the kids from.

As a spectator, you'll witness the rare phenomenon of a mother, *and* a father, *and* their kids playing together as a nuclear family. Imagine that! This is a family town, in the complete meaning of the word. Everywhere you look, you'll see parents walking together and pushing strollers, entire families holding up traffic while riding their bicycles, with the father in the lead like a pied piper and the kids following like ducks in a row, down to the youngest one on training wheels.

Driving around the neighborhoods in Ashland can be quite an entertaining experience to the discerning eye. You'll see nostalgic sights like old-fashioned lemonade stands tended by kids with freckles and missing front teeth selling warm, unidentifiable liquids, and little kids playing pretend dress-up on the sidewalks. You'll also see pretty teenagers playing *for-real* dress-up on the sidewalks, nearly causing whiplash incidents!

As if Lithia Park isn't enough outdoor recreation room for a town of only 20,000, Ashland has several *more* parks, one of which has a fountain-spray area for kids to cool off in, and the other has a public pool. There is a YMCA with an Olympic-sized pool, and the university has a pool as well. No dogs are allowed in the public parks, but there's a special dog park, where dogs and their people can run around and socialize. It's a lively and popular place.

There is no shortage here of baseball and football fields, running tracks, and tennis courts.

Ashland has two post offices (one main, one substation), two fire stations (one on each end of town), two fitness centers, an impressive public library, a hands-on science museum, a fish and wildlife forensic lab (the only one in the world), a major art museum, and thirty art galleries. To top it all off, it has a warm and wonderful hospital, with a special birthing center.

This is the little tourist town that *could*, and *did*! It supports thirty-five B&Bs (bed and breakfasts); fifty churches and synagogues; ninety-five restaurants, cafes, and other eateries; bars galore; sixteen coffee houses; twenty-five motels and hotels; a dozen barbers; and seventy-five beauty salons (and there's *still* enough hair to go around!).

There is a nice balance of sixty real estate brokers and thirty lawyers! You can't have one without the other.

We even have our own phone book, featuring any local photographer who wants to compete for the annual cover photo. In Ashland we have a tight communal bond, but we're quick to reward individuals and their contributions. The *Sneak Preview*, a local weekly newsletter, annually publishes a special issue called "The Best of Ashland" that acknowledges superior performances by businesses and individuals who serve the community. Patrons' votes are tallied (the townspeople) and everyone strives to get mentioned in that issue.

The *Daily Tidings*, Ashland's own newspaper, features a weekly supplement, *The Revels*, that lists all the entertainment going on in the area. There is an outstanding and friendly senior center and several assisted-living facilities, as well as transportation for seniors who don't drive. A public transit system runs from dawn to dusk for anyone who chooses to ride a bus around Ashland, or to Medford and back.

Time magazine listed Ashland as one of the top ten retirement destinations in the US. (1999). The university hosts a large Elderhostel program offering a wide variety of educational programs open to people fifty-five and over.

Ashland is the home of the Shakespearean Festival, which made its debut in 1935 and has been going strong ever since. A half-million tourists visit Ashland every year. Shakespeare's plays are performed from February through October in three unique theatres…a 1,200-seat outdoor Elizabethan stage, the 600-seat Angus Bowmer theater, and the 300-seat New Theatre (formerly the Black Swan). Another venue, the Oregon Cabaret Theatre, a beautiful renovated church with stained-glass windows and tiered seating, attracts almost a quarter of a million patrons to its 140-seat dinner theater to watch musicals and comedies.

Tourists spill over into Jacksonville, a nearby restored gold rush town, where they can attend the "Concert Under the Stars" at the Britt Festival. Peter Britt hosts performances from famous national and international musicians in every genre of music. The Britt Gardens are beautifully landscaped grounds where you can sit on the lawn and enjoy a picnic while being entertained from the outdoor stage.

If you tire of wonderful *live* performances and want to see the latest Hollywood blockbuster instead, Ashland has two movie theatres, one on each end of town.

All summer long on weekends there is a colorful crafts fair going on featuring local artisans and street musicians. It runs along a walkway parallel to the creek, where you can saunter and browse and partake of the wares, or you can just meet up with people and socialize.

To encourage bicycling and facilitate getting from one end of our long town to another, the city created a bicycle path (sidewalk) that runs alongside the main boulevard (Siskiyou Blvd.) all the way into town. It passes in front of the beautiful university that covers several blocks and fills 175 acres. Southern Oregon University (SOU) has been around since 1882 (first called a college, but recently changed to a university). About 6,000 students attend our liberal arts and sciences university and school of business. As you might expect, it is a gorgeous campus replete with imposing historic buildings, a spectacular library, and an impressive recital hall.

Ahhh, the recital hall! Ashlanders *love* classical music. The university has a music department it can boast about, particularly its illustrious piano professor and world-class pianist, Alexander Tutunov, from Russia. We're lucky to have such a *biggie* in our *tiny*.

That's the beauty of Ashland—it is such a desirable place to live that it attracts desirable and talented people. Many famous actors, writers, and artists are tucked away in their second homes here, where they R & R before going back to the big city. Bill Phillips, a famous aviation artist featured in the Smithsonian Institute Gallery, lives here year-round and is the nicest *regular* guy you'd ever want to meet.

The median family income here is about $50,000. An upscale, sizable home costs between $300,000 and $500,000, with smaller tract homes going for $150,000 to $200,000. The median rent for a house is $1,000 per month; an apartment, $500 per month (2004). Property taxes are high because we have no state sales tax, but we refuse to vote in a sales tax. Oregonians are smart; we've learned that taxes never go down, even if new ones are introduced with promises and promises to reduce the old. However, the city of Ashland itself dreamed up a special tax to help fund improvements in parks and recreation. When you eat out, a 5 percent meal's tax is added to your bill. Surprise, surprise!

Ashland stimulates the senses, inspires the imagination,

and enlarges the spirit. People have *chosen* to live here (not come here as victims of circumstance) and they are *happy* to be here. The optimism is contagious, and courtesy abounds. A large percentage of the population is well educated, cultured, and industrious. The median age is forty. People are enlightened and sophisticated. Conservation and recycling are big, as is a healthy lifestyle. There is a natural-food co-op for an unrefined diet, and the Grange Co-op if you want even *more* roughage! Massage and yoga are a given.

What makes it most interesting to live here is the incredible diversity and the surprising live-and-let-live attitude in a non-confrontational climate of tolerance and acceptance. Artists and bankers and loggers and farmers all rub elbows at the local hangouts. Ashland has more than its fair share of beautiful women but *seems* to have a shortage of eligible bachelors. (This might explain the seventy-five beauty salons and only twelve barber shops!)

You can sit at Starbucks downtown and watch the daily parade go by or go out at night on a *treasure hunt* to the local nightclubs. As in most cities, the partygoers come out in droves on weekends, when the bars stay open until 2:00 a. m. Almost all the other businesses, though, roll up the sidewalks at 8:00 or 9:00 p.m. (We don't even have a twenty-four-hour cafe!) Ashland is what's called a *bedroom community*, but not in the illicit meaning of the word. In fact, although this town is big enough to philander in, it's small enough to get caught in! I *know*, because I was a waitress here for twenty years, and I knew everybody's business, and everybody knew mine!

The Ashland Springs Hotel downtown (formerly the Mark Antony) is a nine-story, seventy-room historic monument built in 1925. The hotel has recently been renovated into a lush and plush hotel/bar/nightclub combo. There are several other hot spots in Ashland, but you have to ask around to keep up on the latest bar scene. The Windmill Inn on the south end of town is a beautifully landscaped motel complex with facilities to host seminars and other big events.

The town is sparkling clean and constantly being beautified. Business signs of any kind have to sit low and unobtrusively and look classy, not gaudy; it's the *law*.

Traffic is not a big problem in Ashland, except for the continual upgrading of the streets, like the recent work we *endured* when the city installed and landscaped center-dividers along our main boulevards. We locals get irritated, but the results are always so nice that we should be ashamed of ourselves for complaining about something as inconsequential as a five-minute delay in traffic in trade for permanent shade trees and flowering shrubs. We're spoiled.

Driving in Ashland is a breeze—you can be anywhere you want to go in ten minutes. Motorists seem to be awake and aware, probably because they know they're being monitored by the local cops who keep an eagle eye out for even the smallest infraction. There are no parking meters, but if you overstay your limit in a time zone you *will* get a ticket. If you fail to stop for pedestrians, you will be *drawn and quartered*. The police are strict because they have to protect not only the locals but the huge influx of tourists as well. We have a reputation for a low crime rate, so people feel safe here, and we want to keep it that way.

Although we've had very little crime in the past, it is increasing, along with the mass exodus from other states. Everybody loves to be on the *receiving* end of old-fashioned, small-town values and manners, but newcomers tend to bring their big-city attitudes with them, which can manifest in rude behavior. It's rubbing off on some of us who are in the service industry and have to smile for a living, but we're trying not to become jaded.

Our population has slightly overgrown the critical-mass limit of 20,000 required to remain a *nice* small town. A bumper sticker I spotted on a teenager's car last summer reflects my concern, though I couldn't help but laugh. It read: "Tourists Go Home, but Leave Your Daughters!"

It's certainly an energetic city—maybe because of all the coffee shops. You could drink coffee for a living here, and some people do! But if wine-tasting is your favorite pastime, there are several splendid vineyards and wineries in Ashland—and at least three microbreweries.

A person can stroll around this charming village all day, not spend a cent, and still have a marvelous time. There are new-book stores, used-book stores, small cafes, ice-cream parlors, bakeries, confectionaries, and flower shops. Rows of artistically decorated boutiques that tempt window shoppers with eyecandy line both sides of the main street. They display a wide variety of the latest styles in clothing, jewelry, lingerie, souvenirs, and anything else you might impulsively decide you can't live without. The locals are a little frugal, but the tourists spend money—lots of money. Tourism has the greatest impact on our economy, followed by agriculture (orchards) and logging.

People are friendly and cheerful, nice dogs await their masters outside shops and restaurants, and there's a general feeling of well-being and harmony in downtown Ashland. It gives one the sense of security that even with all the trouble going on in the world, things are okay after all, and life is good—at least for now—at least in Ashland.

Ashland is a self-contained, full-service town, but it has its share of self-service people. Carpenters, craftsmen, and inventors are plentiful, and there are over fifty general construction contractors in town. Ashland has its own lumberyard, several cabinet shops, and a great hardware store where all the rugged, good-lookin' guys hang out, and their pickup trucks fill the parking lot. Besides Texas, Oregon has more trucks per capita than any other state!

If you can't find some esoteric thing you're looking for in town, there's always Medford, only twenty minutes away. Instead of taking the freeway, you can cruise down the old Highway 99 (parallel to I-5), which has become the nonscenic but necessary *industrial* route, with car dealerships, mechanics' garages, equipment rental shops, and everything else people *need* but don't want to *see* within their city limits. Highway 99 runs through Talent (population 6,000) which is only five miles from Ashland, then through Phoenix (population 5,000) which is almost a suburb of Medford. Phoenix is the home of the huge *Bear Creek* pear-packing plant.

I can't talk about Ashland without mentioning the railroad, because that's what put us on the map back in 1884 when the first train came through with mail, passengers, and freight. It took two engines to climb the steep track over the Siskiyou Mountains. The convergence of two railways ultimately connected Ashland to San Francisco and Portland. When the final links were built to complete the circuit across the US in 1887, we were connected to the national economy (not just to the West Coast). Freight trains seldom rumble through Ashland's old Railroad District anymore, which has been tastefully restored into a tourist attraction.

Ashlanders are huge on holidays! Each event is a major celebration that involves the whole community.

At Christmas, downtown Ashland looks like fairyland in a Walt Disney movie. *Santa's Parade* precedes the *Festival of the Lights* ceremony at which a million tiny lights go on with the touch of a wand.

Halloween is another biggie that draws skeletons out of the closets from everywhere. People pour into town for the *extreme fun*. It starts with a children's parade of costumes and ends with the entire downtown area cordoned off so people can parade around and show themselves off. It's an exhibitionist's heaven and can get pretty wild, but downtown is patrolled by policemen, who step in only if they have to. The unique and creative costumes people come up with are amazing! It is *the* night to *ham it up in the hamlet,* and everybody *does*!

The whole town closes down to celebrate the 4th of July. It begins with a six-mile foot race early in the morning, then a big long parade, then concessions in Lithia Park all day, ending with a spectacular fireworks display after dark. The city of Ashland doesn't skimp on the 4th of July! It's a day to get sunburned and drunk, and I think everybody achieves that goal!

As in most towns, Ashland provides free meals for anyone who wants to partake on Easter and Thanksgiving. The rich and famous are welcome alongside the homeless and toothless, and it's fun for all.

If you are the outdoor type or the sporting kind, there are more things to do here, and facilities to do them in, than you'd ever have the spare time *for* (in your lifetime)! Here are just a few:

1. Mt. Ashland Ski Resort: Ski Nov. to April; 200 ski-able areas, four lifts, twenty-three trails, night skiing, rental shop, cafeteria, and bar. There are motel and restaurant accommodations nearby at *Callahan's Lodge.*

2. Emigrant Lake: Five miles SE of Ashland on Highway 66. Swimming, boating, sunbathing, RV and tent camping, fishing, and a giant waterslide for

kids.

3. Several mountain lakes with resorts: Howard Prairie, Hyatt Lake, and Lake of the Woods. Fishing, boating, sailing, camping. Howard Prairie, only twenty miles up Dead Indian Memorial Rd. from Ashland, has a beautiful marina, a restaurant, boat rentals, slip rentals, and a place to clean your fish.

4. White-water rafting and kayaking on the Rogue River: Guide headquarters located in the plaza in Ashland.

5. Golfing: Ashland has its own grand and graceful golf course (nine hole, thirty-six par) with driving range, golf shop, and restaurant.

6. Airport: Want to learn to fly? Or already know how? Ashland has its own *adorable* little airport that looks like the one on the children's TV program *Jay Jay the Jet Plane*.

7. Horseback riding: All over the place.

8. Shooting Range: We have it.

9. Hunting, in season? *Yes.*

10. Mountain climbing: Pompadour Bluff, Pilot Rock, Mt. McLoughlin (altitude 9,500 feet)...all within ten miles of Ashland.

11. Cross-country skiing and snowmobiling: areas everywhere.

12. Hot Springs: Lithia Springs Resort with its private natural mineral baths, large communal pool, and campground, is just a mile north of the city limits. RV parks are on both ends of town.

13. Garage sales: Ashland is the *garage-sailing* capital of the world!

Wow! I'd forgotten what a fantastic place I live in. Writing this article has reopened my eyes to everything

I've been taking for granted for thirty-four years. *Sunset* magazine summed it up best by saying, "The town itself is the main attraction" (2011).

Bill Bryson, author of *The Lost Continent*, a hilarious account of traveling across the United States in search of the perfect small town he named *Amalgam*, never found it—but that's because he missed Ashland.

The secret is out. When the stampede begins, I may regret writing this article!

Footnote: I did some basic general research for this article, but it is not intended to be a technical travel guide. My observations and conclusions are subjective. Statistics, mileage figures, and numbers are rounded off for ease in reading.

CHAPTER 23

PROTECT YOUR HOUSE
FROM LIGHTNING

"There's nothing to fear but danger itself"

I f you're a thrill seeker and want to see the greatest
light show on earth, take a late-summer vacation to
southern Nevada. The show is performed almost every

afternoon, is never cancelled by rain, and the admission is free!

A Las Vegas pyrotechnic extravaganza, you ask? No! That's much too tame. We're talkin' Mother Nature. She's the producer, the director, the lighting technician, and the sound supervisor, all rolled into one big anvil cloud. Zeus is the star, and his script is unrehearsed. The hot, dusty desert is the stage, and the show goes on whether there's an audience or not.

I speak from experience. When I was eight we moved from Santa Barbara, CA, to Boulder City, NV, (a small town twenty miles south of Las Vegas) mainly because my dad was skinny (always cold) and liked extreme heat. As an artist, he found stark beauty in the desert's *lunar landscape with sagebrush* and in its unusual cloud formations.

All I remember of the four years we baked there was the searing 120-degree temperatures, the terrifyingly spectacular thunder and lightning storms, and the resulting flash floods that overflowed the street gutters with warm, gushing rivers to swim in. *That* was great fun! But then the sun would come out and dry everything up in a few hours, like water drops on a hot griddle, as if it had never happened.

For a family outing, my dad would load all eight of us into the old Hudson Hornet and speed off (zero to fifty in fifteen minutes) to be right in the middle of harm's way. We'd sit squeezed together quivering with excitement (believing we were safe in our rubber-tired capsule) while the rain beat down so loud it rivaled the thunder. We'd gasp in unison, "OOOOOOH, did you see THAT?" every time lightning flashed, then giggle like crazy.

We didn't know it back in the 1950s, but now they have a name for people like that (storm chasers) and laws called *child endangerment*. We were just trying to have a little family fun!

I still love a good storm, but now that I've grown older and wiser and boringly *safety oriented*, I decided to put lightning rods on my house. The chances of getting hit by lightning depend on location, location, location, so my house, sitting on top of a hill, had me worried. It had already burned down once, so I figured the nominal cost of a lightning protection system would be money well spent.

Last summer I set out to educate myself about lightning and how to outsmart it. I researched at the library and on the Internet and here's what I basically found out.

Lightning 101

Lightning is a spark of static electricity on a gigantic scale, and thunder is the shock wave of expanding air created by that spark. Light travels a million times faster than sound, hence the delay after the flash. If the strike is a mile away, it'll take five seconds before you hear the thunder.

Lightning is formed when raindrops and hailstones, and dust and heat, are all roiling around violently inside a thundercloud (cumulonimbus). Internal winds can reach 125 mph! That's a lot of bumping and grinding! The negatively charged cloud particles coax the positively charged earth particles to "Come on up; I'll meet you halfway." Opposites attract, they race toward each other, they kiss, the sparks fly, and the relationship is over in a split second. Sound like Hollywood? Nope. It's Mother Nature again.

A bolt of lightning can produce from 100 million to a billion volts and deliver between 1,000 and 300,000 amps, and reach temperatures of 50,000 degrees Fahrenheit! Those figures are beyond my comprehension, but what really boggles the mind is that people can *survive* being hit by such a jolt. Every year in the US an average of 200 people are killed by lightning, but another 750 are only *injured*.

One man in Virginia got hit by lightning *seven* times between 1942 and 1977. Unfortunately, his *lucky streak* didn't apply to the lottery—probably because his chances of getting hit by lightning were one in 700,000, and his odds of winning the lottery were one in several million. I would call him the luckiest unlucky man in the world.

Lightning is like most things in life: it will take the path of least resistance and the shortest distance between two points. But unlike a tornado looking for a trailer park, lightning is a little more predictable and controllable. Nevertheless, it has its quirks. Even scientists will admit they can't explain some of its erratic behavior.

There are several forms of lightning, and they *mis*behave differently: There is forked lightning (our biggest concern here), streak lightning (more direct than forked), sheet lightning (jumps from cloud to cloud), high-altitude lightning (weird), ball lightning (totally weird), bead lightning (unexplainable), and St. Elmo's Fire (a creepy glow).

When the clouds aren't fighting among themselves, they like to *socialize* by hovering over populated areas where they can *play* with us.

Lightning strikes the highest buildings and trees because tall projecting objects provide an easier path to ground than the air is. (Air is an insulator; not a good conductor of electricity.) There are approximately 100,000 thunderstorms across the United States each year, causing 10,000 forest fires and billions of dollars in property damage to homes and other structures. Globally, there are one hundred lightning strikes per second, equaling 8,640,000 times per day! That's reason enough to consider a lightning protection system on your house, especially if you're in a vulnerable area.

Here's How It Works

Normally, the earth is negatively charged, but when a thunderstorm passes over, it induces a positive charge below it. Think of it as what happens when you comb your hair straight up and it stands on end following the comb.

A lightning rod's positive charge actually rushes upward at 60,000 miles per second to meet the negative charge. A leading expert on lightning wrote that the *stepped leader* (a fork in the zigzag) is *unaware* of the lightning rod until it is about 150 feet above it. That's when a spark from the tip of the rod jumps up and closes the circuit. The resulting flash happens within 1/5,000th of a second upon contact.

All the experts assure us that a lightning rod does *not attract* lightning; it's simply there to dissipate the charge if it *does* strike. But if the conducive conditions are only 150 feet above your house, it probably *is* going to strike!

The system on your roof provides a designated path for the current to travel down and into the ground. The general consensus among scientists is that rods improve your chances of diverting a hit, but there is no absolute guarantee of total protection. Lightning doesn't always follow the rules. If you receive a huge direct hit, they say *all bets are off.* Knowing that, I still think it's cheap insurance, especially if you do the labor yourself, as I did. Right or wrong, I have the peace of mind of knowing that at least the odds are in my favor now. And if I'm wrong, I'll never know what hit me!

Where to Find Help

I shopped around on the Internet for a supplier and chose Automatic Lightning in Wausau, Wisconsin to order from (2004). I emailed them a photo of the house and they superimposed the system on it via an illustration and sent instructions along with my order. All the materials they sold me are Underwriters Laboratories (UL) approved.

There are many good licensed lightning protection providers on the Internet (and a few in the yellow pages of your phone book) who will do the installation for you. I chose the do-it-yourself approach, saved a lot of money (labor is always more than I can afford), and it was not complicated. If you are afraid of heights, though, that's a different story—I don't know which would be worse: getting hit by lightning or falling 20 feet off a roof!

I bought everything mail-order except for the ground-rods (they are 8 feet long and heavy to ship), ground-rod clamps, polyurethane caulk, plumber's tape, and small odds and ends. All these items were cheaper at the hardware store. The entire system was $400—not too bad for a lifetime of protection.

The System

A lightning protection system consists of five components:

1. Rods (air terminals) placed every 20 feet or less along the roof ridge.
2. Main conductor (down cable)—a heavy duty braided copper cable containing thirty-two strands of #17 wire.
3. Secondary conductor cables branching off from main cable to stovepipes, etc., to prevent *side-flashing* (jumping off track) of lightning on the way down.
4. Lightning arrester (surge protector) installed in the house's electrical panel to divert surges into

the ground rod.

5. Ground rods (copper-clad iron rods ½-inch diameter by 8 feet long, driven into the earth to guide the lightning harmlessly into the ground).

All materials in the system must be corrosion resistant. If you choose copper *or* aluminum, stick with your choice. Dissimilar metals in contact with each other plus moisture will corrode and eventually fail. Any weak link in the chain will compromise the integrity of the whole system.

List of Materials and How They Are Used

This list is for the standard lightning protection *I* used. Your system may have different requirements and need additional materials.

- 200 feet of copper conductor cable at @$1.09 per foot (reasonable from Internet suppliers, but twice that price from the local hardware store because they don't stock it in volume). The footage depends on the house size.
- 40 copper cable clips (adhesive style) to secure cable to metal roof every 3 feet. They are glued on the roof with polyurethane caulk.
- 1 twin-parallel copper crimp to branch off main cable to metal stovepipe. (Copper T's are also available.)
- 1 bonding lug to fasten cable to stovepipe (bronze or copper) after drilling small hole in stovepipe.
- 1 small roll of copper *plumbers tape* to use as a strap to go around the stovepipe to secure cable against stovepipe for better contact in case bonding lug works loose. This was my own idea; I used a stainless steel bolt, nut, and washer through the tape's holes to cinch it tight.)

Dorothy Ainsworth

- 4 bronze swivel-mounts with 4 screw-in 12-inch copper rods (the air terminals). Mounts have adhesive base to be attached to roof with polyurethane caulk.
- 2 copper-clad grounding rods—one for each end of the house on *diagonally opposite corners*.
- 3 ground-rod clamps to tightly connect cable to ground rod. The third one is to connect the house's original ground rod to the lightning system's ground rod via the braided cable. Bronze or copper acorn style clamps work well.
- Whole-House Protector (surge protector) installed in electrical panel in house, connected by heavy wire to the panel's ground rod, dissipates possible surges into the ground.
- 2 to 3 tubes of polyurethane caulk (waterproof, weather resistant, and bonds better than anything I've ever used, but very sticky-gooey until it sets up).
- Several ½" copper U-shaped pipe brackets and small copper nails to attach the cable to the wood beams and logs, on its route down from the roof. I used plastic straps to attach the cable to the rain gutters.

Installation

Installation was very straightforward. First I glued all four swivel-based rod brackets in their places just down from the ridge, about 20 feet apart, starting not more than 2 feet from the edge of the roof, as instructions dictated. I could have chosen brackets that *straddled* the apex of the ridge, but I didn't want to drill holes in my metal roof.

While up there I also glued on all the copper cable

crimpers 3 feet apart that would hold the wire in place as it runs along the roof.

My son and I then worked together unrolling the heavy wire up from the ground, along its designated path on the ridge, and down the other side to the ground again. We adjusted it just right so equal amounts were hanging down from each end—waiting to be fastened to the ground rods. The cable was slippery, so we temporarily secured it here and there on the roof with duct tape while we made our adjustments.

Then, moving along the ridge, we guided the cable onto the crimper brackets, pushed the tabs down to permanently secure the cable in place, and at the same time secured the cable to the four lightning rod brackets as they came along in the path.

Eric secured the short cable that teed off from the main cable over to the stovepipe with the bonding lug and plumber's tape. Then I let him do the *fun* job of screwing the four air terminals into their brackets. He adjusted them to point straight up and tightened the nuts with a wrench. Then we got off the roof and both went *whew* in relief at being on level ground again!

He went on his merry way, and I climbed the ladder again to continue snaking the wire down, down, down along each end of each roof (north and south), around the 2-foot overhangs on the eves—no *tight* bends allowed in the cable—and down the rain gutters, through the decks (via small drilled holes), and over to the ground-rods driven 8 feet into the earth (one on each end of the house). To drive them into my rock-hard soil, I rented a ground-rod jackhammer from the local rental shop ($20 for two hours) and that remarkable tool worked great.

I crawled under the house and attached a cut length of the braided cable to the house's existing ground rod, then connected the other end to the lightning protection system's ground rod. That activated the *whole-house protector* I had already installed in the electrical panel.

The protector comes with easy instructions—but don't forget to turn the power off first! It would be ironic to get electrocuted while installing a lightning protection system! But then there's the old saying: "Tragedy plus time equals comedy." *Future* relatives would have some good laughs telling the story about what happened to *Grandma* back in 2004.

More Information

There are a few more things to know about lightning: Its extreme heat can cause fires (duh), but not if it stays on course through the thick, multi-stranded wire. There isn't time for it to catch the roof on fire in 1/5000th of a second. However, lightning can jump around if it can find an easier path to ground. It's not uncommon for these *side flashes* to occur even if you have a protection system. If you are on the phone, a side flash may find *you* more *attractive* (pun intended) than a plain ol' skinny wire, because you are 66 percent water, full of electrolytes, and you're holding a wire to your ear!

The best and cheapest way to protect all of the electronic equipment in the house is to *unplug* it during a storm. Even a full-fledged lightning-protection system will not guarantee against damage to stereos, TVs, appliances, computers, telephones, and antennas, especially if you get a direct hit.

Incidentally, cars are relatively safe if you put your hands in your lap and don't touch anything metal.

Closing Thoughts

This article is simply a primer on lightning and an account of my own experience in installing a protection system on my particular house. I don't claim to be an expert, and I have acquired only the knowledge it took to do a satisfactory job on my own house—not enough to advise others exactly how to do their projects. But the information is readily available if you get on the web and do your own research.

What I can say, now that my job is done, is that the protection system is barely noticeable on the house, it was not a difficult project, and the installation is quite do-able for any adept do-it-yourselfer. I'm confident that the system will do what it's supposed to do *if* the time comes, so lightning is one less danger I have to worry about.

But now there's another one! I've been watching the science channel on TV lately, and almost every astronomy program warns us that distant objects and flying debris, hurtling through space, are headed our way. Yikes! I think my next big purchase will be a *meteor helmet*!

CHAPTER 24

BUILD A SMALL SHOP AND
GARDEN TOOL SHED—CHEAP

Shed framing, 6'x12'

My friends jokingly call me the Winchester Woman because I am forever building new structures on my property or remodeling old ones. What may appear to be *property development gone wild* is simply my attempt to create a place for everything and put everything in its place. I think I'm still okay; I haven't built any stairways to nowhere—yet.

I had a log house to live in, a piano studio to play in,

and two small sheds for storage, but I had no shop for the construction tools and no shed for the garden tools. Everything was either covered by a tarp in the yard, with a rattlesnake hiding underneath, stuck under the house gathering black widows, or leaned against a wall getting fried in the sun. And if I wanted to build something in the winter, I had to work on it in the house. It was time to get organized.

I'm a single working gal barely making ends meet, so I have to watch every penny. My MO for outbuildings is to use low-cost materials and do the labor myself but finish them off in such a way as to be fairly attractive. Stud-frame construction is so straightforward and uncomplicated that almost anyone with rudimentary skills and a few basic tools can do it. I tend to build as simply and as easily as possible, but the bottom line is *sturdy*.

The 12' x 16' shop took three months to build in my spare time, and the 6' x 12' toolshed only one month—just a blink of sawdust in the eye—and now they're forever useful on a daily basis. They cost $1,500 and $600 respectively, which amounted to about $500 per month in extra expenditures for four months. It stretched my budget, but at least I avoided the expense of a building permit. (In my county a permit isn't required if the structure is under 200 square feet.)

I checked prices at the local Home Depot and found a comparably sized 6' x 12' shed *kit* for $2,000. It was a shell, unfinished inside and with no insulation. I built mine, completely finished inside, for less than a third of that. I can only imagine what the shop would have cost had I hired it done!

My first step is always visualization, which leads to inspiration, which ultimately leads to a lot of perspiration. I sketch a little plan on scratch paper using standard dimensional lumber as my guide (to eliminate waste and complications), make a list of materials, drive to the lumberyard in my old pickup, and get started. When loading and unloading materials, sawing, drilling, hammering, bending, lifting, climbing ladders, panting, and groaning, I pretend to be at the fitness center getting a full-body workout—in Levi's instead of tights—without leaving home or paying a membership fee. Trouble is, I miss gawking at the good-looking guys; my only social life is provided by the dog.

The nice thing about working alone at a snail's pace (I *am* slow and deliberate) is that I have time to think ahead. I don't plan every detail on paper, but let the process dictate what to do next. I frame a doorway, for instance, to fit an odd-sized recycled door I've been saving. Same with windows. If I'm not sure how to make a stud-frame corner so it has a nailing surface for the inner-wall sheathing too, I look it up in a how-to-do-it book. I fasten everything together with screws, so if I have to take it back apart, I can. Screws hold better than nails, and using a drill is less trauma to the joints than pounding with a hammer.

I just keep plugging along, measuring carefully, sawing straight, and making sure every step is plumb, level, and square. As hard as I try, I still make mistakes, but ultimately the job gets done in a reasonable amount of time, looks good, and serves its purpose. I love beauty, but I'm also practical; I try to combine the two concepts on a shoestring budget—*backwoods home* style.

Part I: Shop

There was an existing concrete slab on the property poured years ago for something that never got built, so I used it for the shop foundation. With the highest grade of heavy-duty construction adhesive available, I glued pressure-treated 2" x 4"s around the 12' x 16' perimeter of the slab. Next I built the frame with 2" x 4"s at 2 feet on center (OC). I sheathed the framed walls while they were down on the floor *before* erecting them into place. Then I fastened the raised walls with 3-inch screws to the pressure-treated (PT) base-plate every 12 inches, and to each other at the corners. The next step was putting up the 2" x 6" rafters at 2 feet OC and the important rafters ties. The 2" x 6" ties at 4 feet OC spanned across the tops of the walls to stabilize the structure, and provided a nailing surface for the ceiling boards.

I wired the building inside the wall cavities by tapping into an existing circuit breaker in a nearby outbuilding. After installing the fiberglass insulation, which also covered the wiring, I put up the inside 4' x 8' sheets of 7/16-inch oriented strand board (OSB) sheathing. Then I put up 1" x 12" x 16' pine ceiling boards for a touch of beauty, and also to serve as a strong wood surface from which to hang the fluorescent light fixture.

I roofed with inexpensive rolled roofing—quick and easy.

I used an old recycled glass-paned door as the back door of the shop and built a 4' x 7.5' door from 1" x 4" cheap utility-grade pine for the front door opening.

Last but not least, I built a long, narrow deck set on piers, with pressure treated 4" x 4" runners fastened to the top of the piers, and topped it off with 2" x 6" Douglas fir (DF) decking.

When all the construction work was done, I cut 2-inch-wide battens out of leftover OSB sheathing and screwed them on vertically 12 inches apart for a decorative board-and-batt look. I then painted everything inside and out, including the floor, for a light-colored clean look.

The final work entailed installing L-brackets and shelving to hold all the tools, paint cans, and hardware supplies. I used old recycled I-beam floor joists (BCIs) for the shelves. They have a built-in lip so things can't fall off the edge—and the price was right (free from a local contractor's building site). Mission accomplished.

Part II: Garden-Tool Shed

I leveled a conveniently located spot as best I could by hand and then drove my pickup to a landscape supplier and got a cubic yard of construction-grade sand. Sand is a good base because it has 100 percent compaction if left undisturbed under a building. It didn't take long to unload it and distribute the piers on the bed of sand in their approximate rows. Using stakes and strings as guides for squaring and leveling the piers with each other, I put more sand underneath the low ones and wiggled the high ones down into the sand. The perimeter strings kept me inside the foundation's 6' x 12' boundary.

The next step was a piece of cake—setting the pressure-treated (PT) 2" x 4"s in the pier slots and connecting the perimeter all around with PT 2" x 6"s.

I decked the floor framing with DF 2" x 6"s and laid out the first wall frame on the nice flat surface, fastening the studs to the top and bottom plates at 2 inches OC with 3-inch screws.

Just like the shop construction, I built all the 2" x 4" wall frames while they were down on the floor, then erected them on site and fastened them to the floor with screws, and to each other at the corners. After I stood the back wall up *plumb*, I braced it on each side with a diagonal 1" x 4" attached to the top side of the back wall and the low front-side of the platform, until I got

the sidewalls up. I wanted double doors, so I put up a 6"
x 8" x 5' header over the 5-foot opening and supported
it with an extra 2" x 4" stud (called a *jack)* fastened to
the door-frame stud on each side. Headers provide roof
support over wide spans.

Rafters were next: 2" x 4"s set at 16 inches OC. Hurricane ties on both ends secured them in place.

I sheathed the outside walls and the roof with OSB
and put the fiberglass insulation in. Then I sheathed the
inside of the shed and even the wood floor with OSB—to
protect it against dirty tools, grease, and oil. I can remove
or replace the OSB anytime, and the wood floor will stay
fresh and clean underneath.

I built a ramp out of PT 2" x 4"s and decked it with
DF 2" x 4"s.

To match the shop that's only 50 feet away, I made
2-inch-wide battens out of OSB to repeat the theme of the
board-and-batt look.

I bought two narrow old doors from a builder's bargain
outlet for only $10 each and decorated them with OSB Xs
cut out of four single sheets of OSB (only $6 each) stacked
on top of each other, marked with a template, and cut all
at once.

I splashed a coat of paint on the entire structure, inside
and out, and again roofed with cheap rolled roofing.

I installed a door latch, then U-brackets to cradle the
garden tool handles so the tools can stand up in a row
along the back wall.

I'm still moving the tools in a few at a time as I dig
them out from their hiding places all over the property.

It feels so good to be organized!

Cost of materials, generously rounded up to cover any
overages (2007):

SHOP:

Framing for walls and roof. $350
Sheathing for entire shop (40 sheets of OSB). . .$250
Insulation (R-13 fiberglass) $150
Pine ceiling (optional). $150
Electrical wiring and materials $200
Doors and hardware $150
Rolled roofing $50
Paint $50
Shelving brackets. $50
Deck. $100
Total **$1,500**

Note: For a shop on a pier foundation like the shed's, add $300.

SHED:

Sand. $25
Pier & PT beam foundation (4" x 4"s & 2" x 6"s). . . .$125
Floor decking (DF 2" x 6"s). $75
Framing for walls and roof (all 2" x 4"s. $100
Sheathing (15 sheets of 7/16" OSB). $100
Insulation (R-13 fiberglass) $50
Rolled roofing $25
Paint $25
Doors and hardware $50
Ramp $25
Total **$600**

CHAPTER 25

BUILD A TREE HOUSE

Zane's tree house

There's nothing like a grandchild to bring you out of your comfort zone. There IS no middle ground. It's either down on your knees or up in the trees. When Zane was four we played on the floor, but when he was five he took to the sky, and that's when this grandma decided he needed a tree house.

His Uncle Eric offered to help build it and volunteered to do the hardest part of the construction. He was inspired to get involved, not only to do something special for his nephew, but because it was a perfect opportunity to be a kid again himself. I'm sure a lot of moms and dads out there feel the same way, but whatever the motivation, building a tree house is a fantastic family project.

The Planning Stage

I live on ten acres and have three big oak trees on my property. We chose the best one of the bunch for accommodating a tree house. It had a double trunk and five major outstretched branches, like an open hand just waiting to hold a tiny house full of squealing kids.

Eric took measurements and sketched a simple plan dictated by the shape of the tree and the orientation of its thicker vertical arms and smaller forked horizontal limbs. The main load would be supported by the five leaders coming off the huge trunks. The platform would have to be strong and sturdy but flexible enough to sway with the tree in a breeze. And all this would be 12 feet off the ground. Eric's reasoning was: "Why build house in a *tree* if you're not up high enough to feel a little giddy?" Made perfect sense to me.

We decided on a 6' x 8' clubhouse on a 9.5' x 12' base, with the house set far enough back on the platform to create a 4-foot landing at the top of the ladder for kids to come and go with ease. The house would be surrounded by a 20-inch-wide deck with 36-inch-high railings and safety netting all around, except for access to a fireman's pole on one side and a slide on the other. A vertical ladder close to the trunk would keep it looking streamlined and give the kids a real workout going up, up, up after the easy rides down, down, down.

Additional playground equipment would include knotted *Tarzan* ropes hanging from thick horizontal limbs, and a big swing suspended by ropes long enough to create an arc that could catapult a daredevil into the next county!

The tree house would have a door as well as screened window openings to keep mosquitoes out on hot summer overnighters, but with shutters to close on cold, rainy days. A hinged bed/table platform with a flat military style mattress would fold up against the wall when not in use.

Division of Labor

I could tell that Eric was itching to get started, and his enthusiasm was infectious, so I appointed myself the *gopher* to run after supplies, trek back and forth with tools and boards, and try to throw said tools up to the *monkey* perched in the tree. "Try" is the key word. Eric miraculously avoided injury from my many spastic attempts (and they were worth a lot of laughs), but I finally had to use the ladder to expedite the process. Zane and his mom were coming to visit soon, and I had promised them a big surprise!

Things to Consider

Building a low-positioned tree house is no problem, but building a tree house *way* up high is logistically challenging. Planks have to be hoisted up with ropes or carried up ladders (think *Swiss Family Robinson,* 1807) and then leveled and fastened while straddling branches and pushing against thin air to put screws in with a cordless drill (*Swiss Family Robinson,* 2007).

The initial work can be downright uncomfortable. I noticed on several occasions that Eric's feet would be facing one way, crammed into narrow crotches in the tree, and his body would be twisted in the exact opposite direction, like a tornado had flung him there. We concluded that there is no need for yoga classes when you build a tree house.

Tips and Techniques

Every family's tree house project will be unique, but what follows are some basics we learned:

Pick a tree that has easy access and is close enough to the house for safety reasons, or at least within earshot to hear cries for help, which sound different from the usual cacophony of screaming and laughing. Adult supervision is mandatory for young children.

Pick a healthy tree and don't damage it—tree wounds do not heal well. Never girdle the trunk or a branch with a tight rope or chain or wire, or cut the bark away all around it. Girdling will kill the tree.

Screw as *few* lag bolts as possible into the tree to secure the first 2" x 6" or 2" x 8" supporting plank of the platform, be it a rectangle, square, triangle, trapezoid, or whatever. Then lash or screw the other framing members to that plank and to each other to finish the framing. Cut away just enough bark to make a flat spot for the lag bolt and its washer.

Trees continually grow, and they move every which way in the wind, so your joinery has to be able to withstand some flexing. If your floor is a rectangle, this can be achieved by securing only *one side* of the rectangle (a 2" x 6" or 2" x 8" on edge) to the trunk and/or to a vertical limb of the tree with ½" x 4" or 5" lag bolts, but the other three sides have to be *free floating*. Those three boards that complete the rectangle will rest on 3-inch heavy-gauge L-brackets that are attached to the tree with shorter, less-invasive ¼-inch-diameter screws.

When the tree moves, the three unanchored boards of the rectangle will ride and slide on the flat surfaces of the L-brackets. You may have to place shims or blocks behind some of the brackets to fill in gaps (curves or dips in the tree) to get the bracket out to where the board *can* ride on it.

It's important to keep everything plumb, level, and square as you go along—as best you can. A string level works well, or you can use a long, straight 2" x 4" with a level on top of it, or a laser level, to span greater distances. You may need a helper for this initial step of the project—to mark the tree while you hold the level.

After the rectangular frame is secured, you will fill it in with a grid of floor joists, straddling vertical branches here and there if you need to. Then you'll top it off with plywood or planks to complete the platform. Eric had to custom fit his floorboards around several vertical trunk-like branches. He *scribed* the circular cutaways to ensure accuracy, then, using a jigsaw, cut them a little larger to allow for tree growth. These massive, nonstructural *trunks* coming right up through the deck add to the Zen-like feeling that you and the tree are *one*.

If you will be circling a single trunk with framing members that radiate out to support your floor, you won't have to worry about the challenge of multiple trunks and vertical limbs that move independently and exert uneven stresses on a structure that could ultimately pull it apart. Eric's ingenious solution to our problem required extra work and accuracy, but the tree house has stood the test of time, through many seasons of high winds and snow loads, without any damage.

Building Materials and Finish Work

Keep in mind the platform is the base of the whole structure. To distribute the weight and keep the total weight of the structure down so your tree won't have to creak and groan, spread the load over as wide an area as possible. After all, it *is* alive. Use the smallest dimensional lumber you can get by with and still maintain strength and durability; even lightweight materials add up. To avoid waste and save time, labor, and money, use common-sized lumber and sheathing whenever possible.

Eric used 2" x 6"s 16 inches apart for the floor framing and 2" x 6"s for the floorboards themselves. He used 2" x 4" studs 24 inches apart for the walls and 16 inches apart for the rafters. He sheathed the structure (walls and roof) with ⁷⁄₁₆-inch oriented strand board (OSB), which is commonly used for construction nowadays because it's lighter and cheaper than plywood. Then he roofed with inexpensive asphalt shingles.

To add a touch of English Tudor style to the house, I fastened narrow battens (cut from OSB) vertically a foot apart on the exterior walls.

The inner walls aren't insulated, but I caulked every crack and spray-glued 1.5-inch-diameter foam-pipe insulation to every seam where wind might blow in. Then I caulked the tubes securely in place.

When that was completed, I painted inside and out with *tree-trunk-gray* so the little house would look like an integral part of the tree. For contrast I painted the battens a lighter shade of the same color and the deck a darker shade.

Together, Eric and I fashioned railings from ¾" iron pipe and fittings and attached them with pipe flanges screwed to the outside planks (rim joists) of the platform.

Eric had fun building the door out of utility-grade 1" x 4"s lamination style: One face is all verticals, the other face all horizontals. The two faces are fastened together with a lot of screws. This method is strong, *doesn't warp*, and can be cut to any shape you like. To allow taller *kids* (i.e., adults) to fit through without ducking, ours was custom cut to the gable roof angle.

Details

The heavy-duty wooden ladder was supported off the ground by piers precast with brackets. This ensured that the bottom of the legs wouldn't rot. (We had recessed the piers into wet concrete on a pad we poured in place.) The ladder also doubled as an extra support for the platform.

The galvanized 1.5-inch-diameter fireman's pole (for small hands) was also set in a deep hole filled with concrete that Eric mixed in a wheelbarrow and poured in place. At the bottom of the pole is a large area of soft sand for the kids to land in. The pipe fittings that connect the pole to the deck also support the side of the platform that has the longest free-floating span.

The slide is built from ¾-inch plywood and 2" x 6" runners. The surface is factory-painted sheet metal, for a nice slick surface. (Galvanized sheet metal is *not* good for sliding on.) I built it at a 35-degree angle so it would be fast but not too fast. Metal pipes are bolted to the lower end of the slide and set in concrete for support. The slide is 24 inches wide and 12 feet long, but the length of your slide will depend on the height of your tree house platform.

The swing seat is a piece of 2" x 10" that's 24 inches long, with holes set 2 inches in from each end to put ¾-inch knotted ropes through, and suspended from a branch above with that rope.

I came across a perfect-sized carpet remnant for $5 at a garage sale and glued it to the tree house floor to keep wind from whistling up through the cracks, while providing a soft place for the kids to play on indoors.

We rigged up an old metal bucket to a block and tackle with ropes to create a dumbwaiter to go from ground to deck so the kids could transport food, toys, and my little dog "Peaches" up and down all day long. This contraption was the biggest hit of all!

Total Cost of Building the Tree House

Cost of materials—about $500.
Cost of labor—one sore arm from throwing like a girlie-girl.

Two Works in Progress: Ours and Mrs. Robin's

Last summer while building the tree house, we got the chance to observe a mother robin raising three consecutive families in a nest hidden deeply in a hole in the upper tree trunk close to where we were working. We respected her privacy but couldn't help peeking down the hole with a flashlight occasionally to watch the progression from blue eggs to tiny naked babies with wide-open beaks, to little pin-feathered creatures fluttering out of the hole, to fully feathered robins flying away—all in a span of only two weeks after the eggs hatched. A birds-eye view of the life cycle of *three* nests of robins was a serendipitous and delightful gift from nature, not unlike what we all witness as our *own* kids (and grandkids) are growing up.

Closing Thoughts

Eric keeps reminding me that this high-rise *Room with a View* isn't just for children. We adults and our fine *un*feathered friends might want to reserve the *Old-Oak Hotel* once in a while just for a change of scenery—to read a book, have a picnic, spend the night, or howl at the moon. In the event that happens, I made a sign for the tree house door: "No Kids Allowed"—with a backwards "s," of course, so the kids can read it.

CHAPTER 26

TEACH YOUR KIDS TO USE TOOLS

Zane, six, building a fort

Kids have an incredibly low boredom threshold. That's why they are so attracted to the fast-paced virtual world of TV and video games. Their little coconut heads are compact computers just waiting to be programmed. They are born with a built-in operating system consisting of a hard drive (genetic predispositions and yet-unused storage vault) and lots of RAM (for processing everyday experiences). They can readily accommodate all the specialized software and files of information that their parents can lovingly import. If *you* don't program their brains, somebody else *will*. The giant sponge analogy fits best; kids soak up whatever comes along.

I believe in teaching kids from a young age some practical real-life skills—such as how to cook and sew and build things using real tools. When my grandson Zane was just three we started with hammering nails into a 2" x 6" board that had tiny predrilled holes in it. That way he could get the nails started without frustration, then wail away on them with a small but *real* hammer. (Of course, he was never done until *all* the nails were gone.) After some practice, he discovered on his own that he could hit the nail head better if he used the hammer with one hand instead of both. Look out!

At age four he graduated to using a small cordless drill to predrill his *own* holes, then put screws in the board. It wasn't long before he perfected the technique for successfully driving them home. He learned the drill had to be held straight up and down or the driver bit would slip out of the screw head, the *trigger* had to be *feathered* a little as the screw went in, and he had to have his weight pressing down on the drill by being in the right position in the first place. I continually reminded him never to put his hands anywhere they could be injured if he missed his target, and monitored him closely every second. Using the forward and reverse buttons was his favorite thing, and good exercise for his brain. I could see the wheels turning each time he paused to contemplate which button did what. He was a quick study, and his coordination developed to an amazing degree by age four and a half.

When he was five we sawed boards with fine-toothed handsaws, used clamps to hold them in place, and learned how to use sockets and wrenches on nuts and bolts to fasten his contraptions together. We assembled pipe fittings for fun, but also for the hidden lesson of righty-tighty, lefty-loosey.

Zane is almost seven now and looks like a pro when using tools. He draws his own plans of things he'd like to make, and we collaborate on the feasibility of his ideas, which are usually outrageously creative but impossible to build. We end up reaching a compromise, which sometimes involves tears, but it's all part of the learning experience of being realistic if you're going to be a do-it-yourselfer. Then I help him measure and mark cut-lines with a carpenter's square, and we proceed with caution. Recently, with close supervision, I let him use the electric jigsaw to cut his boards to length.

We work on a project, try to finish what we set out to do, clean up the site, and put the tools away. Zane knows I'm a stickler for perseverance, so he can't just run off when the going gets tough. In the planning stage, I take into consideration his attention span, but if I miscalculate, we find a good stopping point. Grandma is flexible because, after all, I'm there for *him*. It's not about *me*.

Kids are extremely capable—much more so than we think they are or give them credit for. Biology itself dictates the true nature of children: I've never met a child, even an older baby, who didn't want to *do it him or her self*, whatever *it* is. Children are adamant about that, and we, as parents and grandparents, should take heed of it and restrain ourselves from being overly helpful.

Kids appreciate acknowledgement and moral support, but they need to suffer their own mistakes and celebrate their own successes. I believe we unwittingly rob them of the self-esteem and confidence that comes with *real live* accomplishments by doing too much *for* them. If we give in to their demands for instant gratification, it can retard the development of their character.

The *process* of creating something with their own two hands, and sticking with it until it's finished, is infinitely more valuable than the object itself. The object is just the frosting; their inner growth and satisfaction is the cake.

Kids need to *earn* their *own* approval. All the *I-love-you's* and praise in the world from the outside in doesn't do it, although encouragement definitely helps spur them on. Confidence and self-esteem are earned in small increments over time, and there is no shortcut to feeling good from the inside out.

A sensitive child can be damaged if a well-meaning parent isn't careful, so it's very important to use suggestions instead of criticism during the teaching/learning process. Hurt feelings can be more devastating than a cut finger; the finger will heal. Patience (beyond belief) is mandatory when working with small children.

Every chance I get I have Zane help me in the kitchen. From the time he was three and a half we made pies and cookies and bread—all from scratch. Zane held the apples with a fork with one hand while, with the other, he sliced them with a sharp paring knife. No problem—no accidents. I was the monitor lizard. He rolled out the pie dough with a rolling pin and fluted the edges all around the top crust with his tiny fingers, while his tongue stuck out on one side from extreme concentration.

Sure, it's more work than sending the kids off to play or to watch TV while you make the pie yourself, but the *experience*—teaching them how, the giggling that ensues during the process, and eating the pie together after it comes out of the oven—is priceless!

We all love those old-fashioned movies and stories and pictures of moms and grandmas in the kitchen with the kids laughing and getting in the act. Well, you can create your *own* good old-fashioned memories by doing exactly that with your own kids in your own kitchen. It can be quite the bonding experience.

A Case in Point

One hot summer day when Zane was five we decided to make strawberry smoothies in the blender. We went to the store in my old granny pickup and bought an entire flat of fresh strawberries and a half-gallon of vanilla ice cream. We were *thinkin' big*!

We rushed home, washed them, cut the stems off, cut them in half, and piled them into the blender. Zane was on his regular booster stool at the butcher block, helping every step of the way. We were a team! I let him press the *grind* button over and over so we could fit more and more strawberries in. Oink! Oink! Next we added some ice cream and a little milk and put the lid on. Then Zane kept pressing the loud whirring *liquify* button (his favorite of course) until the delicious pink frothy concoction was bubbling out of the lid.

He was leaning *waaay* over against the block to stabilize the vibrating blender by hanging onto its handle with *both* hands. We were drooling and licking our lips anticipating how good it was going to taste, when all of a sudden Zane's stool slipped out from under him and the blender went along for the ride. Our precious strawberry smoothie splattered *everywhere* like a giant paint ball! Zane ended up flat on his back in the middle of the mess with pink foam dripping from his eyelashes.

We were frozen in absolute shock—for a few moments. Then we laughed...and laughed...and laughed...until our bellies ached. To this day we call ourselves *The Disaster Team*.

Going to McDonald's to buy a ready-made smoothie? Not very exciting. Our memorable experience? *Priceless*!

Zane and I do all kinds of things together. I've let him steer my old truck (since he was two) when going five miles per hour on my dirt road. I've allowed him to sew on my 1929 Singer sewing machine since he was five. He learned to thread it, sew in a straight line, and use the reverse lever to bind the end of the seam.

Déjà vu. His mother made her first little apron on a Singer Featherweight when she was a featherweight herself—at six. Son Eric was a mad scientist, and I encouraged it. He loved microscopes, telescopes, experiments, and the piano. Cynthia was into gymnastics, springboard diving, guitar, and horses. Everything was *real*—including the chemistry explosions *and* the horse sneaking (coaxed?) into the house when I wasn't home!

One thing I know for sure is that kids lose interest fast in plastic toys and/or tools that don't *do* anything. They like to be challenged, and they seem to lose respect for anything that can't potentially *hurt* them. As soon as they instantly figure out that a big yellow plastic saw can't cut their fingers or the furniture, they throw it down and run off to stick their finger in a light socket. It's nature's way.

Mom and Dad's *stuff* is infinitely more fascinating because adult tools aren't toys. That why I encourage parents to introduce their curious kids, who want to feel *all grown up*, into the world of working for some of the things they want and actually creating them out of raw materials.

The most important point I want to *emphasize* is that

every child is a unique individual with his or her own interests, abilities, personality traits, and timetable for learning. And every parent has his or her own parenting style and interests and things to teach that may have nothing to do with hammering and sawing. Steven Spielberg's mom gave *him* a movie camera to play with when he was a child—and we all know the rest of the story.

It's all about being *tuned in* to your children's interests and talents and giving them the special time and attention they crave, while at the same time providing the opportunity to learn real-life skills and feel good about their accomplishments. What could be better than *that* combo?

Anything that keeps kids active and productive and learning I am all for, but energetic activities should be balanced out with plenty of downtime for reading and playing and loving. Daydreaming can be just as important as busy work—for us too.

Closing Thoughts

Parents know their own children best. If you think your child isn't ready to handle certain tools without injury, I wouldn't recommend doing some of the things I let Zane do. When teaching your child how to work with tools—whether in the kitchen, the shop, the garage, or the great outdoors—I can't stress enough that you should provide patient guidance, close supervision, and sensible safety precautions above all other considerations.

My motto for working with kids is, "Hover, but don't smother." Accidents may happen, but so far *The Disaster Team* has had only one biggie piggie mishap!

Note: You can see a video of three-year-old Zane making an apple pie at www.dorothyainsworth.com.

CHAPTER 27

BUILD A HYBRID GO-KART FOR KIDS FOR $150

Zane "Andretti" Cruz

G randma Clara used to delight in telling us the story of our dad's first complete sentence at age two when he received a toy car for Christmas: "It's got *gears!*" I guess it was the *way* he said it, with the long, drawn-out emphasis on *geeeeers* that made it so memorable—and laughable.

Little did they know at the time, but his enthusiastic burst of joy over those little wooden cogs revealed his interest in and passion for all things mechanical that would manifest itself in creative projects and inventions throughout his life (1914 to 1994).

He ended up with six kids and worked as an auto mechanic to feed his hungry horde, but that didn't put a damper on his creative side. When he was home he was forever building boats, painting beautiful oil landscapes, and making sure all six of us were happily *mobile*. Being a mechanical genius of sorts, he prided himself on never having to spend any money to keep us on wheels. (As the sole breadwinner for eight, he didn't *have* any money.)

We enjoyed a *poor-man's fleet*: doodlebugs (motor-scooters) for the older kids and go-karts for the younger ones. He built them out of lawnmower engines, drive-chains, and *geeeers*. At age seven, I remember riding my gas-powered doodlebug over to Lota Jean's house to play, and she would try to keep up with me on her fancy bicycle. Mom called her "the poor little rich girl" because she had *everything*—but a doodlebug. I had *nothing* but a doodlebug—and a really cool family.

We all grew up and graduated to cars and motorcycles and had kids of our own, but some of us carried on the family tradition of scrounging for parts and building something from nothing. Even if whatever it was ended up looking like a contraption, at least it worked, and we had fun with it.

My older brother Gene—professional deep-sea diver, astronomer (telescope maker), builder, artist, cartoonist, writer, poet, musician, and tinkerer/inventor—added *grandfather* to the list a few years ago.

When his grandson turned five, he decided to build him a go-kart in the low-budget Ainsworth tradition. But not just any old go-kart—a *hybrid* go-kart! *Gene would go green* just for the challenge of it. He also wanted the project to be a learning experience for the little guy, so he could see how an engine works and how the linkage is hooked up to drive the wheels. To give inquisitive kids something to ask questions about, he wanted the parts visible (moving or not).

When I visited my daughter, Cynthia, and then seven-year-old grandson, Zane, in Hollywood in the summer of 2008, we went to visit Uncle Gene just to ride the go-kart. It was great fun and well worth the hundred-mile drive. The *jalopy* runs on a lawn-mower engine but can be switched over to run quietly (and slowly) off the battery if a younger child is intimidated by the sound and speed of the gas engine. Zane tried both and found the gas-powered mode to be as fast as he dared to go.

Gene said he'd be happy to share the sketched plans and how-to info with *Backwoods Home* magazine readers, so in this article, with his help, I'll do my best to basically illustrate how to build this thing. The specs and photos will have to tell the story.

Please note that you will need some degree of mechanical understanding and ability, and some experience and skill in using tools, to construct it. This article is simply the documentation and illustration of a prototype that Gene fashioned out of new and used parts as he went along. It cost only $150.

Feel free to alter the dimensions and make any other changes you want to customize it to fit your needs. If you have money to burn, you can make this go-kart as fancy as you desire. Build a body, a sheet metal cowling and fenders, and add paint and pin striping, or anything you else you might dream up.

Basic Construction Specs

1. CHASSIS: 1-inch box steel tubing for main chassis and 2-inch channel iron for rear cross member;

⅝-inch plywood for floorboards. All steel members are welded (best way) but could be bolted together if welder is not available.

2. ENGINE: 2-hp Briggs and Stratton gas engine with centrifugal clutch (lawn-mower engine). *Not* a rotary engine, but the self-propelled type of lawnmower engine. Get any size hp engine you want. Gene wanted a small engine without too much power—for a young child. Common sizes are 3 to 5 hp. You can find 2-hp engines only in older lawnmowers. At top speed it runs at 3,600 rpm, but with the 4-to-1 pulley ratio, it runs at 3,000 rpm and delivers about 1.5 hp. The pulleys determine the *gearing*: how fast it takes off and how fast it goes. A 5-to-1 pulley ratio would have a faster top speed.

3. ELECTRIC DRIVE: Delco-Remy 30-amp, 12-volt DC generator, which acts as a 12-volt DC motor when armature and fields are excited by a battery-supplied 12-volt current (hence *generator/motor*). The generator/motor is limited by the 12-volt battery output so it produces only about ½ hp, just enough to give a small child a thrill. If you can make room for it, use a 12-volt DC battery from an electric-start riding lawn mower, or a large motorcycle battery, or a regular car battery.

You might wonder what the difference is between an electric motor and an electric generator. The answer is technically *no difference*. If you connect a 13-volt generator to a 12-volt car battery, it'll run just like a motor with a slow-turning shaft. Apply mechanical power—hook it up to the gas motor via pulleys and a belt off the shafts—and it works as a generator that recharges the battery because the shaft is now turning fast.

The catch is, you have to put a voltage-regulator between the battery and the generator. The regulator has two relays inside it. One relay keeps the generator from over-charging the battery when the shaft is turning fast and the other relay disconnects the battery from the generator when the shaft is turning slowly and starts to drain the battery. Hence the name, *regulator*. By flipping a switch, this *hybrid* go-kart works in either mode.

4. WHEELS: Fronts are 7-inch-diameter ball-bearing-type wheels on independent steering axles made from a 1.5-inch-diameter steel rod. Rears are 10-inch-diameter wheels on ¾-inch iron pipe. Both sets have hard-rubber tires, but air tires offer a smoother ride if you have a bumpy road.

5. DIMENSIONS: Approximately 2 feet wide and 4 feet long, but you can make it any size that will accommodate all the parts and accessories to work in unison in a practical compatible design.

6. COMPONENTS:
   - On/off toggle switch for electric motor drive.
   - Voltage regulator for charging battery when in gas-engine mode.
   - Voltmeter and ammeters for monitoring battery voltage and charging rate. When I asked Gene why it has a voltmeter *and* an ammeter, he said the voltmeter shows battery *voltage* during charge and discharge mode; the ammeter shows *rate* of discharge during electric motor mode, and *rate* of charge during gas-engine mode. Be sure to get a *center-off* ammeter.
   - Chain drive with 4-to-1 sprocket ratio and centrifugal clutch for the gas engine.
   - Electric V-belt drive with 4-to-1 ratio on pulleys for the electric motor/generator and for battery

charging.

- Brake (hand brake): a V-belt drag-type (sheave) on rear axle, activated by cable and pull-bar. A sheave is a pulley with a V-belt loosely around it, with the opposite side fastened to the frame and rear axle. When you pull on a lever or press on a foot pedal, it puts friction on the sheave and acts as a brake.
- Tie-rod-type direct-ratio steering on front independent axles.
- Spring-loaded aluminum bumpers front and rear made from 2-inch angle stock.
- 12-volt DC headlight and switch.
- Seatbelt, roll bar, and stepped-up seat on back for adult passenger.
- Squeeze-bulb air horn or electric horn with a horn button (easy to wire to the battery). The latter are plentiful at wrecking yards. Funsies for the kids!

Construction Sequence

1. Assemble and weld chassis frame.
2. Mount axles, wheels, and steering linkage to shaft and steering wheel.
3. Mount large pulley, sprocket, and brake drag pulley on rear axle pipe.
4. Install gas engine and motor/generator. Align small pulley and sprocket with counterparts on rear axle.
5. Mount voltage regulator gauges and switches. Wire to battery (#10 wire) and install headlight and horn (#16 wire). Headlight and horn are optional but look *cool* to the kids.

6. Weld seat frame and roll bar. Mount seats.
7. Install plywood floorboards.
8. Install bumpers.
9. Ride, Sally, ride!

Suggested Sources for Materials:

1. Engine: lawn-mower repair shop, want ads for cheap used lawn mowers, or recycling yards at the dump. An ideal bargain would be a discarded riding mower that had not only the engine but the front axle and steering mechanism still intact.
2. Generator/motor: auto parts store or generator/alternator repair shop, wrecking yard, or recycling yard at the dump.
3. Battery: Walmart, lawn-mower shop, automotive department in big variety store, or wrecking yards. If you can't find a *good* used one, buy a new one with a long life you can depend on.
4. Wheels: Ace Hardware or from lawn mowers in recycling yards. For a softer ride, use air tires (tube tires) instead of hard rubber tires. Look for either.
5. Belts and pulleys: Ace Hardware or automotive shops, such as Napa Auto Parts.
6. Chain sprockets and chain: lawn-mower shop or recycling yards.
7. Box tubing and channel iron: welding supply, but cheaper at scrap-iron yards or iron-and-steel works. (See yellow pages.) Ace hardware, Home Depot, and Lowe's have assorted-angle iron and aluminum.
8. Plywood: lumberyards and other building supply places, such as Home Depot and Lowe's (open weekends).

Dorothy Ainsworth

9. Wire: Napa Auto Parts, Lowe's, Home Depot, and hardware stores. Use #10 copper-stranded wire where indicated on the wiring diagram (including ground wires) and #16 copper-stranded everywhere else. Stranded is easier to work with than solid.

10. Switches: Install a 20-amp switch (somewhere that's handy) between the two wires from the battery terminal and the armature terminal on the voltage regulator. Make sure it's a *momentary switch* (spring-loaded) so when it's released, it kills the engine instantly. The headlight switch can be a 2- or 3-amp toggle switch, and the horn a 2-amp button switch.

Scrounge materials anywhere you can think of. With a little luck and ingenuity, the go-kart shouldn't cost over $150.

Buckle up and wear a helmet.

Good luck, and happy motoring!

CHAPTER 28

EAT WELL BUT SPEND LESS:
High-Energy, High-Nutrition, Low-Cost Diet

If you eat like there's no tomorrow, there won't be

I was raised on beans and I still love 'em. My mom figured out how to feed her impoverished family of eight on almost no money. She cooked a pot of beans *every day*. She bought bread, milk, margarine, potatoes, and occasionally some meat, but that was about it. We had a garden for greens and kept a few chickens for eggs. Her idea of variety was deciding which type of beans to cook each day: pinks, pintos, or limas.

We lived in southern California off and on from 1942 to 1960. Back then, oranges, tomatoes, and avocados were abundant and free, and we ate our fill daily. In fact, we were *so* healthy and robust there were never *any* doctor bills. Some people would call it luck, but I attribute it to our peasant diet—and all that vitamin C.

Mom let us dip into the simmering vat of beans *whenever* we were hungry, night or day. It wouldn't spoil our dinner—it *was* our dinner.

To supplement the beans, especially in winter, she would fry up huge skillets of raw grated potatoes with celery and onions and we would each wait our turn to get a big sizzling slab (browned and crispy around the edges) on our plate as fast as she could cook each batch. We could feel the heat rising to our flushed faces as we refueled. Talk about energy packed—we were jet-propelled!

Note: Beans are rich in protein, complex carbohydrates, and cholesterol-reducing fiber. One cup of dried pinto beans contains 7 grams of protein, 60 percent of your daily requirement of fiber, B vitamins, and eight essentials minerals, including lots of calcium and iron, and much more. All this for only 25 cents and 100 calories. Mom was smart!

Beans keep well. I stored 25 pounds of pinto beans in a bucket with a tight lid for twenty-seven years (forgot I had them!), but when I finally cooked them in 2002, the soup was perfect. Nobody would have guessed they were vintage 1975.

How to Eat Well on $6.50/Day

In this article I'm going to share with you how, to this day, one person can live on about $200 per month in food—

good, nutritionally dense food, that, to me and anyone I cook for, is downright delicious.

A typical day for me starts with hot cereal I call *cruel gruel*: seven-grain cereal mixed with thick-rolled oats (*neigh*) from the bulk-food department of a local grocery store that consistently has the lowest prices in town. With milk and a little butter on it, my breakfast costs about $1 and is very filling. I would be just as happy with two scrambled eggs and a piece of toast, totaling only 50 cents.

Lunch may be a can of tuna (58 cents on sale) on one slice of dense wheat-berry bread, wrapped in lots of dark green romaine lettuce, burrito style. Along with it I sip *or* guzzle a glass of V-8 juice, depending on how much time I have. A five-ounce can of tuna supplies about *half* of the average person's daily protein requirement. Lunch total: $2.

Dinner is a big tossed-green salad, and I mean *big*! And extremely *green*—and *red* and *purple* and *orange*, replete with all the nastiest members of the cruciferous family: shredded cabbage, broccoli, cauliflower, etc. (I don't waste money on pale iceberg lettuce.) I use a low-cost homemade dressing that is really tastier than it sounds: oil, vinegar, tomato sauce, a pinch of sugar, and a few spices. After first gorging on salad to assuage my appetite (*moooo*), I cook a little piece of chicken or fish or some form of beef (usually 10-percent-fat hamburger), or I have soup or beans. Dinner total: $3.

If I feel like a snack before bed, I eat a small bowl of raisin-bran cereal or a tablespoon of peanut butter and honey.

Note: Dinners are a breeze if you plan ahead on the labor-intensive *necessities* such as salads. I make a bus-tray full every Sunday and dip into it all week.

I know, I know, it doesn't sound like the all-American

diet, but it illustrates how a person can actually flourish on good, unrefined food for a few dollars a day. I'm single now, so I can eat as I please, but if you have a family, I know very well that you have to provide bigger and more diversified meals.

However, the experts now say too many choices are making Americans fat, so a person or a family can actually get used to and even come to enjoy fewer choices and still have a well-balanced diet. I happen to *know* that's true, and when you're really hungry, even beans taste like steak!

One other thing I know for sure: We should not waste money on *empty calories*, especially since we're in a recession (as of 2008) that may turn into a depression. If you're not vigilant and discriminating in your choices, the cost of food for your family can be a huge percentage of your income. It's imperative during this recession that you strive to get more nutrition for your dollar.

Everything you put in your mouth should be densely nutritious, with few exceptions—such as when you have an occasional sweet tooth you cannot deny. I understand this (I'm no angel), but even my choices of desserts have redeeming value health-wise.

My Short List of *Nays* If Your Budget Is Tight

- No eating out (one large pizza can cost $30, the same price as a 25-pound bag of beans that will feed a hundred people!)
- No take-out (Chinese food can cost $25 for two, plus the tip!)
- No white (bleached) refined flour or white bread
- No sugary boxed cereals (*puffed nothings*: air, fluff, and sugar)

- No prepared frozen dinners (not even!)
- No packages of cookies and puddings—make 'em from scratch (chemical-free)
- No junk food—period! (I know, that's harsh, but you can make your *own* healthful and delicious sweets.)
- No soft drinks (*ever!*) and no sugary, watered-down juice drinks, including lemonade. Sodas are dangerously full of sugar and chemicals and have no redeeming value whatsoever, and they are expensive. The latest research says *diet* soft drinks in particular are toxic, especially to small children.
- No expensive snacks such as potato chips, corn chips, and crackers with labels that show high calories, high fat, and high salt.
- No hot dogs, lunchmeat, or anything else containing killer nitrites and high levels of saturated fat. Read labels.

My List of *Yays*

- Always splurge whatever extra money you might have on fresh fruits and veggies in season. They aren't a luxury; they are a necessity.
- If fresh is not in season, buy (or produce for yourself) canned or frozen fruits and veggies.
- Buy in bulk (dry grains, beans, brown rice, nuts) and save about half the price. Store in sealed containers.
- Stock up on canned goods on sale (Walmart, Costco, Winco, Food 4 Less, etc.).
- If you have no time or inclination to make your own bread, buy the densest whole grain you can find. My favorite is Oroweat's Honey Wheatberry.

- If your family likes bread at every meal, buy a compact, portable bread-making machine ($50 to $100) and get as creative as you want with flour, grains, nuts, brans, and seeds. You simply put the ingredients in and the machine does the work (including the baking), and you have fresh bread in one to two hours. You'll save lots of money; *nutritious* store-bought bread is $3 to $5 a loaf.
- A deer in the freezer is like money in the bank. I'm not a hunter, but during a recession getting a deer is a great idea. You'll have a freezer full of meat, and venison is lean, clean protein.
- I'm not a farmer, but I believe in planting *edible landscaping*. Even if you live in town, plant fruit and nut trees in your yard and enjoy the free harvest every season. My one almond tree produces a year's supply of almonds—every year!
- Keeping a few chickens (three or four) is easy to manage and will probably provide more eggs than you need for a small family. Eggs contain the highest quality protein there is besides mother's milk, which means *all* the essential amino acids. They also contain thirteen essential nutrients, including vitamins A, B, D, and E as well as the minerals calcium, iodine, and iron. One large egg contains 6.5 grams of protein, is only 75 calories, and costs about 15 cents. Do your family and your budget a favor by serving lots of eggs. Some studies now say the lecithin in the yolk emulsifies and counteracts the fat and can even reduce cholesterol absorption in the bloodstream. But no matter what the controversy is, there's no doubt that eggs are the cheapest super-food there is for growing children.

Tip: Without a noisy rooster, even if you live in town,

keeping a few hens in a backyard pen or letting them range free in a fenced yard won't disturb anybody. I find them delightful.

Cooking for a Family When Short on Time and Money

I've always been in a recession financially (single mom/ waitress), so cooking healthfully on a shoestring budget is my area of expertise. Here are some suggestions for a few good quick and easy meals and desserts:

1. Bake a plain chicken in the oven along with some baked potatoes. It takes five minutes of preparation and an hour to bake. Serve with something green or yellow. Meal for four: $8

2. Make a vat of spaghetti sauce, but not *ordinary* spaghetti sauce. Add every vegetable you can get away with into the hamburger-laden tomato sauce: chopped celery, bell peppers, onions, finely grated carrots, zucchini, mushrooms, finely chopped broccoli, garlic if you like, sliced olives, even finely chopped kale and parsley. Use lots of Italian seasonings, and a combination of stewed tomatoes, tomato sauce, tomato paste, and even mild salsa. Start out with a *big* pot! The more veggies you add the higher the level rises, but keep in mind that they *will* cook down in an hour and will be deceptively camouflaged in the sauce (if you have picky eaters).

Bonus: Now you'll have it on hand for spaghetti and/ or lasagna whenever you want to cook the noodles or your choice of pasta. Grate a little cheese on top and you'll have a tasty, substantial meal with some left over to freeze. It's so loaded with goodies that the only side dish you might complement it with is tender frozen peas. If you buy a large 5-pound *value-pak* of hamburger, this meal will serve eight to ten people. Cost: about $20.

3. Tuna gravy is quick, easy, cheap, and *very* tasty, and can be served on toast or fried potatoes. You simply brown oil and flour in a frying pan, add milk (canned milk diluted with water is good too), stir like crazy so lumps don't form, generously add a few cans of tuna (one per person), and stir some more. Side dish: salad, peas, corn, or green beans. It's satisfying to the core. Meal for four: $6.

4. Another hearty meal that requires almost no time but baking time is an inexpensive cut of beef or pork (such as a chuck roast). Put the meat in a baking pan and cook for about an hour, then add veggies cut in large pieces: unpeeled potatoes and carrots sliced lengthwise, then celery and onions. Bake it all another hour, and it's ready. The veggies simmer in the roast juices. What could be easier and better than that? Meal for six: $10.

5. There's always turkey, and it's always comparatively cheap. Why not bake a turkey *without* the trimmings as often as you please? It makes its own gravy (with a little flour added). Serve with mashed potatoes (real ones) and veggies. Turkey sandwiches for lunches are the best, and *your* sliced turkey won't contain preservatives such as nitrites (known carcinogens) as do the expensive packages of sliced turkey. You can find turkey on sale during the holidays for about $1 per pound. Buy two or three if you can and freeze them for the off-season.

6. Same with ham. Cook a whole ham (on sale), use it for sandwiches, or to flavor the beans (bone and

all), or cut it into small pieces to add along with sautéed vegetables to breakfast omelets.

7. If you and the kids like waffles or pancakes, I recommend Krusteaz Wholewheat & Honey Complete Pancake Mix. I add extra eggs and milk for protein. It's really a superior product and a superior alternative to white biscuit mixes. (Note: Cornbread also has more nutritional value than white biscuits.) Breakfast for four: $4.

8. I'm a big soup-maker. Beef (or pork) barley soup and chicken soup are the ones I'm most *famous* for. I start with simmering the cut-up pieces of chicken (usually breasts or thighs), beef, or pork (cheap cuts), for at least an hour to make them tender and create flavorful broth. Then, as you might imagine, I load the soup with finely chopped veggies and add the cooked noodles, rice, or barley last (so they don't end up overcooked). Soup for several days: $10.

9. If you're gone during the day, buy a large slow cooker for $20 to cook beans in and let them simmer on low all day. Dried beans or dried peas are $1 per pound and one pound will feed a small family. Bean soup or pea soup for four: $1 without meat, $3 with meat.

   For a change of pace, you can make chili beans by adding hamburger sautéed with onions, celery, bell peppers, and chili powder. Chili beans for four: $5.

10. Any kind of meat (or tofu) and veggie *stir-fry*, served over brown rice, is excellent for lunch or dinner. Plan ahead and cook the rice in advance, and you can whip up this meal in fifteen minutes. Stir-fry for four: $8.

Sweet Stuff

The desserts I choose to make are as healthful as possible but at the same time wonderfully delicious. If you're in the mood for dessert, you don't want sweet-tasting particleboard.

1. My favorite is carrot cake, and I'll venture to say my recipe is a good one! (See recipe.) I add more finely grated carrots than the law allows, chopped walnuts, and golden raisins. I top it off with cream-cheese frosting whipped with powered sugar and a few drops of vanilla. It gets rave reviews for moistness and flavor, as does my apple cake (similar ingredients). Large carrot cake: $12. (Not cheap, but worth it.)
2. When making an apple pie (or any kind of pie), I don't mess around. Why go to the work to make pie dough for only a small pie? I make fruit pies in a deep skillet with a long handle that I bought years ago for camping trips, and it barely fits in my oven. It has a 16 inch diameter and is 3 inches deep, which means more fruit and less crust (healthier).

   I don't bother to peel such a large number of apples; I just slice 'em thin—at least a dozen. I add sugar (white *and* brown), flour or cornstarch for thickening the juice, a few squirts of lemon juice, some apple cider, cinnamon, sometimes raisins and/or walnuts, and always a few drops of vanilla (the secret ingredient). I bake it 'til it's bubbling out the top crust and all over the bottom of the oven. When I smell smoke I know it's done! (In truth, I line the bottom of the oven with aluminum foil.) Large deep-dish pies using fruit from my own trees: $6 per pie.

Apples keep very well in a cool, dry place and are versatile. It's so easy to make applesauce, a child can do it, and baked apples make themselves.

Anywhere in the country where fruit trees and vines grow well, there are farms where you can pick fruit, veggies, berries, grapes, and nuts yourself. You are charged by the pound or the bushel, and prices are very reasonable compared to grocery stores. If you plan on canning, it's the only affordable way to go. If you have friends with fruit trees or your own trees, there is no reason to pay for summer fruit at all. Waste is a terrible thing—something to seriously consider in a recession—so use all the free fruit you can get. My four apple trees bear so heavily every year, I end up taking bushels and bushels of the smaller apples to ranches and stables for their horses.

We have blackberries growing everywhere here in Oregon, *just for the pickin'* in late summer and early fall. Needless to say, everybody gorges until they're purple in the face (literally). The berries are free and can be picked in excess…and canned, frozen, or *jammed* for wintertime.

3. Pumpkin pie is particularly healthful. It consists of just pumpkin (squash), eggs, canned milk, moderate sugar, and a little cinnamon. It's almost like eating your vegetables as a dessert. Two standard-sized pies from a large can of pumpkin: $8.

4. Another quick dessert is pudding: lemon, chocolate, or banana. It takes about ten minutes to make from scratch with cornstarch and sugar. You can pour the bubbling lava on a *plate* to cool faster if you just can't wait! I never made my kids wait, and

we even licked the plates when our spoons failed to scrape up the last of it. "Oink oink." It costs less than $2 to make a medium saucepan full.

5. Granola is also one of my specialties, and I make it when the kids visit, or for any good excuse. I mix a multitude of ingredients, from oats, sunflower seeds, and nuts to coconut, raisins, and everything else imaginable into a sweetened-with-honey *batter*, which *glues* it all together. Then I spread it out on a large cookie sheet and bake it to golden brown. Even before it cools, the stampede begins. It's *so* much cheaper to make and *so* much more nutrient-dense than store-bought granola that there's no comparison. You can almost consider it a meal! Large sheet of granola: $10.

6. Homemade oatmeal/raisin and peanut butter cookies are also energy-packed, healthful treats. I use lots more oats, and much more peanut butter, than any recipe would dare to call for. When I cook and bake, I pay no attention to rules.

7. Make real-fruit popsicles for the kids. They're full of natural vitamin C and are much more nutritious and delicious than store bought.

8. Buy an electric orange-juice and lemon-juice juice-maker. They are unbelievably cheap ($10 to $15), and their motors are so strong it's virtually impossible to overheat them. (Believe me, I've put it to the test making quarts at a time of orange juice for *years*.) There's just nothing like fresh-squeezed orange juice, and this easy *squeezer* is my favorite kitchen appliance.

9. Invest in a regular-type juicer and/or blender (Goodwill or on sale) and make fruity smoothies, especially in the summer with free or u-pick

orchard fruit—instead of buying soft drinks or *Koolaid* (sugar-water).

Save Money on Food at Walmart and Costco

Whenever I go to Walmart, I stock up on the food they carry that is consistently priced much lower than in the grocery store.

My list (2014):
- Raisin Bran: $1.98 per box, compared to $4.98 per box at the grocery store. It's *very* good raisin bran and has enough raisins to choke a pig. As expensive as raisins are, I don't know how they sell it for less than $2!
- Tuna: Every grade of tuna you would want (dolphin-safe albacore to various chunk-lights) and name brands are sold at about half the price of regular market price.
- Macaroni and cheese (the original fast food for emergencies) is only 58 cents a box.
- Condiments like mayonnaise, mustard, and catsup are cheap, as are jars of pickles.
- Sugar and flour are sold at substantially reduced prices.
- Coffee is *not* cheap anywhere, but *is* a little cheaper at Walmart. Again, I'm no angel—I like coffee with lots of cream and sugar in it!
- *I recently bought a case (12 cans) of Wilderness and Comstock cherry pie filling (another weakness) for only $2 per can—*half* the regular price at the grocery store.
- Spanish peanuts are a real bargain at $2 per can.
- The food that gets my vote for the biggest bang for your buck (certainly containing the most energy) is

Adams Peanut Butter (crunchy or smooth), which consists of peanuts and salt *and that's all*. It's definitely a survival food and can be stored in the refrigerator or freezer for a long, long time. It's basically protein and fat (the good kind) and the best pick-me-up I can think of—and longer lasting and healthier than a cup of coffee. Mix it with a little honey on a slice of wheat-berry bread, and it'll tide you over for hours.

Tip: Stock up on several large jars when they're on sale. The regular price is less than $5 per jar. That might *sound* expensive, but when you consider that you need only a tablespoon at a time to do the trick, it's *cheap*. What you don't ever want to do is buy *hydrogenated* peanut butter (the common kind). It'll clog your arteries with saturated fat.

- I buy all my paper goods—and other everyday kitchen, bathroom, and office supplies—from Walmart or Costco. Walmart carries the *Great Value* brand, and it really *is* great. Their GV plastic food wrap is only $1.98 for 200 feet. It's good quality for an unbeatable price. I'll never go back to paying $4 at the grocery store.
- If you're feeding a large family or having a houseful of hungry relatives come to visit, the best bargains I've ever seen are in the *institutional canned goods* aisle of any supermarket or grocery outlet. *Gallon cans* of beans, fruit, and vegetables are unbelievably cheap. I recently bought a gallon of pineapple chunks for $4, and a gallon of pear halves and apricot halves for $6.50 each. The fruit is minimally processed and has no sugar added. I was impressed with the high quality of everything I stocked up on.

- Here's a great way to get free honey: If you have the type of land and a location that bees might like (south facing), allow a local beekeeper to place his hives in a small area on it, in trade for a nice supply of honey each year. I recently received my six annual quarts of beautiful *liquid gold* from the professional beekeeper who does *all* the work while I sit around eating bread and honey! Honey value: About $100.

Closing Thoughts

Eating a healthful diet is like an inexpensive insurance policy called preventive medicine. Health *is* wealth.

Even if you have a few bad habits, it is possible to retrain your palate to prefer *real* food. Nutrient-dense food leaves you feeling so satisfied and stabilized you just won't have the cravings for junk food.

The trick is to plan your schedule so you don't get so hungry you'll devour anything in sight, such as greasy fast food. I recommend carrying a can of Spanish peanuts in the car as a ready snack for you and the kids—so you aren't tempted to screech into McDonalds. *Spanish* are the least expensive peanut you can buy. They are tender and moist and stabilize blood sugar instantly.

My *big three* survival-food winners are beans, eggs, and peanut butter (or other nuts). They all keep well (except eggs), so stock up on them—just in case. And don't forget to store some water—just in case.

You can save a lot of money going green and going natural. Many people are enlightened and already have a good diet, but it wouldn't hurt to spend even fewer precious dollars on food during this recession, and without compromising health. You can have a balanced diet *and* a balanced checkbook!

Dorothy's Carrot Cake Recipe

2 cups flour
1 cup dark brown sugar
1 cup white sugar
2 teaspoons baking soda
1 teaspoons baking powder (optional)
1 teaspoons salt (or less)
1 tablespoon cinnamon
1 teaspoon ginger or pumpkin pie spice (optional)
4 large eggs
1¾ cups of vegetable oil (important measurement)
1 tablespoon vanilla extract
4 cups finely grated carrots (don't skimp)
1 cup chopped walnuts
1 cup raisins (dark and/or golden)

Beat eggs and oil together until frothy. Gradually blend in dry ingredients (flour last). Add carrots, nuts, raisins, and vanilla. Blend well with mixer on low speed.

Pour into large oiled rectangular baking pan 9" x 14" (easy way) and bake at 350 degrees for an hour, or use two oiled 8-inch round pans for a layer cake and bake at 350 degrees for 45 minutes.

Do not overbake or it won't be as moist.

Cool for an hour. Then frost with cream-cheese frosting made with ½ cube butter (softened) mixed with two 8-ounce packages Philadelphia cream cheese. Beat in 2 cups of powdered sugar and 1 teaspoon of vanilla extract.

The only thing left to say: "Yum"—with your mouth full.

CHAPTER 29

GARDEN SPACES FOR
SMALL PLACES

Jill and the Beanstalk

"When the world wearies, and society ceases to satisfy, there is always the garden" (Minnie Aumonier, 1865). That's true, but so is this

228   *Dorothy Ainsworth*

one: "If your budget is lean and you want something green, there's always the garden." I'm more practical than poetic, but on second thought, we both have a point.

Why Have a Garden?

What could be better than a garden as an excuse to play in the dirt, think and meditate, get some sun and exercise, and give nature a chance to show its stuff? During this recession a garden in the yard is better than money in the bank, and much more profitable. A handful of seeds can produce a pantry full of organic food for winter.

A garden is an amazing study of life itself. You can show the kids where food comes from by marveling with them over the miracle of poking tiny seeds into the dirt and seeing them come to life in a week or so right before their eyes. And if you aren't too squeamish, you and the kids can study bugs and worms and insects while you are down at their level. It's a perfect opportunity to explore the fascinating and sometimes startling microworld you thought was only on the Discovery Channel. When you meet eyebrow to antennae with a Jerusalem cricket (potato bug) you'll know what I mean!

Audrey Hepburn said: "To plant a garden is to believe in tomorrow." It's a fun challenge to play the optimistic chemist who mixes soil, compost, water, and seeds together under the sun in hopes the experiment will spring to life and flourish. If you do it right, you'll end up with not only tasty, nutrient-rich food to eat but thousands of seeds for next year's crop. Nature is incredibly bountiful: "Tickle the earth with a hoe and it will laugh with a harvest" (Douglas Jerrold, 1803). Well, it's not quite *that* easy. Let's get to work.

Where to Put Your Garden

First of all, you don't need acreage to grow most vegetables and fruits. You can have a customized garden almost *anywhere* that you can fill containers with soil and have enough sunlight drenching your plants for at least six hours a day—even on an apartment deck. Many edibles can be grown beautifully in wine barrels cut in half, or deep cedar planter boxes, window boxes, hanging baskets, terra cotta pots, plastic pots, or any other well-drained container—even an old bathtub or wheelbarrow. You can put casters on wooden containers and roll them around to follow the sun or make a simple wooden box with long legs like stilts so you can harvest herbs at waist level.

If your growing space is extremely limited, you can put up trellises along a fence or wall or garage and grow vines and sprawling plants such as cucumbers, squash, and pole beans—*vertically.*

I built an 8' x 8' freestanding 2" x 4" frame and covered it with lattice to hide the unattractive pump house for the well. I planted climbing roses along the bottom, and within a few years they grew into a solid wall of gorgeous pink blossoms. The same could be done with edible vines.

If you have a yard, front *or* back, and all you have growing is grass, it's time to get practical and creative and use some of that taxed property to grow *food* instead. In some cases a lawn is a luxurious waste of space and water, and it yields little in return for all the time and energy you spend mowing, fertilizing, aerating, watering, raking, and removing dog poop. Why not raise something besides a crop of unwanted dandelions? Raise your neighbor's eyebrows instead—be the first in your neighborhood with a front-yard garden!

Sure, it might be unconventional in a subdivision in

town, but when it comes down to saving big bucks on fruit and vegetables, who cares? It *is* possible to design a very attractive front-yard garden that meanders around the yard with grass trails in between raised beds and pots of flowers and herbs here and there as colorful accents. Draw it out on graph paper, and you'll see how beautiful, functional, and educational *edible landscaping* can be. You could make history, combining botany and biology with geometry. Remember crop circles?

Why *Raised* Beds?

If you have a backyard with southern exposure, you can build a two- or three-tiered set of raised beds along the fence or against your house's concrete foundation and grow the same amount of vegetables as on flat ground but concentrated in a long, narrow strip. Not only that, the deep soil and the heat and water retention that happens with one tier against the other, make for unusually advantageous growing conditions.

Tiered raised garden beds are easy to access for weeding and tending so they are kind to backs and knees. A fifty-foot run of three tiers adds up to 150 square feet of garden space. That's a lot of tomatoes, snow peas, carrots, bell peppers, onions, beets, radishes, parsley, chives, and lettuce—all in a 3-foot-wide swath of your yard!

You can use rocks, stones, concrete blocks, bricks, railroad ties, synthetic lumber, or weather-resistant lumber for these terraced beds or any other raised beds. If you use standard lumber, the back section will be about 30 or 36 inches high, depending on whether you use three 1" x 10"s or 2" x 10"s or three 1" x 12"s or 2" x 12"s stacked on edge for the back section. The middle section will use two boards stacked on edge, and the front section will use one.

Use tie bolts (½" galvanized threaded stock with nuts and washers on each end) to hold them together so when filled to the brim, they don't bulge with the weight of wet soil.

Note: I've hammered ½" rebar into the ground to hold 24-inch-high walls made from three 1" x 8"s of old cedar fencing (standing on edge), and it worked great.

You'll have to haul in a load of topsoil and some soil amendments, but that will be a one-time expense. It costs about $25 per cubic yard locally (southern Oregon). You may already have some or all of your own soil to use, but be sure it's rich enough. Nutrient-rich organic soil is the single *most important ingredient* in having a successful, productive garden.

Raised beds offer many advantages to limited-space gardening and can produce an abundant harvest for the average family. Beds can be anywhere from 2 feet to 5 feet wide (4 feet is ideal) with working space around them (footpaths), but a tomato bed can be as narrow as 1½ feet. Several beds of varying lengths can be placed almost anywhere they'll get enough light and sun exposure, preferably oriented north/south.

Because they warm up sooner in the spring and keep producing into the fall, raised beds can extend your gardening season.

The beauty of raised beds and other self-contained gardening techniques is that you can't accidentally step near your plant roots and compact the soil, as can happen when weeding a conventional garden plot. Roots need to *breathe* in order to absorb water and nutrients.

Because the beds are raised, you won't have to prepare the ground soil, except for laying down some kind of gopher and mole control such as hardware cloth, small-holed chicken wire, or other metal mesh on it. Cut the mesh long enough to curve up the inside surface of perimeter boards at least 3 inches and staple it in place. If your bed will be resting on hard clay ground or worse, you may need to put down a few inches of gravel first to ensure good drainage. In the case of impenetrable ground, the gopher mesh probably won't be necessary—famous last words!

Then you simply fill the forms with topsoil, and you're good to go. An optimum garden soil is made up of two parts fertile topsoil, one part fine compost, and one part sand, all mixed well and allowed to settle in the forms after being saturated with water. Every year thereafter you can continue to enrich the soil by adding compost and manure and other conditioners such as wood ash, blood meal, and bone meal.

Special Projects for Kids: Corn and Strawberries

Corn is a fun crop for kids to plant and tend because it grows fast and tall. They can hide in it for fun and make scarecrows out of the stalks in the fall. It should be planted in squares or blocks for water retention and good pollination—*not* in long, skinny rows. It will tower over the other veggies and deplete the soil, so it should be planted in its own bed, where it can't shade the garden and drink up all the water. Early hybrid varieties are smaller and mature faster in shorter growing seasons. Stagger your plantings two weeks apart from warm spring until midsummer so the corn doesn't ripen all at once. Keep in mind that corn is greedy; it loves lots of heat and water and a nice breeze to pollinate its tassels. Run rows north and south for maximum sun. Figure one to two good ears per stalk.

Strawberries are easy to grow, and they adapt to almost any kind of container. They send out runners and propagate themselves continuously, but they also welcome a helping hand to divide them up and transplant them anywhere and everywhere. "Strawberry Fields Forever" aren't just the lyrics of a Beatles song—they are a reality when you let strawberries have their way. What could be better than a *surplus* of strawberries? It's a thrill for even *very* young children to pick the bright-red berries out of the patch with their tiny fingers and eat 'em on the spot.

But this article is not about *what* you should plant and *how* to grow it, but to encourage you to build raised beds and to use planters and containers to grow your garden *in*. Raised beds facilitate what is called *intensive gardening*—meaning increased yields, improved quality, and efficiency. You'll have more control over every aspect of the garden work: planting, watering, fertilizing, weeding, thinning, pruning, removing pests, and harvesting, not to mention smelling and tasting. As I stated before, the extra elevation makes the garden a pleasure to tend, without crouching and straining. If you ever *do* have to resort to your knees, strap on cheap foam knee pads from the hardware store or the Grange Co-op (in Oregon) ($5). They work great and are totally comfortable. I even wear them in the house when I'm scrubbing the bathtub or cleaning the oven.

Building the Beds

Beds made from conventional lumber are easy to build and require only the most rudimentary carpenter skills. You can use just about any old and gray lumber you can find, or you can buy garden-heart (cheapest) redwood planks or cedar fencing from the lumberyard. My raised beds are made from regular 2" x 10" DF (Douglas fir) in standard lengths because I had a pile of culls lying around unemployed. The soil is rich under the beds, so taller sides weren't necessary. The fir won't last as long as redwood or cedar, but I can switch when it starts to rot. Right now beautiful DF lumber is cheap, cheap, cheap at the lumberyards (only $0.20 a foot in 2008).

The end boards of your rectangle or square are joined to the side boards with 3-inch Sheetrock screws. It's a good idea to put a couple of 90-degree brackets inside each corner, but I used extra screws instead. Note: To prevent splitting, always pre-drill screw holes close to the *ends* of the boards.

For more strength, you can place a vertical 4" x 4" or 2" x 4" inside each corner to fasten the horizontal boards to. If you want to anchor your bed to the ground, build it upside down, taper the ends of the four corner posts, then turn it over and drive those pointed legs into the ground. Use a small sledge but put a protective board on top of the corner to pound on.

Raised wooden beds can have 1" x 2" vertical stakes easily screwed to their sides to hold translucent plastic sheeting for heat retention in early spring and for starting seeds or tiny plants—creating what is called a *cold frame*. Later on, those same stakes can support bird mesh to protect young plants until they mature. To discourage dogs from jumping in and digging, you can string plastic tape around the garden perimeter (against the stakes) to support bird mesh or translucent plastic sheeting.

Another method to support mesh or sheeting is to place a row of arched ½" PVC pipes over the top of the bed—greenhouse style if you like. Just fasten the ends of each bendable pipe to the insides of the beds with little U-brackets. Brackets are cheap, and so is PVC pipe. Clip the bird mesh on with clothespins.

Railroad ties, logs, timbers, or beams can be laid up corncrib style (stacked) to make very attractive raised beds. But do not use pressure-treated wood; the poisonous chemicals that preserve the wood will leach into the soil. I would recommend lining the bed with 6-mil. plastic or some kind of waterproof barrier where soil comes in contact with creosoted railroad ties.

Raised concrete-block beds are impervious to decay and easy to set up. Just haul in a predetermined number of recycled or new 8" x 8" x 16" blocks (cost is about $1.30 each locally) and stack them one, two, or three high, fill the rectangular beds with soil—including the voids in the blocks—and start planting.

Note: To scare away unwanted grazers you can set up a laser-beam *deer-activated* sprinkler in any garden.

Mulching and Composting

I mulch everything with straw to conserve water from evaporation and to trap heat. It keeps mud from splashing when you water and discourages weeds from starting. It costs about $8 a bale (2010), and one or two bales will mulch several beds.

I recommend reading *The One-Straw Revolution*, a book by Masarobu Fukuoka about the importance of mulching to conserve water and to create a microbiotic environment for optimum yields. His popular book, a best seller in 1978, is about a fascinating and enlightening method of natural gardening that makes perfect sense (common sense) and requires no weeding. His basic message is how important it is to protect the soil from direct sunlight, which kills on contact the good and necessary microorganisms that are exposed on the surface.

It's a good idea to start your own compost pile in a corner of the yard where it's partially hidden but close enough to the kitchen door to make it handy to throw organic scraps onto it daily. Compost can be made on open ground by heaping up layers of organic matter such as grass clippings and leaves and kitchen scraps, but a simple slatted bin or lattice bin is more sanitary. It is self-contained, easy to erect, and easy to partially disassemble when you want to turn (aerate) the compost from time to time, and it's ideal for protection and ventilation. The bin can be as small as 3' x 3' and still be adequate to supplement the soil in a few raised beds or a small garden.

Fruit Trees for Small Spaces

It's possible to grow fruit *trees* even where there seems to be no room available. You can grow them against a wall, fence, or house, and prune any branches that dare to grow in any direction but laterally. A trellis or lattice against a concrete wall will provide wood slats for tying off and training young branches. The pruned trees or vines are called *espaliers*, and they are the product of a beautiful and unusual growing technique creatively used in tight spaces by professional landscapers. Edible espaliers that are easily trained to grow in one plane include almond, apple, apricot, cherry, peach, pear, plum, nectarine, and citrus. If I may use a noun as a verb, I say, "Espalier away!"

Closing Thoughts

I love the concept of a community garden where a group of friends (one country mouse with property and several city mice with ambition and energy) work together and share a garden space, share the expense, share the work, and share the harvest. It's a great way to get together socially, involve the kids, talk, laugh, gossip, share ideas, and get some exercise. And saving money on organic food by growing it yourself is just plain smart.

Last Word

Say *no* to giant zucchinis!

A sure way to get shunned is to grow more than *one* zucchini plant, then try to give away the bulbous, club-shaped tonnage to family, friends, and neighbors—and when *they* run for their lives—to strangers. My advice is to never *ever* plant more than one zucchini! They are so cute when they're little...

CHAPTER 30

VEGETARIAN LOVE

"Carrots in love"

G randma Ruth's version of an old poem:

Do you carrot all for me?
My heart is soft as squash.
For you are such a peach,
With your radish hair and turnip nose.
You're the apple of my eye.
If we cantaloupe, lettuce marry anyhow,
For I know we'd make a pear.

Printed in honor of my adorable mom, Ruth, who lived to age ninety.

CHAPTER 31

SELF-RELIANCE ESSAY

Shaving the crown off a rafter

Self-reliance is a mind-set. If you have it, you are on your way to independence. If you don't, it would be in your best interest to develop it. It requires the conscious effort of replacing an "I need help" attitude with an "I can do it myself" attitude.

I was lucky; I acquired it at an early age by default. I grew up in a large family with no money for anything but the barest necessities. If we wanted something extra, we had to work at an outside job to get it. We didn't resent that reality; it was a given. There was no sense of entitlement in our family. We were raised with the philosophy that nobody owed us anything.

An example of the self-reliant mind-set already in place when I was five is illustrated by my first day of school. I got on the bus with my brothers and sisters and felt happy and proud that I was all grown up and on my way to school—until my older sister left me at my classroom and disappeared. I loved the learning part that day, but it was overshadowed by being worried sick about how I was going to find my way home (five miles away). It never occurred to me that I could actually ask for help to find the right bus at the end of the day. I truly believed it was solely up to me to figure it out, and if I didn't, I would be spending the night in the dark parking lot.

Don't get me wrong; this isn't a sob story. My mom did an amazing feat just getting all six kids on the bus in the morning! Because I had been so eager to start school, it didn't occur to her that I would be fearful that day.

Nevertheless, the sense of abandonment I felt is seared into my brain and probably contributed to the lifelong desire for security I still have. Strangely enough, the way I handled my problem that day is the same way I handle problems now—by taking personal responsibility to exhaust all options before crying for help.

I did manage to get on the right bus, and I remember feeling really good about finding it all by myself. Therein lies the silver lining of self-reliance. When you achieve even a modicum of it, you feel good about yourself. This concept is the basis for the Outward Bound program for wayward teenagers—and it's a great success. When you set realistic goals and actually achieve them, the payoffs are huge. You earn your self-esteem while becoming self-sufficient at the same time. In the process you will be doing something almost every day that you fear or is difficult and that will get you in the habit of overcoming your own self-doubts. You may have to grit your teeth and embrace the challenge, but it's so worth the journey and the result. Shakespeare said, "Our doubts are traitors, and make us lose the good we oft might win by fearing to attempt."

My parents did their best, by example, to instill good values in us, including a strong work ethic. Sometimes poverty is a blessing in disguise because it can foster creativity and gumption. Although we were financially poor, we were rich in every other way.

A parent's most important responsibility is to prepare the kids to survive independently in the world.

Back in the late 1940s, work experience happened automatically. I had my first real job at age eight (during the summer), babysitting two small children and doing the lady's housework, for 50 cents a day.

At age eleven, I ironed for 50 cents an hour on Saturdays and mowed lawns for neighbors so I could buy fabric at three yards for $1. I made all my own clothes on a treadle sewing machine and felt warm with pride as I twirled around in each new outfit while Mom beamed and lavished praise.

Little did I know I was developing an ability to look at raw materials and flat patterns and instantly visualize the three-dimensional finished products. I would someday do the same with lumber and blueprints.

By age twelve, Mom let me take over much of the family cooking because I was good at it, enjoyed it, and I wanted to.

My first waitressing job was at fifteen. I used my earnings that summer to pay for all my own dental work—and felt good about it.

We all draw conclusions from our own experiences, so naturally this essay is subjective, but I think there are some absolutes about human nature that can be applied universally. I strongly and unwaveringly believe that accomplishments alone build self-esteem, self-respect, and self-reliance.

Unconditional love, parental praise, and the approval of peers don't do it. Actual skills learned and deeds accomplished—no matter how small and insignificant to others, but meaningful to you—does do it. The glow of satisfaction that comes from earning your own approval is like magic.

Parents who give, give, give to their kids mean well but are actually robbing their kids of earning their self-esteem. I was taught early on to either rely on my own resources to create what I wanted or have nothing at all.

There are degrees of self-reliance, and even a little bit is better than none, but let's assume your goal is extreme self-reliance—like mine was. You move to a small town, buy five to ten acres in the country, build a house, develop your own water supply and septic system, and possibly go off the grid for your electricity. You have a few chickens, assorted dogs and cats, and a nice garden. You work at a job you like (ideal) or one you don't like (survival), and simplify your life to the point that you can spend every extra cent on developing your property.

I still drive an old truck; my arms are my power steering and the windows are my air-conditioning. I buy clothes at Goodwill; my fashion statements are more functional and comfortable than intentional. I eat plain, healthful food (cruel gruel), wash my dishes with the hose when I have to, and I don't give a hoot about what anybody thinks. That's another mind-set to achieve (freedom from the shackles of convention), but you can't fake it. It comes with the territory—literally. When you become a landowner, start actually achieving your goals in tiny steps, and can visualize the end result, all of a sudden it really doesn't matter if your hair is messed up and you have dried caulk under your fingernails; you're on a roll. You'll have more important things on your mind—like survival.

Obviously, there are some personal requirements for becoming self-sufficient: You have to want it badly, and you have to be in pretty good shape. You'll end up in excellent shape, but you should be fairly healthy to begin with. It helps to dream big and visualize what you want; that's what keeps you going—but focusing your energy on the task at hand is what makes it happen. Have a plan and a list of goals and start transforming wishful thinking into labor.

You are smarter and more capable than you think. You can't learn if you don't try. If a task looks daunting, get started anyway. Take it one step at a time. Dream big but take baby steps. Write down a plan. List your priorities. Number them. Start in with whatever it takes to get started. You want to design your own house? Go downtown and buy graph paper and a ruler. Go to the library or magazine rack and look at house plans. Ideas will snowball. The mind does funny things when you give it a problem; it keeps on working overtime. In fact, you can't shut it off.

It's important to begin with something tangible. Make a model. You'll see there's no big mystery in putting a house together. A three-dimensional structure always looks bigger than the parts, but a house is just one board put up at a time. I built my house one log at a time. Then it burned down and I rebuilt it one more log at a time.

To achieve self-sufficiency, you have to delay gratification. You can taste a pinch of cookie dough, but you'll have to wait for the cookies. The only instant satisfaction you're likely to get for a while will come in tiny increments, like hammering a nail in straight without bending the head over with the last whack. Your pleasures will come in small dosages, like when you smash your finger with said hammer and your boyfriend kisses it to make it better and playfully musses up your hair.

Each little job is an end in itself but is a stepping-stone to the next level. You'll be living in the moment but working like hell for the future. Some of those moments won't be happy, but they'll be meaningful. Real happiness is found in the everyday struggles and the little peak experiences you can glean from them. Hsun-Tzu said: "If there is no dull and determined effort, there will be no brilliant achievement." I don't know who in the heck Hsun-Tzu was or even how to pronounce his name, but he was a wise man. Progress happens in tiny increments. And when you are the one doing the work, each little accomplishment is a big deal.

In spite of the struggle and occasional pain, you can learn optimism. Whistle while you work. If you are lucky enough to have a partner, joke around. Try to see the funny side of everything; laugh it up. You have the power to shift your moods and attitude. It's all about taking charge of your life. When you know you are it, and there won't be any so-called help, something will spark in you. Only ask for help as a last resort. You'll never know how strong you are until you put yourself to the test.

The worst thing that can happen to a person is to be paralyzed by indecision, inertia, and fear of making a mistake. Time lost by procrastination and excusitis can take years out of your life.

Sometimes you have to do what doesn't come naturally, and that ain't easy. People who read my articles and see the house I built call me a ballsy chick and a gutsy lady. That couldn't be further from the truth. I'm actually quite wimpy and hesitant to try new things, but if I want something badly enough, my drive overrides my fear. Years ago I raced motorcycles (flat track and motocross) because we had a motorcycle shop, and my husband wanted me and the kids involved—it was good advertising. I am not by nature an aggressive, competitive female. I was terrified at first, but so motivated to please my husband that I donned my leathers and left-foot skid-shoe every weekend and actually got good enough to win some flat-track races, even against men! I'm telling you this story in case you are a woman who can't even imagine doing something like that. I couldn't either—until I tried.

I had been raised with traditional 1950s values: The woman is the caregiver; she makes dinner, bears and rears the kids, and makes her husband happy. That's all fine if you aren't sacrificing your very soul to do it. My marriage turned out to be so one-sided I eventually had to get out, but if I could break free to develop my potential and become self-reliant, anybody could.

At thirty I was a divorced woman with two kids to support on a waitress's earnings and no child support. And, as aforementioned, I was a girlie-girl and a fraidy cat. But there was one thing I was never afraid of: work—hard, tortuous work. I believed fervently that I could create what I wanted (within realistic financial and physical capabilities), and I didn't care how long it took. I didn't get started until I was thirty-eight, and now, thirty-five years later, I'm still working at it.

No one is confident about everything—certainly not me. I learned by mistakes and failures (Darn! I cut that board ½" too short!). I had years of oops and darns. I learned that if you can accept your mistakes, it will free you to take more risks. Trying until you get it right is how most of us learn things. Perfectionism leads to procrastination and paralysis. You have to cut yourself some slack—just don't cut yourself! A job done reasonably well is good enough.

My quest for self-reliance, which included having my own home, was my passion. Because I was inspired with possibility thinking, the self-discipline aspect took care of itself.

I strongly believe in never taking the easy way out if it means selling even the tiniest piece of your soul. Nature is a great equalizer. You reap exactly what you sow. There's no way out of the formula; it's written in stone. It's human nature to take the easy way if there's an easier way, but if you give up your decision-making power and your acquiring-skills power, you pay a dear price: You have to live by someone else's rules, someone else's taste, someone else's choices. Now that I have been able to uncompromisingly be true to myself, I would loathe going back to being the obedient one, with someone else in charge.

Every time you are confronted with a new task that requires learning a new skill—hit the books. That's how I learned everything I know—by reading and practicing. If I can do it, you can do it—whatever it is. Even if you have money, do it yourself. Harrison Ford repairs his own fences and makes furniture in his shop. There's a reason for this: it is profoundly satisfying. There is no shortcut to get that feeling, and no substitute for it.

I wish I could tell you it's easy, but it's not. Nothing worthwhile is ever easy. I'll cite my son as an example: Envision a giant pyramid underground filled with a billion musical notes, and only the top is sticking out of the sand where Eric sits at a grand piano. He's playing a Beethoven sonata—beautifully, powerfully, with great manual dexterity, speed, and passion. That's just the tip of the musical pyramid; it took thirty years of practicing to get to that level. How did he achieve it? One note at a time, fueled by his passion for classical music and his desire to "do the composers justice" (his words). If you would like to see and hear Eric play, go to www. pianoamp.com.

The moral to this story is to find what you are passionate about, and the self-discipline will follow. Because the payoffs increase steadily and proportionally to the effort, discipline is habit forming. You just can't put a price on the payback you get from being true to yourself and working your buns off, or on the enjoyment it ultimately brings.

Happiness is having your own approval—by never selling out and never giving up, and getting good at what you do (judging yourself by your own standards). The word "success" usually means somebody's else's evaluation; measure success by your own measuring stick. There are doers and there are braggarts. Confidence should never be confused with arrogance; they aren't even related.

I must give my lovely daughter equal time by using her as another example of being true to one's self. Cynthia wanted to become a photographer, so she bought a camera, read a manual or two, and started right in. First she practiced on friends. Then she had a few successful shoots to prove to herself what she already intuitively knew: that she had a natural eye for beauty, light, and composition. She advertised her services, began to attract clients, built a great reputation, and the rest is history. It took a lot of courage and a belief in herself to get started. She was a model and an actress, but she knew in her heart of hearts that her true desire was to be on the other side of a camera. Now she does what she loves and is using her earnings to buy a little ranch and become self-sufficient and have all the horses she wants (her other passion). In 1998 she was chosen by *Cosmopolitan* magazine as one of the year's top sixteen "Fun and Fearless Females." She is totally self-taught. If you'd like to see some of her work, go to www.smalleyphoto.com and www.wildhorsesandwestern

art.com. This is another example of the principle that if you pursue what you like to do, everything else falls into place.

It's not a luxury to be self-reliant anymore; it's becoming a necessity. Your very survival could depend on how well prepared you are to live without any outside help for weeks at a time. Sadly, but predictably (due to our giveaway programs), we are becoming a nation of needy dependent people or just lazy dependent people who are willing to give up personal power to let the government take care of them. Too many sheeple will take the easy way out if it's offered.

Dependence is a baaaad idea. It could prove to be fatal. It's the wrong mind-set to expect help with everything and fail to take personal responsibility for anything. They say "a kept woman earns every penny" and "marrying for money is a hard way to make a living." Well, I feel the same way about the government providing handouts to keep us under its control. I don't want the government to be my master.

I cringe at the thought of socialism taking over this country. I want to be responsible for my own life and be free to make my own choices. I want to learn my own lessons and suffer the consequences of my own bad actions or choices. I also want to be able to reap and keep the rewards of my own labor. If I want to share my fruits with others, it should be my choice. I don't want to contribute my hard-earned money to undeserving people on the dole. Reckless generosity is found only in people who are giving away someone else's money!

Change is growth. If you are widowed or divorced, it's a perfect opportunity to become self-reliant. Even if your new circumstance was forced upon you, use it to come into your own as an autonomous individual—a party of one.

Once you achieve self-reliance and the self-confidence that goes along with it, you'll be more apt to pick your equal in the next relationship, instead of falling prey to the wrong guy just because he helps you in a weak moment. Working on your self-reliance is a lot better position to come from than being helpless. You might say, "I don't have time. I have kids. I have to work for a living." That's excusitis. I know you can do it, because I was in that exact situation, and I was able to do it. It all hinges on establishing priorities and sticking to the plan.

Don't wait to find the right person—work on becoming the right person. Push the play button. Quit rewinding. When you break out of the gravitational field of collective mediocrity, you may risk being alone for a while. Embrace it. The great 18th century writer and philosopher Goethe said: "Boldness has genius, power, and magic in it." "You can remain a flower in a vase, with unopened petals, or you can be a free-spirited wildflower in the wind, holding onto dear life by your roots, but also feeling the sun in your face when the storm passes." (Anon.)

I had a great partnership with a prince of a man for several years. We were equals: I was twice his age, and he was twice my size! We were a perfect match for ten glorious years. There's nothing more wonderful than being in a relationship with the right person, but nothing more terrible than being in a relationship with the wrong one.

If you are lucky enough to have a wonderful mate, you can still become incredibly self-reliant if you make a conscious effort to do so. To this day, I tend to let a man take over if there's one around; it's biology and conditioning. It's also nice to have manpower around; men are a lot stronger. But if you find yourself single and alone you can manage anyway.

A friend who is a single mom sent me an email recently

telling how she moved a washer and dryer up steps and into her house all by herself. She said, "When you don't have might, you tend to use your wits." She continued: "I just walked them step by step, pushing one corner, then the next, until they were in the spot they needed to be. It's all about balance. If you find the balance point, you can almost spin and pivot things around without feeling the weight of the object!" I received her email when I was in the middle of writing this chapter, and it illustrated my point precisely. I am so proud of her; she's learning how to be self-reliant.

If you have a mate, and he's working in the shop or on the house that he's building for the family, don't stay in the kitchen and bake cookies. They're delicious, but you already know how to bake cookies. It's time to learn some self-reliance skills—just in case he has a heart attack (possibly from too many goodies you've already baked for him over the years).

The division of labor between husband and wife in a family is great, but this article is about self-reliance and survival skills. There's only one way to learn them, and it's by doing.

Surprise him! Not with a new Victoria's Secret negligee, but with the carpenter's belt you secretly bought. Put it on with all the trimmings (tape measure, pencil, small square) and go out and say, "Where do you want me to start? I'm ready, willing, and almost able. Teach me, baby!" He'll be shocked. It'll be fun—and a great beginning to developing an equal partnership. (Your husband should also learn to cook.)

It has been customary for the man to build the house and for the woman to pick the drapes. Heck with that! I want to design AND decorate the house. I once went out to dinner with an adorable pauper. He said, "Order anything you want, honey—you're buying."

I always remembered that humorous line. But it's true: "Design anything you want, honey—you're building!" So I did.

If you do have plenty of money and can hire everything done—and can buy all the goods and supplies needed to survive in your home and custom-made bomb shelter— remember this old saying that has a provocative twist to it: "The real measure of a person's character isn't how well he or she does in bad times, but how well he or she keeps striving in good times."

In this new age of terrorism, we can't afford to sit on our laurels anymore. If you have the option of taking the easy way out, say, "No, thank you. I want to do it myself." Like a good Girl Scout, "Be prepared."

Because of my upbringing, I can't not do what needs to be done. I'll never feel comfortable with feeling too comfortable. I'm glad I got started thirty-five years ago on my plan for "future" self-sufficiency and security. That future is now here.

I urge you to get started on the road to self-reliance. Time is not a renewable resource!

CHAPTER 32

THE ART OF SCROUNGING:
Get Building Materials at
Bargain Prices or Free!

Free piers but heavy labor

Don't let a little thing like not enough money keep you from building your dream home. You can get richer in more ways than one by *spending yourself*! Think of your journey as the difference between taking the freeway in a Mercedes—if you're wealthy and can hire everything done—or taking a dirt road in an old pickup—if you're financially challenged and do all the labor yourself. You can still get from here to there; it'll just take longer. I know, because I'm still driving the same old pickup I bought twenty-five years ago for $800 (it was old THEN) and I have managed to build sixteen assorted structures in my spare time, while working as a waitress earning $1,200 per month.

By plugging along all these years, I have increased the value of my property from $40,000 to over a million dollars, and I'm still working on it. My secret? Tunnel vision, energy and drive, and scrounging building materials like crazy. What I *didn't* have was any building experience, but because I paid as I went along, I had plenty of time to learn as I went along. Progress was slow in both categories, but what seemed like mission impossible ended up mission accomplished. How did I learn to build, and how did I afford it? By reading how-to books, using common sense, employing the monkey-see monkey-do method, and incorporating other peoples' surplus into all my livable structures. If I can do it, *you* can too.

We live in a land of plenty. This is a great, opulent country. Consumers keep the economy going, but even people on subsistence-level incomes like myself can benefit immensely from what others cast away—such as their old stuff that isn't even old yet but is tossed out to make room for their new stuff. Garages are so full there's no room for the family cars! Sometimes you'll see couches and tables set out in yards with signs that say "free." American homes are overflowing.

Scrounging is the art of looking for building materials wherever you go and sometimes finding them in unlikely places. If you are *itching* for a bargain, the world is a great big flea market. It's not about being a cheapskate; it's about being smart and saving money, and at the same time recycling what would have gone to waste. And in my *self-righteous* book of virtues, waste is immoral.

It takes some keen observational skills to be on the lookout for what you want and the motivation to ask for it—the motivation being you have no extra money.

Figure out what you need at any given stage of your building project and cultivate a roving eye as you drive around and notice what appears to be discarded stuff: lumber, fencing, pipes, roofing, tarpaper, Visqueen, rebar, concrete blocks, bricks, windows, pallets, etc., piled around houses and businesses, and even near Dumpsters. Screech to a halt and ask if it's for sale or if you can have it free for hauling it off. You'll be amazed at how many people will welcome you to take their clutter away.

Take a drive around town just before trash pick-up day, and if you spot some goodies, ask the homeowner for permission to take those items they had set out for the garbage truck to haul off. Be sure to get there before *The Terminator* (garbage truck) beats you to it.

Get on the phone regularly or go in person and ask at hardware stores and paint stores if they have a collection of assorted reject paint and stains they'd like to get rid of (wrongly mixed colors or whatever). They always *do*. Usually they have five-gallon buckets as well as one-gallon cans. I've bought almost all my paint and stains for $5 per gallon this way. And they've even added some pigment for a small fee to achieve a color I wanted, just to get rid of their stash that's taking up storage room.

Go to carpet outlets looking for slightly damaged carpet (a faded streak or tear or some imperfection) and ask what their rock-bottom price is—or make an offer. My carpet was a color apparently nobody but me liked—burnt orange—so they marked it down to only $6 per yard. It was brand new and excellent quality—made for heavy traffic in casinos and hotels—and is still in great shape after ten years of wear and tear.

Visit linoleum and tile dealers and other big outlet stores for slightly damaged goods as well. Tile stores almost always have fantastic sales on batches of tile they're trying to get rid of to make room for new stock and the latest trends. Sometimes they have boxes of free tile out back.

Check out window and glass companies for glass with imperfections such as a tiny scratch or a speck between the panes. I had all the double-paned windows for three of my log structures made from *used* glass at half the cost of new, and I can't tell the difference. I am presently storing a large load of expensive low-E (energy-efficient) double-paned windows that were given to me by a contractor whose wealthy client changed her mind on her fenestration (window plan) and paid for the change. My son, who is building his own house, will make his window openings to accommodate them. It will save him hundreds of dollars.

Manufacturing plants and cabinetmaker shops sometimes have a by-product you might be able to use. I used to get redwood sawdust for my landscaping needs from a place that made hummingbird feeders and other items out of redwood. I would leave my truck under their chute and drive it home when it was full. I used the attractive redwood mulch in rock gardens and walking trails all over my property.

Lumberyards have bargain bins and slightly weathered lumber that doesn't appeal to the average customer, and sometimes broken bundles of shingles and shakes, outdated siding, unpopular fencing styles, and huge cracked and weathered beams nobody wants because they aren't *pretty* anymore.

You can hire a portable sawmill owner to come to you and cut dimensional lumber planks or beams from your own trees with a Wood-Mizer or TimberKing mill (to name a couple). With his Wood-Mizer, my neighbor cut my true 2 inches thick by 16 feet long rafters for the piano studio I built.

Buy old gray timbers and have them shaved down to size with a portable saw mill. I bought a huge load of timbers for only $250 per 1,000 ($0.25 a board foot compared with new timbers at $1 a board foot) and had another *mizer-man* trim them down to 9" x 9"s with *his* Wood-Mizer. It cost me only $100 for his time and labor (just a few hours), and I had all the ridge-beams and top-plates I needed for my large log home. The mill worked beautifully, and its thin band-saw blade left almost no sawdust in its wake.

Flea markets are treasure troves of everything imaginable and some unimaginables that you impulsively decide you can't live without. Estate sales and auctions are also chock-full of tools and supplies and furniture galore. Estate-sale outlet stores can be found in the yellow pages and are great places to visit regularly because they are constantly being replenished. Estate sales at homes are usually advertised in the newspaper or *The Nickel*. Widows are notorious for getting rid of their late-husband's workshop full of power tools and hand tools in one fell swoop by calling an estate liquidator or placing their own ad.

Fund-raising bazaars and giant swap-meets are also places to find excellent bargains and a diverse array of household goods and building materials. Watch the newspaper for announcements and dates.

Frequenting Goodwill, the Salvation Army, and other secondhand stores is a good habit to get into. While you wander around looking, develop the skill of *possibility thinking* or, better yet, *adaptability thinking*. That's the ability to see something made for a specific purpose and imagine using it for something entirely different and unrelated. I used a futon couch frame from Goodwill ($5) for my kitchen sink counter-top framing, and it worked beautifully.

The Nickel want ads reach thousands of people. Peruse yours weekly for fantastic bargains (particularly appliances). Whenever you need something specific (such as a tool) or general (like assorted lumber), put in your own "wanted" ad for a nominal fee (about $3 for a short ad).

Craigslist on the Internet is an excellent resource for finding almost anything you are looking for cheap or free, or *post* to "wanted" what you are looking for. People *will* respond, and you can negotiate the price.

Go to garage sales every chance you get. You'll find the bargains of your life at yard sales and moving sales, and you'll have a great time socializing while you're at it. A garage sale is like a big party in somebody's front yard, and everyone in town is invited! People are engaged in laughing and dickering, gossiping and snickering, and having fun playing the negotiation *game.* I've witnessed people trying to get a 10-cent item marked down to a nickel. The owners are hell-bent on getting rid of *everything* they set out and toward the end of the day sometimes say, "Just take it away!"

If you're not particularly athletic but become a frequent wheeler-dealer at garage sales, you can boast that *extreme garage saling* is *your* sport!

Builder's Bargain Centers are aptly named. They really *are* full of bargains. I've bought smooth solid-core doors to be used for computer tabletops—and multi-paned doors joined together to make French doors, and any other doors needed—for $20 to $30 each from the local place that sells *seconds* (imperfect materials).

A popular renovator/recycler in Medford, Oregon, has made a business (Morrows) out of organizing and selling unusual building materials from demolition sites and twentieth-century houses. Materials include lumber, claw-foot bathtubs, and vintage fixtures, all at bargain prices. But once you go in, the array of unique items is so extensive and diverse that it's hard to leave until they kick you out at closing time!

My all-time favorite place to *shop* is the *city dump.* *Sinks and seagulls* nostalgically come to mind when I remember trips to the dump. Regretfully, it is now just a *transfer station* and there's no more scrounging allowed, but in its heyday, it offered a half-acre of good stuff to paw through to your heart's content. A few years ago I purchased all my beautiful, white-enameled cast-iron sinks for $1 apiece at the dump. I still have several saved for future use.

If you are lucky enough to have an old-fashioned dump near your town, go there regularly on a treasure hunt. You won't come away empty handed, and you'll marvel all the way home at what you scored. The dump is a massive renewable resource and *the* best place to scrounge and salvage. Even the seagulls love it!

Ask for price reductions anywhere you are shopping if the materials look a little shopworn or *distressed.* I recently got a 50 percent reduction on twenty sheets of pink rigid foam insulation from Lowe's because the edges were a little *sunburned.* Their carelessness was my good fortune.

Buy used, or new but dented, water heaters. The dented casings don't matter, but slightly damaged water heaters are sold *cheap.* Turn the dent to the wall.

Appliances are a dime a dozen. Anything you need, from washers and dryers to ranges and refrigerators, sell *used* for almost nothing compared to new ones. Look on Craigslist for year-round bargains or visit a big household appliance outlet store. They are perpetually advertising "Liquidation Sale," "Overstocked," "Going out of Business." (It sounds like what they should be advertising for is a new manager.)

Need a phone line from the phone company's box to your house? If you provide the trench, the phone company will give you all the direct-burial phone line you need. I recently buried 1,000 feet of line—free. Call your local phone company.

Keep your eyes peeled for demolition sights. For whatever reasons, people are constantly tearing down perfectly good structures and building something else. These sites are excellent sources for all kinds of building materials, from siding to large beams.

A few years ago I asked if I could *have* an assortment of *huge* glu-lams (beams) that were piled in an alley behind where a renovation team was turning a grocery store into a movie theater. The 6" x 24" x 50' glulam beam had been the ridge-beam in the store but was now cut up into 12-foot and 16-foot lengths and dumped outside.

The workers said, "Sure, you can have 'em if you can lift 'em," then slapped their thighs and laughed their heads off. I phoned my big, strong boyfriend, Kirt, to come down and load them into my old pickup. He tossed them in like they were made of Styrofoam, and off I sped (0 to 40 mph in fifteen minutes), having the last laugh all the way home. I sanded and stained them and used them for countertops, a pass-through counter, and my dining-room table.

Note: Glu-lam is short for glued and laminated. It is built from dimensional lumber (usually Douglas fir 2" x 6"s) stacked, glued, and pressed together to create a beam of any thickness and length desired. The end result is strong, straight, and quite beautiful.

When you *do* find a demolition site, ask if you can haul off some of the building materials, or offer to help dismantle something in return for the spoils. That's how I got all the old barn hinges for my batten doors, the silvery-gray barn-wood for picture frames and other projects, and a stash of gorgeous 30-inch hand-split shingles they don't make anymore. I'll eventually use them for siding on a decorative wall or on a small building someday. My son is currently salvaging some nice 8" x 8" x 12' timbers from an old outbuilding that needs to be removed from rezoned commercial property. They'll come in handy for a carport.

Almost all construction sites, residential or commercial, are gold mines for surplus building materials. Ask the contractor if you can do some of his post-construction cleanup work by taking away unused random lengths of lumber, headers, versa-lam beams (multi-ply laminated veneers) and partial sheets of plywood that were thrown down by carpenters in a hurry and scattered all over the place. Most builders have time constraints and such a mess to clean up—after a house is built and before the landscaping begins—that they will most likely appreciate all the cleanup help they can get.

Bartering and trading labor and/or goods is always a viable way to get building materials and physical help without any money changing hands. It's good old-fashioned free enterprise at work, and the mutual sharing back and forth can forge strong and valuable friendships.

On one newly purchased lot where the owner was trying to clear the land of debris so he *could* build, I spied a sign that read: "Free Concrete Piers—*You* Haul." I rushed home and got my son and his friend to help lift them into my truck, five at a time, at 200 pounds each. We made six trips to take all thirty of them. I ultimately used them for a large deck foundation, and for the entranceway footings on the studio I built. They came in handy and saved me *tons* of money.

So you don't miss an opportunity to snag something good that you can use now or later, take work gloves and a box of assorted hand tools with you everywhere you go. It wouldn't hurt to also carry with you a liability agreement that states you will not hold the owner of the goods responsible if you get hurt taking them away. Give out a signed copy whenever you need to. People (including contractors) are so afraid of being sued that a signed waiver will assuage their trepidation and possibly cinch the deal; they will feel legally protected.

Cabinetmakers have used cabinets to get rid of after people remodel their kitchens and have new cabinets built. *Those* people have money to burn; *you* don't. Ask to haul away the perfectly good but *used* cabinets. If need be, you can paint them a color you like. Cabinet and furniture makers often have piles of hardwood scraps, such as leftover pieces of exotic woods and high-quality plywood that they are often willing to get rid of. If nothing else, you could burn the kiln-dried hardwood in your woodstove.

Go to lumber mills, if you have any nearby, and ask to see their stacks of lumber and plywood rejects. Retailers want perfect stock, so plywood with a few mislaid plys and slightly damaged lumber are sold at bargain *cash and carry* prices. The mill is happy to break even. They'll even load it for you with their forklift. I've bought most of my *imperfect* plywood over the years at half-price by going straight to the mill for it.

Call electrical contractors and ask if they have *used* electrical boxes, breakers, conduit, and assorted rolls of wire that were left over from a job. Builders put up temporary electrical service boxes then remove and replace them when the house is ready to be permanently wired. The contractor will have to use a brand-new box on his next project, so the old one (like new) gets put on a shelf in a storage facility. That's where you come in.

Keep an eye out for free fill dirt from construction sites where basements are being dug or hilly land is being leveled. The contractor needs to dump it somewhere, and if you're closer than the dump, he'll bring it to *you* instead. To get on the contractor's preferred list and beat out the competition, offer to at least pay for the gas. My son Eric recently had twenty loads of fill dirt from a project in town brought to his building site, to backfill his basement walls, for the price of the trucker's time and diesel fuel. So instead of the usual $200 to $500 for a 10-cubic-yard dump-truck load of dirt, he paid $50 a load. The price of fuel has driven up all construction prices tremendously. There has never been a more mandatory time to scrounge than *now*!

Most nurseries have reject plants in their back lots where they keep their crooked and scraggly trees and bushes and sell them cheaply. A tree is a tree is a tree—it'll recover and thrive after it's planted. At the rate you will probably be developing your property, you won't need immediate landscaping.

Let landscaping contractors or spec-house building contractors know that you'll pick up their leftover sod from their *instant lawn* projects. Ask them to call you before the rolls dry out. I did my own front yard, a little at a time, by acquiring *free* sod this way.

I also asked my friends around town if I could take root cuttings from their weed-like, drought-resistant trees that send out root runners every which way that sprout up, well...like weeds. Now I have beautiful windbreaks of silver poplars and trees of heaven all over my property. The effort was labor-intensive—digging and planting always *is*—but free.

Go to tire dealers for used tires for your garden. They are great to partially bury in the ground and plant tomatoes and other vegetables in, as well as for weed and water control. Their heat-retention quality is great for early spring planting.

Refurbished tools, half-priced or less, are piled high on shelves at Sears Service Centers, just waiting for a second owner to use and abuse them. They come with a *new* guarantee.

Fabric outlet stores and giant discount stores are the places to go for interior furnishings. Yardage and drapery material are sometimes a buck or two a yard. I bought all my heavy-duty cotton duck curtain fabric from Walmart for only $3 per yard.

I highly recommend buying a small trailer to convert to a temporary bathroom facility and placing it near your septic tank so it can be easily hooked up. I did just that when I was building my house and used it for *years*. I gutted it, installed a toilet, basin, painted-plywood shower stall, and 40-gallon water heater. When the house was finished, I put an ad in *The Nickel* want ads and sold it to the first caller for $500 ($200 profit after using it for years). Even *before* it was towed away, I received twenty more calls from disappointed would-be buyers.

If you don't have a septic system installed yet, pick up an old water heater free from the dump or an appliance store, strip it down to the bare tank, paint it black, and set it up on stilts or a platform above where you'll be showering so the water will gravity flow. Whenever the sun shines, you'll have all the hot water you need for bathing.

When I first moved onto my land and was living in

a tent and had no electricity yet, I bought a wood-fired hot tub from the Snorkel Stove Co. I bathed and soaked under a canopy of stars whenever I was dirty, tired, and sore—which was *always*. It was little splash of heaven after a hard day's work.

Another way to save money while developing your property is to put up a clothesline and buy an old wringer washing machine that can be filled with a hose. If you live out in the country, driving to town to a Laundromat burns gas and is expensive and time-consuming.

Apply for extensions on your building permit, so you have a *year* between inspections instead of the allotted six months. That will give you extra time to save up for materials and complete the labor for each stage of your building project that requires an inspection.

If your friends and relatives are insistent on giving you holiday gifts, tell them that what you really want for Christmas or your birthday are building supplies: a gift certificate to the lumberyard or hardware store, or just plain cash to buy materials with. If they want specifics, give them a list of items to choose from.

Closing Thoughts

"Scrounging" is synonymous with "labor," and "free" is synonymous with "sweat." If you want to save money, you will have to *pay* in time and labor. But look at it this way: You are also saving a bundle on not needing a fitness center membership or a personal trainer!

CHAPTER 33

COPING WITH A RECESSION

Winter firewood will warm Kirt twice

We're headed for a *major* recession, and we need to make some *adjustments*—financially and psychologically. We've all been living too high on the hog, spending money before we even earn it by maxing out our credit cards and buying expensive houses and cars that are beyond our stretched budgets. In *any* economy this isn't a good practice. If we can't augment our means, we need to diminish our wants, or at least make a list of priorities and eliminate things we can live without right now. (2008)

A recession means money will be tight, and that rude awakening will dictate that you spend it on necessities, not luxuries. Some of us are spoiled, so it might be hard to differentiate between the two. We'll have to *get real*.

Being creatures of habit, spending can become an addiction, and when it's taken away, we may suffer withdrawals. Next time we're out on a spending spree (if there *is* a next time), we should ask ourselves, "Do I really *need* this?" Try to determine whether it's an emotional need, a physical need, or just a bad habit of convincing ourselves that everything we desire is a necessity. In short, "Shop till you drop will have to *stop*."

We've grown accustomed to life in the fast lane and instant gratification. We get necessities mixed up with *excessities*. Our sense of entitlement tends to prevail over our sense of reality. A *rational* attitude adjustment is not an easy task, but the good news is, we are all creatively rich inside if we muster up the gumption to tap into our inner resources. Every cloud has a silver lining.

We can use this time for personal growth. Instead of seeking out *external* stimuli such as movies and concerts and constantly going places that burn up expensive gas, *stay home* and read a book—for *internal* stimulus. An old Chinese proverb says it best: "A book is like a garden carried in your pocket." What *best* to fill that empty pocket!

We all profess to love rainy days and talk about how we wish we would get snowed in for a week, but have we ever asked ourselves what we would actually *do* if that happened?

Learn to be with yourself. The real business of life is getting to know one's self. Get in shape: jog, hike, and work out. Read voraciously, learn to sew, grow a garden, learn to play an acoustic instrument. Find your inner artist, your inner writer, your inner musician, your inner craftsman, and your inner humanitarian. Do good things. Be a big brother to an unfortunate kid, hold babies at the hospital, read to a shut-in. Spend *yourself*.

Stay home and cook healthful, inexpensive food from scratch, such as *beans and greens*. Going out to eat on a regular basis is terribly expensive, a fleeting experience, and a luxury we can live without for a while.

Do your *own* hair and nails—or *don't*. Designer fingernails, when you're in a financial crisis, should be the least of your worries. Go natural; beauty really does emanate from industrious people doing what they love to do, even if their hair is messed up. My son Eric, a classical pianist, is bald—but that doesn't detract even one *hair* from the beauty and enjoyment of his passionate piano playing!

Not only will we have to cut down on our *own* spending, but we'll have to quit indulging the kids. Yay! It may the best thing that ever happened to them. Instead of deliberately withholding things they want—to *try* to teach them values—we simply won't *have it* to give. What we *will* have is a perfect excuse to inform them that from now on they'll have to "Use it up, wear it out, make it do, or do without" (an old American motto). Kids are resilient and adapt to just about any situation. After they get over the initial shock, you'll see them drawing upon their own imaginations and ingenuity to *create* activities and *make* things they want. They'll learn to entertain themselves. (Now *that's* a novel concept!)

If I sound a little cynical about spoiled, demanding

kids, I guess it's because I *am*. I've seen far too many family members totally alienated from each other. They all zoom around in separate cars to separate destinations seeking entertainment everywhere but home. Then when they *do* come home, they grab some food out of the refrigerator, rush to their respective rooms (replete with PCs and TVs), and shut their doors—with barely a mumble or no greeting at all. I believe a recession will bring family members closer to one another. Everybody will be in the same lifeboat together fighting off the sharks—the loan sharks.

We can show our love for one another by doing things for each other, rather than buying things for each other. *Things* don't make us happy—feelings of love and self-worth and peace of mind do, but those intangibles have to be earned.

Triumphing over adversity is very rewarding. It might not be much fun at first, but nature is a great equalizer. Your initial investment of struggle and a little pain in the short run will pay off in the long run, like compound interest for the rest of your life. People in denial who continue to live on borrowed time and borrowed money will likely crash and burn.

Without any extra money to spend, we'll discover things to do we have never thought of, or have been procrastinating for years. It's amazing what we can come up with when we don't have our usual options and diversions. The famous Dr. Robert Schuller aptly calls it *possibility thinking*.

How about dusting off that old piano in the corner and learning to play it? To illustrate how wonderful it is to know how to play a musical instrument, here's a true account: Recently we had a huge thunder and lightning storm while my son was playing a wild and dynamic

Beethoven sonata. It was nighttime, and all of a sudden the lights went out. Eric never missed a beat—he kept on playing in the dark. It was magnificent! It sounded like an entire orchestra in the pitch-black house. The incongruity of it all was downright comical. When he ended the piece with a giant crescendo, like making his *own* thunder, we laughed uproariously—in the dark.

That serendipitous lesson made me realize how we should all strive to depend more on the things in life that money can't buy—and never *has* been able to buy. We need to develop our special talents and desires that emanate from within us, just in case we're stuck at home with no extra money and maybe no electricity. If everything we're interested in has to be plugged in, it's time for a reassessment. How about lively conversations and discussions with *each other* (a lost art) or with good friends you haven't invited over in a while.

People who have worked on themselves, developed their creativity, and have hobbies and accomplishments and skills galore are the lucky ones who will stay happy and fulfilled through a recession. They have money in the bank—their *memory bank*. Their frontal lobes and other cranial *vaults* have been programmed like computers with skills, abilities, knowledge, and practical experience.

Backwoods Home readers are generally those kind of people—rugged individualists who have *chosen* a lifestyle of self-reliance, independence, and security. The moral of "The Ant and the Grasshopper" fable lives on in the *Backwoods Home* philosophy. "The Little Red Hen" is a close runner-up.

I've been in survival mode all my life (subsistence-level income), so my lifestyle probably won't change at all. In retrospect, I feel fortunate I didn't ever have anything handed to me, thus was forced to develop my potential by working at it. I count my blessings every day with what I have been able to accomplish so far—mainly because I live in this great country of equal opportunity and free enterprise (capitalism). I simply took advantage of it.

Recession or no recession, I don't believe in handouts from the government (socialism), or handouts from one family member who earned it to another who didn't. I'm a firm believer in the concept that you hurt people by helping them too much, unless it's an emergency or there are other extenuating circumstances beyond their control, or unless they are putting in equal energy in helping themselves and the outcome is in sight. Give a leg up instead of a handout.

In America, even during a recession, our standard of living is so much higher than in a third-world country that there *is* no comparison. To put it all in perspective, just think about what we already *have*! When you're feeling gloom and doom, take an inventory. How many pairs of shoes can you wear at once unless you're a centipede?

But we don't have to panic; nothing lasts forever, not even a recession. *This too shall pass*, and we'll each be a better person for it. Until we were tested, we probably didn't think we had it in us to be so resourceful. When it's over I hope we can give ourselves an "A" on our own personal report cards and apply all those good lessons we learned to when times are prosperous again. And they *will* be.

But meanwhile, find the humor in your situation. Laugh a lot! We are not victims—we probably did most of this to ourselves by running up those credit cards and *eating dessert first* one time too many. We have the body we deserve and the bank account we deserve. The blame game is lame. We need to take personal responsibility for our part in it and go forward with some positive changes.

They say there are three types of people: The ones who *let* things happen, the ones who *make* things happen, and the ones who wonder *what happened*? Which one will you *choose* to be?

CHAPTER 34

RED-TAILED HAWKS

Cynthia, four, with Ilka

Ever hear of Galena, Nevada? Didn't think so. I hadn't either until I spent a summer there in 1969. It's an old ghost town about ten miles south of Battle Mountain and forty-four miles southeast of Winnemucca, Nevada. *Now* you're getting the picture—and you're right; the picture is bleak. It's in the foothills above Battle Mountain in the middle of Galena Canyon, which in turn is in the middle of nowhere. When we were there, the population was only five: My husband, Ron, myself, and our two little kids, Eric and Cynthia—and Oscar, an old hard-rock miner who was a permanent fixture. (The population is now ten.)

Galena had seen better days back in the 1870s and 1880s, when it was a hoppin' town that boasted 250 residents and a hundred miners. In the town's short life its mines produced $5 million worth of silver and lead—the latter extracted from its namesake ore, *galena*.

There was also *gold* in them thar hills, and that's what took us there. My in-laws were in the real-estate business in Reno, and as an investment adventure based on pure speculation, they bought the rights to glean whatever gold they could find left in the tunnel and in the tailings from an old mine there. They sent their only begotten son to work the mine for three months or bust. Our home was in Reno, but I didn't mind going along because it was the first (and last) time I would have an extended vacation from waitressing, and the kids were only five and six and would be easily entertained.

We were provided a small livable travel trailer surrounded by tall cottonwood trees for shade. Oscar, who was there to help, was an experienced dynamite-blasting man from a bygone era. He stayed in an old dilapidated building, fought off large Norway rats at night, and showed us the fresh scratches on his legs in the morning. He complained about sleep deprivation from the huge rats stomping their feet all night to communicate and told us that when he challenged them with a flashlight, they'd rear up on their hind legs, make growling and hissing noises, and go for his shins.

Oscar knew how to operate the ore-sifting and ore-washing equipment and how to keep the holding pond full from the natural spring that fed Galena Creek. Ron operated an Allis Chalmers track loader to bring the ore out of the mine, then loaded it into a big dump truck and drove it to a nearby processing shed.

The only modern building in Galena was a concrete-block assay office a hopeful investor built during a previous resurgence of interest in the old mines.

We were determined to bloom where we were planted, so we decided to be very creative and get the most out of our *Summer Lampoon Vacation*. It helped that we were young and in love, healthy and happy, and interested in science and nature.

It didn't take long to discover that this desolate landscape was literally crawling with life. The kids and I scrutinized beetles and bugs, lizards and snakes, spiders and moths, climbed trees, chased butterflies, started a bird nest collection, found beautiful rocks and precious stones, and played in the runoff water from the mine tailings. Eric and Cynthia had gold fever too—well, fool's gold fever—and they got rich quick by filling leather pouches with shiny mica.

There were old, deserted houses to browse through, caves to get lost in, and mine shafts to fall into everywhere we explored.

We even caught trout by hand in a narrow stream with overhanging banks. The wary fish would hide up under the overhang in the roots, and that's where we would be able to get a grip on them. But grabbing a slippery fish and hanging onto it are two different things. While we squeezed and giggled, they slimed and wiggled—until they catapulted out of our hands like greased lightning! It wasn't easy, but we managed to catch enough for a big fish fry.

My only complaint about the desert was the heat, so I cut my long, thick hair as short as possible, and the kids and I wore bathing suits (or less) most of the time. There was nobody around to see us except Oscar, and he was busy fighting off real or imaginary rats (depending on how much he'd had to drink).

Ron had always been interested in raptors (birds of prey), had read several books on falcons and hawks, and was particularly interested in falconry. He hoped that someday he would have the opportunity to try out his knowledge and actually train a hawk to hunt. As serendipity would have it, a mother red-tail had made a nest about fifty feet up in one of the cottonwood trees by our trailer. We'd hear her familiar raspy, shrill cry all day long as she flew to and fro bringing food to her babies.

After we got settled in for a couple of weeks, Ron decided to climb the tree and take a look in the nest. Just in case there were *two* fledglings (birds old enough to learn to fly), he took along a pillowcase to nab one. Up, up, up he bravely went while the kids and I waited nervously at the bottom and warned him, "Hurry, here she comes!" Sure enough, there *were* two feathered adolescents in the nest (six weeks old), so he grabbed one and stuck it in the bag and scrambled down the tree, just before the screaming mama swooped down to peck off his nose. This was no nursery rhyme moment! (We learned later that red-tailed hawks do not attack people and will generally flee rather than defend their nest.)

Ron had prepared to *keep the hawk* in falconer's style if his bird napping was successful. He had converted a small outbuilding into a hawk house, bought jesses (leather straps) for its feet and had a .22 revolver to hunt rodents with. We named our beautiful girl Ilka, a Hungarian name that we simply liked the sound of.

Ron and I *manned the hawk* regularly (part of its training to learn to stay on its master's arm) by taking turns walking with it loosely lashed to our held-out wrists and/or fists. If it jumped off, it fell straight down, flapping and hanging by the jesses, and was swooped back up onto the wrist by a special technique described in the training manual. Ilka quickly learned to stay on the wrist. The rest of the time she stayed in the hawk house, ate her hand-delivered meals, and watched everything going on around her. She was basically trouble free and nonaggressive, and she seemed to enjoy the attention we gave her.

Because they are so common and easily trained as capable hunters, the majority of hawks captured by falconers in the United States *are* red-tails. But by law, people are only allowed to take them in their first year, before they are locked into uncooperative adult behaviors. They are also protected by state and federal laws and the US Migratory Bird Act. A falconer has to get a permit to harbor a hawk. We learned that the hard way (more about that later).

A falconer releases his trained hawk to perch in a tree or other high vantage point and flushes out the prey (sometimes with a dog). Then when the hawk kills the prey, the falconer has to track it down and trade the bird a ready-to-eat piece of flesh (usually from a previous kill) in exchange for the new kill. The experts say that hawks develop no loving bond with their captors but will *work for food* and quickly learn to associate the falconer with a guaranteed meal. In other words, a hawk never becomes a *pet*.

The red-tailed hawk is revered in some Native American cultures, and its feathers are considered sacred and often used in religious ceremonies. Falconry has been around for 4,000 years and can be traced to its beginnings in the Middle East and Far East. It used to be a quick way to fetch fresh meat for the family but is now is more of an art than a necessity. In medieval England, falconry became the sport of kings, and having a beautiful, well-trained bird was an incredible status symbol. Falconers were well paid and well respected. Today in the United States there are about 4,000 hobbyist falconers practicing the art.

Red-tailed hawks are one of the most widely distributed hawks in North America. They inhabit open fields, deserts, prairies, marshes, wooded areas, bluffs, mountain forests, small towns *and* big cities, and even tropical rain forests. The northernmost birds migrate south during the winter.

They are very well adapted and hang around their established territory as long as it has a good food supply. About 85 to 90 percent of a red-tail's diet consists of small- to medium-sized mammals such as mice, moles, ground squirrels, and rabbits; birds; reptiles like snakes and lizards; and occasionally frogs and fish.

Their eyesight is eight times as powerful as a human's. With binocular vision they can see spiders and beetles from afar and can spy a mouse from a mile high!

They hunt by swooping down from a high perch, seize their prey with their long, sharp talons, and either land to swallow it whole or tear it to bite-sized pieces on the spot. Sometimes they fly off to a safer place before devouring it.

When not courting and mating, they are hunting or digesting food. In flight, the red-tail prefers to soar, conserving energy by flapping as little as possible. In strong winds it occasionally hovers (kites) on beating wings to remain stationary above the ground but is particularly adept at catching updrafts and thermals to gain altitude, where it lazily circles and glides at twenty to forty miles per hour. When it spots a juicy rodent, it lets out a shrill cry like a steam whistle—which terrorizes and freezes the prey for a moment—then it dives down at speeds up to 120 mph, and seizes it with its talons.

A hawk's talons are dangerous weapons. Once they

grasp their prey, they don't release their death grip unless they *want* to or have been trained to release it for an instant reward (tasty tidbit). There have been cases of a falconer having to have his hawk's talons surgically removed from his arm (or worse).

Red-tailed hawks are sexually mature at two years but usually begin breeding around three years old. They are monogamous (mate for life).

In early spring their courtship is a spectacular display of aerial acrobatics. They literally *fall* in love! The pair flies together in large circles to gain great height while uttering shrill cries. Then the male plunges into a deep dive and immediately shoots up again in an accelerated steep climb, and if that isn't awe-inspiring enough, he repeats it over and over again. Then the lovers interlock their talons and spiral toward the ground—not unlike a wild and crazy couple who get married while skydiving—but the hawks *don't* crash-land.

Six to eight weeks later the female lays one to three eggs in the large stick nest that the couple constructed following the consummation of their marriage. Incubation takes about a month and is maintained almost entirely by the female, but the male hunts for both of them and brings food to the nest for her. When hatched, the young are covered with soft white down. The babies (called eyases) will eat beetles and worms, and of course rodents that Mom and Dad rip into little pieces and poke down their throats.

They remain in the nest for up to forty-eight days, keeping both parents incredibly busy. During the last ten days or so, the overgrown teenagers appear as large as the parents. They practice flapping their wings and balancing in the wind on the edge of the nest, preparing for the *moment of truth* when they will launch themselves into the air. They become completely independent of their parents at about ten weeks old.

The next year the couple will stay in their territory and use the same nest or rotate usage with their other old nests. They repair the large, flat, shallow nests with sticks and twigs about ½" in diameter. Over the years a nest can grow to measure 3 feet wide and 3 feet deep if it is situated in the crotch of a large tree.

An average red-tail weighs from 2 to 4 pounds, is 17 to 22 inches tall, has a wingspan of about 4½ feet, and—if all goes well—a lifespan of twenty years.

The female is nearly one quarter to one third larger than the male. Adults have dark-brown and auburn plumage on their backs and wings, but their undersides are light with a mottled and streaked chest and belly, and a sprinkle of cinnamon down the neck and upper chest. When they are soaring overhead, you can see that familiar broad, rounded, russet-red tail, hence the name. Their strong legs and feet are yellow with three toes pointed forward and one aft. They have a hooked beak with holes (nares) in it like nostrils so they can breathe while eating. Their beautiful, piercing eyes are yellow-gold in youth but turn amber with maturity.

Sometimes a hawk is chased and heckled by a mob of smaller birds that feel threatened by its mere presence in their territory. It works! A biologist friend recently informed me that not only can the little birds outmaneuver the hawk and peck at it mercilessly, but they try to poop on its feathers. Poop can be disastrous (deadly) for a hawk. It cannot afford for its feathers to get wet and dirty, so it escapes their attacks as fast as it can.

Because they are larger than most birds, you can easily spot red-tails perched along the highway on telephone poles and fence posts. They are opportunists and have adapted well to human habitats. When they seize their prey and stay on the ground to eat it, they puff out their feathers, flare their wings in a hovering arch, and fan out their tail, to guard their meal. That is when they are the most vulnerable, so they *dine and dash* as fast as they can—and don't even bother to leave a tip!

When their crop is bulging, they may not hunt for a day or two. The crop is a pouch, halfway between the mouth and stomach, where the food is stored and gradually released to the stomach. When all the juices and nutrients are extracted, the hawk coughs up a lightweight *casting*, which consists of hair, little bones, and anything else not digestible. The casting material also cleans the crop before it's expelled. To maintain its health, a hawk *has* to eat whole animals, including their blood, guts, organs, and all the *trimmings*. It would die on steak alone.

We had to regularly hunt for our captive hawk. Ron was busy working the mine, so I had to do some of the hunting. I am *not* the Sarah Palin type. I hate killing animals, or *anything* for that matter. One extremely hot day, wearing only a bikini, I donned my holster, gun, and a little game bag, and set out to find a small bird to shoot for Ilka's dinner. The kids were napping in the trailer, and Ron was nearby in case of emergency, so I ventured about a half mile away and reluctantly shot a robin. On the way back, seemingly out of nowhere, I saw what looked like a dust devil coming right at me. Squinting my eyes to see a little better in the glaring sunlight, I could tell that it was a truck barreling up the dusty dirt road. Surprise!

It turned out to be a desert ranger making the rounds in his designated godforsaken territory. He screeched to a halt in a cloud of dust and asked, "What do have in the pouch?" I said, "A bird." He said, "Let me see it." Upon examination he determined it was a *songbird* and *insectivore*—both against the law to kill. He asked, "Why did you shoot it?" I foolishly said, "For our hawk." That did it!

He got out his ticket pad and wrote up *two* citations, then told me to get in; he would drive me back to the trailer so he could see the hawk with his own two beady eyes. We were busted! It was against the law to harbor a hawk *and* to kill a robin. While he was checking out Ilka, I excused myself and ran to the trailer to hide our little pigmy cottontail we had as a temporary pet in a cage. I was afraid having Bun-Bun would be off-limits too. (I found out later it *was*!)

Mr. Gruff Ranger turned out to be an okay guy after all. He gave me just warning tickets and said to come into the sheriff's office before my court date—he would prepare a permit for us. The very next day the kids and I went barreling down the dirt road in our old beat-up Ford Fairlane with the eight-track blaring Herman's Hermits, singing along with "Mrs. Brown, You've Got A Lovely Daughter" all the way to Battle Mountain. (When you're young, everything is fun!) I paid the permit fee instead of a fine and became a law-abiding citizen instead of the lawless songbird killer and hawk-harboring criminal I had been the day before. While I was at it I bought a fishing license, but knew better than to ask if catching fish by *hand* was against the law.

Meanwhile, back at the ranch, a friend had come to visit and thought he was doing us a favor by shooting a bird to feed our hawk. It *would* have been a favor, but he shot not only the wrong kind of bird (a robin again) but the *wrong* robin—the mother of a nest full of babies in a tree right outside our trailer. For a week I had heard them peeping nonstop and saw her flying back and forth all day with bugs and worms. Now she was dead, and I could hear the babies screaming for food. It was *tragic*! Oh, what to do? There was only one thing I *could* do: become Mother Robin myself. And I *did*. The kids and I spent countless hours digging for worms, looking for bugs, and going back and forth to town to buy fresh beef to slice into worm-length strips to poke down their hatches. It was a full-time job, feeding four babies every thirty minutes all day long. The only time they were quiet was at night when I would put the nest in a cupboard and shut the door. But in the early morning if I even jiggled the floor, they would feel the vibration and stick their open beaks straight up and peep, peep, peep for breakfast. It was much louder than an alarm clock, and there was no snooze button!

We managed to keep them fat and happy into feather-hood, but then they wouldn't go away. I *was* their mother; they were *malimprinted*. I had no choice but to take them back to Reno.

It was a long, hot summer, but sadly, it was coming to an end; we were getting ready to pack up and move back home.

Ron had trained Ilka to hunt by using bird wings and other tempting lures on the end of a fishing pole, as was instructed in the training manual. We figured she was finally ready to be set free.

We prepared to turn her loose in a carefully chosen spot with a shallow stream running through it, not far from the trailer. We said our goodbyes and good lucks with tears in our eyes, and then Ron unstrapped her jesses and boosted her aloft and heaved her into the air with all his might. But instead of taking off in a spectacular *born-free* flight as we had envisioned, she flew straight to me, landed on my shoulder, then fluttered up on top my head. Intuitively, we had never feared that Ilka would sink her talons in any of *us* (her adoptive family?), and indeed she did not. She simply skated around ever so gently, trying to balance on the *ball* (my cranium), which was the highest point in her immediate vicinity.

She flapped around for a while, then took off and flew over to the stream to check *it* out. Ron had read that hawks are very particular about where they bathe. The water has to be the perfect depth, width, velocity, and temperature, or they won't dip into it. Evidently, it met all the requirements, and she took her first bath. How lucky could we get! We were not only able to witness such a rare event *in the wild* but to record it with our old silent-movie camera.

After her bath Ron attempted over and over again to launch her into the air for her maiden voyage, but she wouldn't take the hint. She finally hopped back onto his wrist and we all walked back to the trailer wondering what we were going to do with her.

We had valiantly *tried* to set her free—but she would not go. She'd hang out above our trailer on a dead branch and just sit there. Whenever we wanted her to come down from her perch—which was often—we'd put on the glove and hold it out with hamburger or some kind of dead meat hanging from it and she'd immediately swoop down with great accuracy and finesse, land on it, and eat. The kids loved this game even though she was so heavy they had to support her with *both* arms.

The day came to leave Galena for good. We packed up our menagerie and headed home. We decided we would keep Ilka in a backyard hawk house (mews) until she was ready to fly the coop on her own. And I had found a home for the robins—my mom said she'd be happy to provide a safe haven for them in her fenced and shady backyard.

All went well. Ilka seemed happy in suburbia and the totally tame robins followed Mom around like she was the pied piper. They even went through her back door and into her kitchen, where they'd jump up on the table for scraps. She'd had *six* kids herself and missed being mother bird, so she *encouraged* it! They eventually learned to fly and perch in her trees but never left her yard.

Ilka finally flew up, up, up and away one day after eating a fat gopher, and the last I saw of her, she was a tiny, dark speck in the bright-blue sky over Reno, Nevada.

The summer of '69 was a memorable one indeed. Nobody got rich mining gold, but when the kids started school in September, they surely had plenty to talk about in "Show and Tell."

Note: You can see a video of Ilka at www.dorothyainsworth.com.

CHAPTER 35

BUILD A SMALL CABIN

"The pointy end of the nail goes in the wall"—Red Skelton

If you could use some extra space in the form of a small studio/cabin, and if you know how to use basic tools, I have just the project for you. I call it my 2-2-2 plan: 200 square feet, 2 months to build, $2,000, and I might add: 2-cute.

Years ago I built a 16' x 16' storage platform 100 feet downhill from the house my son and I are building for him. We piled stuff on it and covered it with a huge silvery gray tarp to reflect heat and shed rain. It looked like a beached whale, but that's what I wanted: a low-profile temporary storage area to blend in with the weeds.

We've since moved most of the stuff into the basement of Eric's almost-finished house, so there sat the platform still covered by the tarp but with only one hump in the middle. It had served its purpose but was now an eyesore and I wanted to get rid of it.

Then I got to thinking. I had built it with a strong pier and girder foundation and a thick subfloor. It not only looked like a whale, but it could have supported one!

It seemed a shame to tear it all down, so I decided to build a little cabin on it. In my county one can build a 200-square-foot structure (or less) without buying a permit. A 12' x 16' building would fit on the 16' x 16' platform—with a strip left over for a narrow deck off the back.

The timing was perfect because our big delivery of sugar-pine siding for the new house was delayed six weeks, the fall weather was beautiful, and I felt up to the task. I didn't have the extra cash in a bundle, but I knew I could charge all the materials at Home Depot on a twelve-month interest-free account, so there was no good excuse to put it off.

Once started, it took on a life of its own and ended up being one of my favorite projects of all the structures I've built over the past thirty years. Because it was small, it took shape in a hurry, and each phase of construction was almost textbook perfect. I buried a heavy-duty electrical line over from the main panel at the house to supply the studio with a 20-AMP service for lights, a small heater, and my computer. In only two months of spare-time labor and $2,000 in materials—some new, some used—it was completely finished.

I now have my own quiet office with a beautiful view. It's well insulated, has a clean white interior belying its rustic exterior, and two tiny decks. It's away from distractions when I feel like writing or organizing my thousands of photographs—or just sitting on the back deck with a cup of coffee and gazing across the beautiful rolling hills.

Foundation and Floor

The following instructions are for building a 12' x 16' cabin on uneven ground, but you can make it any dimensions you want and on any kind of foundation you want, as long as it's under 200 square feet. (Check with your building department to make sure the "under 200 square feet rule" is legal in your county.)

1. Stake out your site, then level and square it with "batter boards" and strings (Google simple batter-board instructions).

   If you are lucky enough to already have level ground and can use regular wood-topped piers, or want to pour a level concrete foundation, build a simple floor frame out of 2" x 6"s and skip to Step 5.

   Note: For uneven ground I recommend using adjustable pier brackets, which are like mini-jacks if you want to hasten and ease the process of "leveling the playing field." Use piers with a hole in the middle for the threaded bolt on your adjustable bracket to go into.

2. Set your evenly spaced piers no farther apart than 4 to 6 feet. You don't need to level them with each other if your ground is sloped because you will be using PT (pressure-treated) 4" x 4" uprights cut at various lengths and put in the adjustable pier brackets to compensate for any differences in height.

3. Once you get all the 4" x 4"s close to the same level (your future floor level), attach another type of bracket to the top of each one (see photo), which

will create the channels to slide the 16-foot girders into. I made my girders out of pairs of straight 16' x 2" x 6"s screwed together for ease in handling and because they were affordable (common dimensional lumber is cheap these days). The catch is that two 2" x 6"s on edge are only 3 inches thick, and the bracket holds a 4" x 4", so a ½"-thick plywood spacer has to be put in each bracket to fill it out (see photo).

4. Level all the girders to each other by jacking up the adjustable brackets to meet your level strings going every which way but loose (you don't want loose). All it takes is a wrench on the large nut to run it up or down the threaded bolt to adjust the height.

5. Install your 2" x 6" floor joists at 16-inch centers between the girders with joist hangers, or, if you want your building higher, on top of the girders. If you choose to put them on top, you must put blocking (spacers) between the joists at their halfway point and also cap off the joist ends with 2" x 6" rim joists to stabilize them.

6. Now you're ready for the subfloor. I recommend thick T&G OSB (¾" or ⅞") because it is inexpensive compared to plywood. It should be screwed down every 8 inches around the perimeter and every 12 inches along each floor joist (snap chalk lines).

Framing and Sheathing

1. I used 2" x 4" studs on 16-inch centers for the walls and 2" x 6" rafters on 2-foot centers for the roof and 2" x 6" rafter-tie members every 2 feet (called ceiling joists). I sheathed everything with

4' x 8' x 7/16" OSB because it was only $6.50 a sheet and I knew I'd also be putting a layer of 1" x 12" sugar pine siding on the outside walls (to match the main house).

2. I bought a slightly imperfect 36-inch door with a jamb at Builder's Bargain Center for $99. It was solid straight-grained Douglas fir and had six window lights in the upper half...just what I wanted. I hung it without incident and installed a lockset.

3. I installed two 2' x 4' flange-mount windows from Home Depot (on sale) in the framed openings (very easy). I chose medium-sized windows to save on heat and cooling.

4. After attaching the electrical outlet boxes to the studs and running the wires to each outlet, I installed R-13 fiberglass insulation in the walls and between the rafters, using an electric stapler. Then I sheathed the interior (including the ceiling) with more 7/16" OSB and screws.

Note: I used OSB mainly because I did not want to deal with Sheetrock and all the cutting, mudding, taping, sanding, and texturing involved. I also wanted a wall I could hang a shelf or a picture on or stick a nail in without using special fasteners.

The penalty for avoiding Sheetrock was to have to caulk every seam and joint and use trim in the corners and where the walls met the ceiling, but it was still easier than messing with Sheetrock!

Paint, Carpet, and Trim

1. Before installing carpet I filled all the screw holes in the walls and ceiling with wood-spackle, using

a putty knife, then painted the whole interior with two coats of off-white paint. The first coat was an excellent quality primer to seal any off-gassing from the OSB. Then I rolled on regular interior paint very generously to fill all the tiny crevices in the OSB. The result looks like a subtle texturing job.

2. Fortunately, I had stored a sizable roll of beige carpet for years (a free gift) and was finally able to use it. I squared it up with a straight edge and utility knife and fitted it to the floor in a dry run. I then covered the rough subfloor with smooth ⅝" particle board and counter sunk each screw-head so I could glue the carpet down (no pad). I used a nontoxic carpet adhesive; the process went smoothly, and the carpet fit perfectly.

3. After laying the carpet, I installed baseboard, corner molding, ceiling trim, and window trim. I painted all the trim with bright semigloss white for contrast against the flat white walls. White on white would help bounce light around from the two windows.

4. Next came the ceiling light and porch light installation (quick and easy). My retired-electrician friend Russ advised me to put a secondary circuit-breaker box inside the studio, and he wired the switches for me so if I trip the breaker by overloading the plug-outlets, the lights will remain on. Brilliant!

5. I finally closed the door on the interior job and went outside to do some real work. First off, to create a vapor barrier behind the siding, I painted the OSB with bargain-priced mismatched paint from the hardware store, instead of using expensive Tyvek house-wrap.

Note: Some of my other storage buildings sheathed

with OSB are simply painted with two coats of exterior paint and have held up for years. Siding is an optional expense.

Roofing and Rain Gutters

1. I roofed with three-tab asphalt shingles—one step up from the my usual poorman's rolled roofing on outbuildings—so the roof would look fairly attractive when viewed from Eric's front window.
2. Rain gutters were imperative because the roof pitch drained over the front door and the back deck. I bought dark-brown vinyl gutters and downspouts and all the trimmings from Home Depot (inexpensive) and installed them in a day.

Decks and Siding

After the roofing job, I built a small entrance deck on the place. I used some old concrete piers I already had and constructed a 2" x 6" frame on them, and I used more DF 2" x 6"s for the decking itself (only 25 cents a foot).

For the back deck, I attached two 4' x 8' sheets of 1⅛" subfloor plywood (end to end) to the 3-foot strip left over on the original platform, and painted the heck out of it with deck paint. The now 4-foot wide by 16-foot long deck is cantilevered out a bit but strong and usable. I capped it off all around with 2" x 12"s and installed a cedar railing. The twenty railing posts were only $1 each at Home Depot. I laid them down on an old sheet of OSB and prestained them using a small garden sprayer.

I built two sets of stairs, one at each end of the long deck, for convenience, but also for my ten-year-old grandson, Zane. He and his friends (and the dog) can chase each other up one side and down the other like the cartoon characters they are.

Eric's 3,200 feet of 1" x 12" sugar-pine siding finally arrived by boom truck, so I set about installing some of it on the cabin first. It was good practice and only took three days to complete. I found that the batts took as much time and effort to install as the boards! Using a small table saw, my friend Russ helped me rip an inch off the width of all the 1" x 4" x 16' utility pine boards I bought to make narrow batts (20 cents a foot).

After I drove in the last of hundreds of 2-inch star-headed bronze-coated screws, I slapped on some cedar stain, snapped a few photos and the labor is now history—except for sharing the story so you can do it too!

Closing Thoughts

This multipurpose studio/cabin could be used for just about anything that doesn't require running water, such as: a sewing room, music practice room, artist's studio, writer's den, massage "parlor," yoga and meditation space, dance studio or exercise room (put up mirrors), hobbies of all kinds, plain old storage, or an office. It's a place where you can leave home without running away. Everybody needs a space like that. If Herman Cain wants to follow MY 2-2-2 plan, he can have one too (2011).

CHAPTER 36

DROUGHT-TOLERANT
LANDSCAPING

Landscaping around piano studio

What would a homestead look like without any trees? Mars comes to mind: barren, windswept, desolate, and uninviting. There would be nothing alive to climb on, play hide-and-go-seek behind, sit and read a book against, or have a picnic under. There'd be no shade, no birds, no fruit and nuts, no autumn leaves, no branches to hang a swing from, and no bark for lovers to carve their initials in and revisit when they're old. Oh, and no oxygen to breathe!

Trees are the magnificent culmination of evolutionary genius. They run on solar energy and give back oxygen, so not only do they decorate the earth, but they clean the air. They help slow climate change by absorbing carbon dioxide, and they conserve topsoil. In the world of solar technology, plants of any kind are waaay ahead of the game of harnessing the sun's rays, and their diversity of leaf design is mind-boggling.

Note: According to the Arbor Day Foundation, a mature leafy tree produces as much oxygen in a season as ten people inhale in a year!

Landscaping decisions are tough and what we get is not always what we would aesthetically prefer, but each plant we choose has to fit the soil and climate conditions we have to offer. In this article I will tell what trees and bushes I chose for my property, and why.

Leland Cypress

When I bought ten acres back in 1981 on the hot, thirsty side of Ashland, Oregon, all there was on the land was star thistle, poison oak, buckbrush, and a couple of old live oaks that looked half dead. I was determined to change all that, so for starters, as soon as I drilled a well and hooked up a hose, I bought fifty 1-gallon-size Leyland Cypress trees at $5 each and planted them 5 feet apart along the front of the property that runs parallel to the road.

I would have liked to buy larger trees, but with more time than money, I had no choice but to be patient. I was too engrossed in developing the property and building a house to do anything but VISUALIZE what those tiny trees would look like someday. That elusive "someday" is now here and the trees are 10 feet wide and 50 feet tall—

in fact, SO tall that the power company had to trim them from their lines last year! They provide a thick barrier against traffic noise and fumes and are a gorgeous sight to behold.

Leyland Cypresses are drought resistant, insect resistant, deer resistant, and the fastest growing evergreens there are (about 2 feet a year). They are low maintenance, grow almost anywhere in any kind of soil, and look lush, plush, and beautiful. They form a dense privacy screen and a formidable windbreak. They even keep free-range errant cows out of my yard!

Leyland Cypresses thrive well in zones 6 to 10, but their kissin' cousins, Thuja Green Giants, hold up better in colder climates, zones 5 to 8. They both like plenty of sun and do best in fairly well-drained soil, but then, not many species of trees like wet feet all the time.

Southern Oregon only gets 20 inches of rainfall a year, so I store well-water in a large holding tank and let gravity do its drip-irrigation all over the property via a maze of inexpensive ¾" poly-pipe, with an ice-pick hole punched wherever there's a plant. This poor-man's system works great, and I've had very few casualties even during extreme drought years.

Deodar Cedar and Juniper

The Deodar Cedar is another evergreen that does well under harsh conditions. I found that out "the easy way" by buying a 4-inch seedling in a 4-inch pot for $1.79 at Sprouse-Reitz thirty years ago (now extinct like Woolworths). I poked it in the ground where I could keep an eye on it and water it with a cup, and now that eye has to look 60 feet up to see the top. Before long I'll need binoculars! Others I've planted have taken off with the same rapid growth. Their sweeping branches hang elegantly like flared skirts with lacey edges of velvety new growth. The needles are soft and touchable, and the wood is fragrant. They are beautiful trees, and I highly recommend them.

Every once in a while a tree chooses me. A small juniper with its tiny roots intact jumped off a logging truck as it went by my property and I scooped it off the road and stuck it in the ground. Now it's a huge and handsome bluish-green tree with juniper berries galore on it. If I were a drinker I could make my own gin!

Poplars

I'm too busy multitasking to fuss over any ONE task (such as landscaping), so whatever I plant better be able to mostly take care of itself. Drought-tolerant Hybrid Poplars fit that description, so I bought 20 of them at $10 each back in the eighties and planted them 12 feet apart along the west side of my future house site. The house is now finished, and they provide shade in the summer and dazzle us with golden leaves in autumn that create a natural bed of mulch when they fall. (No, I don't rake leaves!) I planted some evergreens behind them so when the poplars are bare, Douglas Firs, Ponderosa Pines, and Blue Spruces take over the job of wind protection.

Poplars send out runners (surface roots with new shoots sticking up), so I took cuttings with a sharp shovel and transplanted dozens of them all over the property and around a pond fed by a windmill. Those lucky trees at the pond got all the water they could drink, so they've grown HUGE and now provide a cool, heavenly oasis where the dogs and kids hang out when it's a hundred degrees in the summer.

A combination of evergreens and deciduous trees chosen for practical as well as aesthetic reasons grace the land with plenty of seasonal color and a variety of shapes, sizes, and textures to gaze upon: globes and ovals, wide spreading, columnar, open headed, pyramidal, and weeping. Alternating the two types in the same row or with one row behind the other provides backup wind protection in the winter.

Another drought-resistant tree is the Silver Poplar. Twenty-five years ago, I took root cuttings from a friend's yard (yes, I'm the Root Bandit) and planted a double row of what looked like scrawny little stems poking out of the ground along the road that curves around a piano studio I built. From those tiny starts grew long, graceful trunks supporting high branches filled with shimmering leaves that sway in the breeze. The leaves are green on one side and white on the other and they quake in the wind like their close relative the aspen.

I have since taken cuttings from those second-generation trees and let nature help me create even more beautiful windbreaks in other problem areas, such as near my son Eric's house. I used a tight row of Leyland Cypresses again to deflect the strong winds coming up his hill from the southwest, and I planted a row of Silver Poplars in front of them for color and shade in three out of the four seasons.

A local nursery had a rare sale on 10-foot Lombardi Poplars several years ago, so I bought fifty of them at $10 each and planted them 8 feet apart along the northern boundary of my property. I ran 400 feet of irrigation polypipe along the fence line, and those trees are now about 30 feet high. Their fall color is breathtaking!

Tree of Heaven

Another friend offered me root cuttings from what most nurseries call a *weed* but is one of my favorites: the Tree of Heaven. Talk about drought resistant; this one gets the prize! You can propagate them anywhere and they grow rapidly into big, strong, widely branched shade trees similar to Black Locusts. The multifingered *pinnate* leaves (resembling a feather's design) are delicate-looking as they hang from slender stems, but don't be fooled; these trees are tough!

I planted ten of them strategically around the property where I want *big* shade and they are here to stay. Everywhere I look around town I see these survivors growing and flourishing where no other plant would dare to tread. Some have more than one trunk and support canopies that are 60 feet high and 40 feet wide. (Originally from China, they were used in medicine and for hosting silk worms.)

They are called *invasive*, but that's exactly what I want where nothing else will grow without being pampered. Their life span is only about fifty years, but they continually colonize by sending out root sprouts, and the seeds have *wings*. That means free labor!

Bamboo

Bamboo is another plant that has a bad reputation for being invasive. I say, "Bring it on!" It will only spread if it gets a surplus of water, and on this dry land it doesn't. Dense *walls* of Golden Bamboo surround one of my decks, extending the indoor/outdoor living space. The deck is totally protected from wind and sun and the segmented trunks and long, skinny leaves of bamboo are simply divine. It is easily transplanted from root cuttings wherever one wants a beautiful stand of green-and-yellow bamboo that filters the light and offers privacy and protection.

A large stand of bamboo is so impenetrable that you could hack a narrow trail into the middle and clear a flat spot to use as a meditation *room* or a kid's *clubhouse* or whatever. Bamboo is unique, versatile, and fast growing. It comes in many varieties, including timber bamboo, which is used for construction in Asia, and wood products such as flooring. In my opinion bamboo is one of the most visually appealing ornamental plants there is.

Ground Cover

For large and hilly areas, I prefer *rows* of trees and *banks* of ground-cover plants, with accent bushes placed here and there for bursts of fall color. St. John's Wort is a great solution if you have a steep bank and want to prevent erosion. These plants are drought-resistant, fast-growing *creepers* and spread their tangled roots in a formidable grid to hold soil and water. I've covered two such banks with tiny starter plants the size of a quarter (and the cost of a quarter), and now they carpet the banks with a dense layer of soft green leaves. The deer don't like it, but ladybugs and honey bees abound in great numbers when the foot-high foliage blooms with bright yellow flowers in late June.

Maples and Oaks

In addition to the rows of low-maintenance trees, I've been unable to resist buying a few trees for sheer beauty and dazzling fall color. Among those gorgeous trees are the maples. The October Glory is big and hardy and turns crimson red in the fall, and the Autumn Blaze is so brilliant it looks like it's on fire when the leaves turn a phosphorescent red-orange.

I planted a Red Oak for size and longevity, and a Sugar Maple for height. The latest addition to my family of maples is a columnar Karpick Maple, which stands stately like a sentinel at the end of a long row of Red-Tip Photinia planted along the dirt road to Eric's house. Someday it will tickle the sky 50 feet up but remain slim at 20 feet wide. In the fall, its bright red and gold leaves look striking against the deep-blue sky.

Royal Empress and Mimosa Silk Tree

Two other trees that are an absolute must to plant on just about any piece of property are the Mimosa Silk Tree and the Royal Empress Tree. They are both tough and fast growing, but their beauty belies their durability.

The Royal Empress is one of the fastest growing deciduous trees (3 feet a year is common) and will reach 50 feet tall and 40 feet wide in just a few years. The large leaves hang from widely spaced branches, forming a dense umbrella of delicious shade by summer. Oddly enough, the *empress* is late to come to the ball in the spring but stays long after the party is over before letting her hair down at midnight (late fall).

In winter the smooth branches are covered with furry little buds that burst into fragrant pinkish-purple blossoms in the spring, like something you'd see in Hawaii. Its fragrance is a cross between jasmine and gardenia. It grows almost anywhere and has no significant pest or disease problems. It tolerates drought and most soils, and it is a hardwood that lives to an old age. All this in a tree you don't have to baby! It's incredibly beautiful but almost indestructible. Even Oprah got in the act and recommended it.

When I bought mine, it looked like a tiny squash plant with a pliable green stem (trunk?) in a 6-inch container, but it cost $25! I remember thinking: *This* is a *tree*? I really had my doubts—but not for long. It has been in the ground only four years, is 12 feet tall, and it's already spreading its arms far and wide and waving gracefully like a royal empress should. I did it a favor by planting it on the lee side of Eric's house so its huge leaves would be buffered from the wind, and indeed, it is flourishing flawlessly.

The Mimosa Silk Tree—another remarkable beauty— is unsurpassed as a hummingbird *magnet*. It is easy to grow, drought tolerant, adapts to almost any soil type, and can be planted in full sun or partial shade. Its fragrant, hot-pink, tropical-looking blossoms grow in clusters and face *up* like shimmering *cups* offering nectar to be sipped. Its smooth greenish-gray trunk supports a fluttering umbrella of fern-like leaves that is wider than the tree is tall and lends wonderful shade on a hot summer day. I like to sit and watch the *show* where at least twenty hummingbirds at any given time flit around from flower to flower, drinking, fighting, flirting, mating, and singing. I could go down to the local bar and see the same thing, but, no thanks, I'll stay home where it's much more entertaining—under the silk tree.

Note: The Mimosa Silk Tree is another late bloomer. Just when you think it must have died in the winter, it finally shows signs of life in late spring, but it is still going strong in late fall long after all the other trees are skeletons of their former selves.

Flowering Hawthorne and Golden Chain Tree

Two more ornamental trees that offer unusual visual

treats in the spring are the Flowering Hawthorne and the Golden Chain. Both do well up here on the arid savannah. I planted them in close proximity to each other twenty years ago, unaware that they would bloom at the same time and compliment each other as beautifully as a multicultural beauty pageant. The Flowering Hawthorne's tangled *hair* reminds me of a Jamaican's dreadlocks adorned with an extravagance of dark-pink rosettes, and the Golden Chain's bright-yellow pendulous blossoms hang like Goldilocks's ringlets. Side by side, the contrast is stunning!

Fruit and Nuts

Being a big advocate of *edible* landscaping, I planted a small orchard years ago and another one recently. I've found that cherry trees require the least maintenance. Apples and almonds are next, then plums and pears. Apricot and peach trees are prone to leaf curl and other diseases and need to be sprayed and pruned regularly. Apricot trees are the first to bloom in the spring, and their blossoms have to be protected against frostbite. Nothing seems to bother cherry trees. I prefer *standard* Bings because they grow impressively huge and I'm perfectly willing to share the crop on the very top with the birds. I planted one bare-root Bing for grandson Zane the year he was born and they are growing up together—both fourteen this year!

His mother, Cynthia, bought a Spanish Fir as a live Christmas tree for Zane's first Christmas, and they too are growing up together. The Spanish Fir has proven to be a perfectly suited species for this hot, dry land. It is very unusual and exceptionally handsome—just like Zane! (Am I a grandma or what?)

The Halls Hardy Almond and the Hardy English Walnut trees I planted are extremely low maintenance and very productive. Nuts are excellent survival food when all else fails. They store well and are loaded with protein and healthful omega-3 fatty acids.

Shrubs

Ceanothus (buckbrush) is native to this land, so I leave it alone to do its thing. It is also known as Wild Lilac and literally buzzes with bees in the spring, which also help pollinate the fruit trees. It is practically drought proof but fast growing and stickery, so I prune it back on trails or if it gets too close to a structure (fire danger), and that's it. An eye-catching variety called Blue Ceanothus is available at nurseries; the blue is so intense it appears fluorescent.

Pampas Grass is one of my all-time favorite grassy shrubs. It makes an attractive impermeable hedge (the sharp-edged leaves can cut like a knife) but has a whimsical flair and gorgeous spires that burst into feathery bloom in the fall. It is native to southern South America, so it's drought friendly and self-pruning (old spires die and make way for new ones). Because I prefer tall and wide hedges, I always buy the large standard size, but the dwarf variety would look pretty in a smaller yard as well as in containers.

I've had excellent luck with lavendar, lilac, Scotch broom, Oregon grape, burning bush, staghorn sumac, and Rhododendrons. Red-Tipped Photinia is a given; it grows anywhere (even along a freeway) and can be trimmed into a hedge or allowed to turn into a tree (8 feet tall and 6 feet wide). The rich red tips (new growth) that come out in the spring are like eye candy wherever you look.

Forsythia is a large shrub that is the first to bloom

in early spring, with bright-yellow tentacles of blossoms reaching out wildly in every direction and announcing that spring is here (even though the calendar says it isn't).

Rose-hips (good source of vitamin C) volunteer all over the place. Boysenberry and blackberry vines are thickly draped over an old 100-foot-long barbed-wire fence and continue to spread unchecked as long as they get water. Wild strawberries carpet the ground here and there, but I also plant regular strawberries. They propagate themselves by sending out runners, so there's never a shortage. I mulch their beds with straw to withstand the winter.

Flowers

I've chosen flowers that do well in full sun: sunflowers, climbing roses, old-fashioned hollyhocks (think Grandma), morning glories, and my all-time favorite—foxglove (adorable speckled hanging bells). I've planted hundreds of *bulbs*: daffodils, narcissi, poppies, and irises. Every year we get surprised anew when those harbingers of spring poke their pretty little heads out of the snow. Bulbs are one of nature's most ingenious "inventions"!

I adore flowers, but I don't clip their heads off and put them in a vase. I like everything to be free, including myself. Using the land as an artist's pallet, nature herself paints the sloping hills knee-deep in purple vetch and blue lupine every spring. The sight is spectacular! Then when it all dries up, it adds nitrogen to the soil. Beautiful *and* useful—a perfect balance.

The Plan

My landscaping style is pretty *loose*, and I'm certainly not an expert horticulturist. I do some Google research, then just up and plant whatever catches my eye and is recommended for my area (zone). My general philosophy is "let nature take its course" and "survival of the fittest."

There has been no master plan or grand scheme, but I know what I like: beauty, balance, and practicality. I do a lot of artistic visualization as I go along so the overall landscape will end up looking natural and pleasing to the eye. Sometimes I've bought shrubs and trees on impulse (on sale) and figured out where to put them after I got home. Nurseries thrive on plant lovers like me who let "green emotions" run away with their purse! (Warning: It's an easy addiction to acquire.)

My homestead is a work in progress. I water everything enough, fertilize occasionally, and mulch with hay and/or straw for winter. I *should* spray my fruit trees (organic oil spray) and prune them regularly, but I seldom get around to it. Heck, I don't even prune my own hair very often!

Smoke Tree

I'm finally winding down on planting because we're on a well and I'm forced to conserve water—and I also maintain a vegetable garden. But there's a special tree I've always wanted and it doesn't drink much—but it "smokes"! Smoke Trees are like giant shrubs with unusually eye-catching clouds of gossamer pink, white, or purple haze hovering over the inner branches, which are camouflaged by the billowing "smoke." Artists have portrayed them in western desert paintings because they are so unique and enchanting to gaze upon. Once you see one, you'll never forget it.

Closing thoughts

It feels good to look about the land and know that I planted everything on it by digging each hole with a pick and a shovel. It was mildly backbreaking but not bank-breaking. It was tremendous exercise, and I still have the muscles to show for it. That's the benefit-in-disguise of being economically challenged: you HAVE to do all your own work, and nature pays you back with strength, endurance, and a feeling of satisfaction you can't put a price on. About half my landscaping has been free for the digging. I never turn down a green gift from somebody's yard, even if I have to turn red to get it.

By plugging away over the years, I've inadvertently created a diversified ecosystem that is virtually alive with birds (sixty species documented so far) and a multitude of other critters running around night and day. When I first bought the property, only lizards, scorpions, and rattlesnakes were scurrying and slithering around. Now there's an environment that invites and nurtures all kinds of wildlife, and we're all sharing the land and enjoying the heck out of it.

My biggest trees have provided not only shade and fruit but priceless memories (and photographs) of dogs, cats, and kids who have had great fun playing on, under, and around them. Laughter still echoes from the tree house whenever Zane comes to visit. What could be better than that!

My advice to new property owners is to plant NOW and do everything else later. Dig a hole, add water, and nature will do the rest. The labor is short-lived but the beauty and usefulness are forever. Grab your shovel—time is not a renewable resource!

Author's note: I've planted many more species of

trees and bushes than I wrote about in this article, but I described the major ones.

Dorothy Ainsworth

CHAPTER 37

BUILD A BALCONY DECK

Balcony deck on Eric's house

The charm and appeal of a deck is that it lets you go outside without leaving the house. It provides a seamless transition from indoors to outdoors without putting your foot in the dirt, and that makes it feel as good as it looks.

A balcony deck is a pleasant and inviting place to get a breath of fresh air, lounge and sip, pet the cat, read the paper, hear the birds, and enjoy the view. From your elevated perch, you can watch the sunrise, gaze at the stars, or howl at the moon.

In my opinion there's not a second-story room in any

house that wouldn't be enhanced by adding a deck to it. Why not be able to step out onto the balcony deck of your bedroom and stretch and yawn and greet the day— barefoot and in your bathrobe if you like?

Decks extend our living space without costing very much. In thirty years of developing my property, I've added at least one deck onto every livable structure and every storage building—totaling thirteen in all.

My last big project (building Eric's house) took six years of paying as we went and doing the labor ourselves. To get to the finish line a little sooner, we decided to postpone building the balcony deck off the kitchen until later—or never. The deck was in the original plans, and we paid the permit fee for it, but enough was enough. Fortunately, we had planned ahead and left the electrical wiring out of the place in the wall where the door might be someday, and stubbed out two sets of wires for an outlet and a porch light.

After we received the final inspection and occupancy certificate in April 2012, I hung up my carpenter's belt and considered myself retired from construction work. That silly concept was short-lived. Exactly one year later, I took the belt off its rusty nail, rescued a cute little spider from its home in the nail pouch, and started in on the project.

Planning the Deck

Eric's house is nestled into the side of a slope, with the basement buried on the west side but completely exposed on the east side. His kitchen is 8 feet off the ground, sitting atop the basement. The entire east wall is tall, bare, and boring with nothing on it but the kitchen window 12 feet up and the basement door at ground level far over to one side. The house just didn't look balanced without a balcony deck on that side; it cried out to be built.

I figured the deck would not only be an attractive and useful addition to that side of the house but also create a protected area underneath it for garden tools. It would accentuate the good features of the east side: a spectacular view, sunrises and moon rises, delicious shade in the afternoon, rainbows galore in the spring, and—being on the lee side—very little wind.

We decided on a long, narrow deck that would be small and affordable ($10 per square foot) and only take a couple of months to build. I had a 24-foot wall to play with, so I decided to make the deck 18 feet long and 5 feet wide. That way I could use standard lumber with very little waste and still have room to squeeze in a fire-escape stairway off the end without it extending beyond the wall and intruding onto the walkway around the house. The 90-square-foot deck itself would have plenty of room for a little table, some chairs, and a portable barbecue.

It was a cool April, so getting it done before the scorching summer was imperative. I sketched out some detailed plans, made a materials list, and drove the old truck to Home Depot, where I used my twelve-month interest-free charge card and got loaded up, or down—depending on whether you are looking at the height of the load or the flatness of the tires.

Sidebar: I'm a do-it-yourselfer as well as a devout patriot, so to me and many other builders, Home Depot and Lowe's save us time and money by providing everything we need at a one-stop shop. In my opinion they represent the American free-enterprise system and capitalism at its finest!

About Deck Construction

The great thing about retrofitting a deck is that you can do all your hammering and sawing outside without disturbing anybody inside—well, until you cut the door opening in the wall. But that's just one day of inconvenience and mild torture—a small price to pay for years of future enjoyment.

Deck construction is simple and straightforward. There's nothing complicated about footings and piers, bolting or lag-screwing a ledger board to the house, attaching the joists, then laying down the deck boards.

My first step was measuring and remeasuring, then hammering stakes in the ground and running level strings every which way—with horizontal string-levels hanging from them—to lay out the deck on the ground first so I would know where to dig the pier holes. After outlining the squares with fluorescent spray paint, I dug five large and fairly deep holes (44 inches apart) so I could wrestle the piers into them and have room to adjust their exact positions and level them before pouring concrete around them. I used piers with a hole in the top to hold adjustable brackets so I could fine-tune the deck leveling process later if I needed to.

Note: When you build a deck, the most important tools are levels: string-levels, a long level, a medium level, and a short (torpedo) level. The old saw "plumb, level, and square" should be muttered under your breath constantly like a prayer as you work so you won't end up muttering something else when you discover you just built a sloping parallelogram instead of a level rectangle.

Setting the Ledger Board

Next step was snapping a long horizontal level chalk-line on the outside wall *3 inches lower* than the finished floor on the inside. That 3-inch drop-down provides a 1.5-inch step-down from the house to the deck, and allows for the 1.5-inch-thick 2" x 6" deck boards that will be fastened on top of the ledger board later. The resultant 1.5-inch step-down is very important so rain doesn't creep into your house.

I installed all the joist hangers on the 2" x 6" 18-foot ledger board and its corresponding rim joist at 24-inch O.C. while they were still down on the sawhorses. Then I lag-screwed the ledger board to the house making sure it was lined up and squared with the piers and perfectly level from end to end.

Setting the Posts

I temporarily plumbed and braced each 4" x 4" in place in its bracket on top of each pier. Then, working from a ladder, I was able to run a 6-foot level from the ledger board to the post and make a mark to cut the post off level with the ledger board.

After taking the 4" x 4" posts down and cutting them off, I put them back up, rebraced them, and fastened them permanently to the post brackets with screws. I then connected the posts all around with *two* sets of rim joists on all three sides to accommodate fastening long rail posts later.

Then I mixed ready-mix concrete in a wheelbarrow and poured it around each pier. I did this step last just in case I had to make any last minute pier adjustments.

Installing Deck Boards

I put L-flashing along the house side and installed the ten 2" x 6" x 5' joists. Then I screwed down all the 2" x 6" x 18' DF kiln-dried deck boards with 3-inch deck screws and put a coat of natural sealer/stain on them. It was now time to build the deck railing.

Deck Railing

To use the same style railing as the front deck, I bought the identical decorative Gothic posts and picket fencing (Home Depot) and installed it as before—by notching the Gothic posts and screwing them onto the rim joists surrounding the deck, then fastening the fencing to those posts.

Stairs and Handrails

I built a little gate on the stair-end of the deck and then tackled the stairs. To fit the rise and run of the space, they had to be moderately steep, but still within the safety code. They are there mainly to be used as a fire escape, so the handrails are only 27 inches apart, enabling a person to safely and securely hang on with both hands while going up or down. I also put traction strips on the steps—cut from inexpensive composition roofing and screwed down with flat lath-screws.

I cut the stair horses from Doug Fir 2" x 12"s and attached them at the top with metal hangers and at the bottom to a landing. I made handrails out of smoothly sanded 2" x 4"s forming an upside-down "T" (screwed together) for the outside rail. I fastened it flat-side-down to the angled-cut top of 4" x 4" posts set in concrete and used wall brackets for the inside rail. The handrails are strong, supportive, and inexpensive to make.

Door from House to Deck

Now that the deck itself was done, it was time to cut the door opening to fit a quaint little one-of-a-kind 2-foot-wide door I bought for $50 at a builders' discount outlet. It was built from beautiful straight-grain Douglas fir, and had a window in it to let more light into the kitchen, which made it ideal.

Eric cut the opening with a circular saw through the siding on the outside and a Sheetrock saw and Sawzall on the inside. The hardest part was removing one wall stud from the middle of the opening and adding an additional stud on each side.

I then framed it all around with straight-grain kiln-dried Doug fir 2" x 10"s. The three layers of siding, sheathing, and inner wall sheetrock, plus the 2" x 6" framing, added up to 8.25 inches, so I had to rip 1 inch off of each 2" x 10", because a 2" x 10" is actually 9.25 inches. (Rip means cut lengthwise.) I measured and shimmed very carefully during the doorjamb framing process so the door would fit the jamb with only ⅛- to ³⁄₁₆-inch clearance all the way around, leaving just enough room at the bottom for the threshold.

Note: Shims are mandatory for squaring and plumbing a jamb and hanging a door.

I installed the door's hardware and hung it without incident. Everything fit perfectly, including the sweep on the bottom of the door as it brushed over the threshold. I used finish nails to attach molding (stops) all around the doorjamb and framed the outside of the door with siding to match the window frames.

I splashed more sealer/stain on everything and backed down the steps as I sashayed back and forth with the paintbrush—and the job was done.

Building the deck had another benefit: I was now able to finally (and easily) put rain gutters on that tall side of the house without using scaffolding. I may get ambitious and put an awning over the deck before the rainy season begins, but for now, it's barbecue time!

When (pianist) Eric wears his "Go For Baroque" T-shirt, everybody misreads it as "Go for Barbeque," so now he's right in style either way.

CHAPTER 38

DECK OUT YOUR RV!

RV deck, 8'x16'

Just two little words—"Let's go!"—will send any dog into an excited state of anticipation, and *six* little words—"Let's go on a road trip!"—will send me into one. Likewise, anybody who has a family knows that the three most exciting words you can say to a kid are: "Let's go camping!" If you have an RV, all the better; you can get going at a moment's notice, and when you reach your destination, you can "have your comfort and rough it too."

The Long, Long Trailer, a classic comedy with Lucille Ball and Desi Arnaz, comes to mind. It romanticizes the carefree adventures of cruising down scenic highways by day and staying at campgrounds at night, but not until it first gives us a reality check with the unforgettable footage of Desi's towing lesson ending in hysteria: "Trailer brakes! Trailer brakes!"

Which brings up the refreshingly liberating fact (in contrast to the helmet and seatbelt laws) that no special driver's license endorsement is required to take off down the road pulling a 4,000-pound travel trailer behind any old vehicle, as long as all the rear lights are hooked up and a safety chain is attached. The only stipulation in the law is that no passengers are supposed to be in it. "Lucy, you're busted!"

According to statistics, about 10 percent of American families own an RV in the form of a travel trailer or a motor home. Calculated on an average of four people per household, that's about eight million! It makes one wonder whether we hardworking, time-crunched Americans love RVs almost as much for the freedom they represent as for their actual use. Most of the time they sit there unemployed until we have a weekend off or a vacation coming. There's nothing wrong with wonderful dreams of fun to be had and memories to be made, but until we can drive off with it, why not use the dang thing while it's parked at home?

Good Reasons to Buy an RV

The great news is that almost anyone can now afford what used to be a luxury for a few. Buying a "previously owned" RV is one of the best bargains available, and "available" is an understatement! Used RV lot salesmen and Craigslist advertisers are practically giving them away. People are either trading up for a newer model or are broke and need instant cash—or simply don't have the time to use it and want the giant tortoise out of their yard and into yours.

It didn't take much research for me to conclude that supply and demand has created a booming BUYERS' market.

How else can you have a completely self-contained and cozy abode for pennies on the dollar if it isn't a travel trailer? Instead of spending $100 a square foot to build a room with nothing in it, you'll likely pay $100 a *running foot* for a room with everything in it. Those running feet are jam-packed with all the comforts of home: a propane range and oven, a refrigerator, a bathroom with a tub and shower, beds that can be made into couches and tables that can be made into beds, and more storage space and cubby holes than you have stuff to stuff in. Some of the more creative models can sleep eight if you don't mind being a sardine for a night.

Having built a few houses from scratch, I know first-hand how much work it is and how much it costs per square foot for living space alone, not to mention installing fixtures and appliances. On top of the initial cost, to remodel or add a room can be astronomical, and you have to deal with permits and inspections.

If you need a spare room, why not buy a little house on wheels and avoid all that trouble? Relatives who come to visit, or teenagers who always seem to need their "space," will particularly appreciate the "guest house," and it will be forever ready to take to the open road whenever you are.

Shopping for an RV

Applying that practical concept to my own situation, I started looking regularly on Craigslist for just the right RV to suit my fancy and my budget. One day a new entry popped up featuring a 1983 24-foot Skyline Nomad travel trailer that looked and sounded ideal, so I jumped on it (if you snooze, you lose). It was love at first sight—a deluxe bunkhouse model with built-in bunk beds, hardwood floors, and an all wood-grain interior. It was loaded with extras and upgraded replacements, including a $2,000 refrigerator that runs on propone *or* electricity. The owner said, "It keeps ice cream frozen solid," and the efficient air conditioner "keeps the inhabitants frozen solid." After a scorching-hot summer, that alone sold me.

The only thing it needed was an igniter for the water heater ($200 job), and it had wild and crazy eighties upholstery that didn't thrill me, so I negotiated the price down from $3,000 to $2,500, and the owner agreed to deliver it to boot. After having an RV expert thoroughly check it out the next day and give it two thumbs-up ($50 fee), I happily bought it with a promotional low-interest cash advance from my credit card company—and it'll be paid off in a year.

Preparing the RV Pad

I have some acreage, so I picked a secluded area with a pastoral view and called my backhoe/grader guy. He moved a few big rocks and pushed some dirt around to make a road to the spot, then leveled the sloping ground as best he could where the RV would sit ($200 labor). Then I called the rock man and had 10 yards gravel (a dump truck full) laid down on the road and plenty on the pad to cover any mud during the rainy season ($200).

Note: I always marvel at how much amazing work can be done in a short time by a good, fast heavy equipment operator, and what a tremendous bargain it is—when you consider the initial cost of equipment, repairs and maintenance, the logistics of hauling the giant machines to the site on trailers, the gas, the oil, licenses, insurance, and taxes, and—most important to the client—experience and skill. Most excavators are honest and try to be fair, so in my book, they deserve every cent they charge. Amen!

When the RV arrived two days later, I was ready. The seller was kind enough to level the beast, block the wheels, and show me how everything worked, including the adjustable awning.

A source for power and water were nearby, so it would be no problem hooking them up. A septic emptying station is only four miles away at a service station and costs a mere $5. In a pinch, there's a mobile pumping service available for $50.

Planning the Deck

My next plan was to build a deck for the trailer—freestanding, of course, so it could be moved in and out as needed. I sketched a plan, measured and remeasured, ran level strings every which way, sprayed fluorescent marking paint where the piers would be placed, then made a materials list.

I had also decided to create a little yard enclosure around the trailer for more privacy and in case any guests had dogs to secure, so while I was at it, I added cedar fencing to the list.

My usual MO is to charge everything at Home Depot or Lowe's, interest free for a year to eighteen months (depending on the total), so that's what I did this time too.

Small Is Beautiful

Any small, attractive, and *green* all-in-one living space

is the hottest architectural trend in our culture right now. Not that I have ever tried purposely to be *in vogue,* but on this project, I just happened to be thinking small (the RV) and attractive (deck and fence) and green (low energy consumption), so I guess that makes the RV right in style—but what about that psychedelic upholstery? In any case, I've always liked invitingly livable structures with landscaping around them, so I was determined to dress up the RV as best I could.

Building the Deck

The only problem with too many bright ideas is the hard work it takes to implement them. I work alone, and I'm not getting any younger as the years whiz by, but considering my new spending spree *investment,* I couldn't let a little pain stop me now. So down I went on my hands and knees (mandatory for deck building) and started in setting twenty concrete piers into the hard-packed undisturbed soil beneath the gravel.

When I finally stood up as a homo erectus again, I placed adjustable brackets in the pier holes, and fastened 4" x 4" upright posts in the brackets. I had marked and precut the posts so all their tops would be level, but the adjustable brackets would allow me to fine-tune their *levelosity* later. Then I ran 16-foot 2" x 6" joists along both sides of the 4" x 4" posts in each row and screwed them on. Flanking *both* sides was a little overkill, even by my standards, but what the heck—I liked the balanced look.

Thus, the foundation grid consisted of four rows of piers 2 feet apart parallel to the trailer and five rows of piers 4 feet apart perpendicular to the trailer. That meant the 8' x 16' deck would be supported by four *pairs* of joists—making it super-strong and symmetrical.

I tend to overbuild, because, who knows, maybe the deck will be the floor of a little building someday, like the storage platform I built years before that ended up as a cabin floor.

The fun and satisfying part of building any deck is fastening the deck boards down with deck screws, and this one was no exception. It took 35 8-foot kiln-dried DF 2" x 6"s to cover the deck. I capped off the end-grain of the front with a 16-foot 2" x 8" and built some short stairs going down to the yard. Then I waterproofed the beautiful Douglas fir boards with deck stain and snapped a few photos of the finished deck's golden hue in the setting sun.

The Fence

I supported the cedar picket-fence panels with cedar stakes pounded well into the ground every few feet and screwed the stakes into the horizontal fence members (2" x 3"s), then made two gates for convenient access from opposite sides.

The fence is secure enough for what it's for—as a perimeter to surround a grassy yard (I sowed grass seed right away), and to facilitate the climbing tentacles of thirty-five young honeysuckle vines I planted around it, which will eventually cover it and attract hummingbirds and butterflies. Two fence panels (left unencumbered) can easily be removed and set aside when the RV is pulled out.

Closing Thoughts

All told, the RV project cost $4,000—not bad for a comfy accommodation, whether its wheels are spinning or not, and for a back-up shelter that runs on propane and batteries in an emergency situation.

For now, though, the *caravan* (as I prefer to call it) sits in its own little Field of Dreams, waiting for some action. Come summer, it will accompany us to the mountain lakes where we'll go camping, city-slicker style. Daughter Cynthia and grandson Zane have already put in their reservations.

"Build it and they will come"—but I hope *they* will bring a big truck with a trailer hitch! Old Bessie, my 1971 Ford F-100 pickup, won't even *look* at the RV!

CHAPTER 39

EASY AWNINGS

Quick and easy awnings

A window without an awning is like a lamp without
a shade—bare and glaring. In my opinion there's
not a window around that wouldn't look better with
an awning on it. But attractiveness isn't the only consideration; awnings are practical and useful.

They offer shade from the sun, prevent UV damage,
protect from rain, save on heating and cooling bills, keep
birds from flying into deceiving reflections in the glass,
and divert water runoff from going straight down into
foundations.

Back in 2005 I made massive cloth awnings on

iron-pipe frames for a big log house and a log piano studio. They turned out beautifully, but I'm afraid they were more work than the average do-it-yourselfer would be willing to do, even to save tons of money—which I *did*.

Since then, my son and I had built his stud-frame house, which also needed awnings. This time around I decided to make small metal-framed awnings for his modestly sized south-facing windows. They were quick and easy to make and install, so I thought I'd share my design with other shady characters.

The steel frames are made from ¾-inch square tubing and require a welder or a person you can hire to do the welding. Everything else you can do yourself. I was fortunate to have a professional welder right down the road to ask if he would make the frames and mounting brackets for me and how much he'd charge.

I gave him the size of each awning frame I wanted—along with a drawing of the awning design and the length, width, and pitch (35-degree slope angle) of each one—so he could calculate how much square tubing to buy and the time it would take to weld them up and give me an estimate. In short order he said he'd do it for $540 for all six, including the custom-made mounting brackets, and he'd also drill the screw holes.

I was thrilled with the reasonable enough price and gave him the go-ahead. Steel is at an all-time high and skilled welders are not cheap, but I figured $90 each was affordable for frames that will last forever.

He had them all done in no time, and I started in doing my part. As soon as I brought them home I cleaned them with solvent and spray-painted them with Ace's enamel "Warm Brown."

Home Depot and Lowe's have polycarbonate corrugated roofing panels for awnings, greenhouses, and outbuildings, made by Palram Corp. They are durable, lightweight, rigid, UV resistant, chemical resistant, can support a heavy snow load, are easy to cut and work with, *and* virtually unbreakable.

Their "Suntuf" translucent panels have a lifetime warranty, but I chose their non-see-through (opaque) "Suntop" panels, which have a ten-year warranty, because I didn't want the greenhouse effect of trapped heat under the awnings. They may fade a little after the ten years, but could be easily replaced whenever necessary.

The panels come in different colors and lengths, but I chose the easy-to-handle 2' x 8' panels in "Sedona Brick." The sloping surface area of each awning—except for the bigger picture window awning—would be only 2 feet so I could cut the 8-footers in equal increments. I bought four panels from Home Depot at $25 each.

Before I could screw the panels onto each frame, I had to bolt furring strips across the top and bottom. I had a lot of scrap lumber, so I used lightweight, low-profile 1" x 3"s and sealed them with spray paint.

Surprisingly, the various mounting bolts, flat washers, lock washers, and screws really added up at the hardware store and totaled about $50 before I was through!

I methodically cut and installed the wooden strips and the awning material until, one by one, they were all done and ready to put on the house. I placed the panels on the frames so there would be a 1-inch gap at the top and a 2.5-inch overhang at the bottom. I fastened the panels with 1-inch gasketed screws in the trough of each corrugation and snugged them down just so.

The mounting bracket design ended up being a good idea because it has a ¾-inch drop-in channel that holds the awning frame securely to the house horizontally along the top, and the awning-frame *legs* hold it vertically to the house. It ain't goin' nowhere.

All told, the six awnings of various sizes cost an average of $115 apiece. You can't have them custom made and installed for that anywhere.

I hung the awnings at a calculated level where they offer delicious shade but don't block much of the view—just like the baseball cap I wear all summer.

CHAPTER 40

BUILD AN 8' X 12' LEAN-TO GREENHOUSE

Lean-to greenhouse on Eric's house

Just *thinking* about a greenhouse can stimulate the senses. In your mind's eye, you can see the filtered light shimmering down on rows of greenery, feel the moist, warm air, smell the rich soil, and even taste a juicy tomato, now only tiny and green. A greenhouse is a protected and controlled environment that you can create year-round in a small, simple structure that costs only a few hundred dollars if you build it yourself.

THE HOUSE THAT DOROTHY BUILT   329

Imagine that! Your first ripe tomato will only cost $800—but it's worth it, and here's why:

Your miniature Hawaii will allow for 365 days of gardening a year. Summer and fall plants will yield for an extra season, and new seeds can gain a head start for spring planting. Frost, snow, rain, and wind can't touch your precious plants and flowers—or YOU—while you are in the nursery tending your babies and puttering around to your heart's content.

You'll get your initial investment back within a year, and then your greenhouse earns its keep forever after.

Doctors say that time spent gardening in a greenhouse is a great way to relieve everyday tension and stress—and you can do it standing up, which saves your back. They also say diffused light helps to alleviate SAD (seasonal affective disorder) by lifting your spirits and warming your heart. Son Eric calls it "the greenhouse effect"… it's real and it's palpable.

Location, Location, Location

The fact that half of Eric's basement is above ground created a tall wall facing south with nothing on it but two windows up high. It has been begging for a greenhouse since 2012 when we finished it.

Last summer Eric grew cherry tomatoes in pots along the base of the wall. They got fried by the sun, beaten by wind, and the soil dried out too fast each day, but they miraculously produced in spite of it all. To make their life a little easier this year, we decided that an 8' x 12' attached lean-to type greenhouse was the answer to those harsh conditions on the hill, and we began building it in March after the winter storms subsided.

It wasn't a tough project. Just about anybody who

can use basic tools and knows a little about stud-frame construction would have no problem building it.

Building the Foundation and Floor

First off, I dug the pier holes deeper on the highest side of the slope and shallower on the low side. The house had been backfilled with decomposed granite, so the digging was easy. Then I set sixteen piers evenly spaced (four on the long side, 3 feet apart, and four on the short side, 2 feet apart) and screwed short posts into their brackets on the low side. I connected the posts in each row with a 12-foot PT (pressure-treated) 2" x 6", and leveled it before attaching it. The four 12-foot parallel rows were also leveled with each other. To finish off the rectangular layout, I connected the ENDS of the rows with 2" x 6" PT rim joists.

Note: Before attaching anything, I trimmed 3 inches off the four 12-footers to compensate for the addition of rim joists on the ends, so the floor would end up exactly 12 feet long. If the floor is 3 inches too long, it throws everything off and wastes standard-sized materials. It always pays off to think a couple of steps ahead when building with dimensional lumber.

Now there were four 12-foot stringers (joists) 2 feet apart to fasten the deck boards across. I used twenty-six 8-foot 2" x 6" green DF (Douglas fir) boards for the flooring. When they dry and shrink, there'll be ⅜-inch gaps between them to let water and stray dirt fall through as we work and irrigate inside the greenhouse. Some people prefer no floor, but we like a floor.

Framing the Structure

The south wall of the house is basically the back wall

of the greenhouse, but I built an 8' x 12' frame using 2" x 4"s at 2-foot centers and sheathed it with ⁷⁄₁₆ inches OSB (oriented strand board) to fasten to that wall so the board and batten siding on the house would remain unscathed in case we ever want to remove the greenhouse.

I sealed the outside of the wall with exterior paint and then raised it up and fastened it in place with 3-inch screws. Then I covered its front face with three more sheets of OSB and painted that too.

Using KD (kiln-dried) 2" x 4" studs at 2-foot centers, I framed the front wall, then the sidewalls, including a 30 ½-inch-wide door opening (with a 4" x 4" header) on one end of the structure. I found an unusual door at the local Builder's Bargain Center for $89 and it was perfect for a greenhouse. The top half of the door has a dual window that can be opened by sliding the top down or the bottom up, and it was screened on the outside. I installed a threshold, then attached three hinges and a door knob set and hung the door with a ³⁄₁₆-inch gap all around which disappears against "stops" when closed.

I used seven 2" x 6" x 8' rafters spaced 2 feet apart and deeply notched at both ends to keep the roof low and stable at a 15-degree pitch. Brackets hold them securely in place.

After attaching a grid of pre-stained 1" x 3" pine boards spaced 30 inches apart across the top of the rafters and 24 inches apart across the vertical framing, I covered the whole structure with eighteen 2' x 8' polycarbonate corrugated transparent panels from Home Depot. I screwed them to the furring strips with hundreds of 1-inch gasketed screws—one in each corrugation. I chose Palram's "Suntuf" panels because they block harmful UV rays and they are lightweight but almost indestructible.

Note: Because it's a greenhouse and will be exposed inside AND out to sun, heat, and moisture on a daily basis, it's a good idea to stain all framing members as you are putting them up (before each step). It's not only easy and practical to do in advance but looks pretty too. I used Superdeck's "Waterborne" red-cedar stain, which is resin-based but odorless and can be cleaned up with water. The product turned out to be so fantastic, I'll never use stinky petroleum-based stains again!

The Fan and Thermostat

Instead of making vents on the roof (which might leak), I framed in two openings up high on each end of the structure and installed shutters above the door on the windward side and an exhaust fan on the lee side. The inlet-shutters can be manually opened on hot days to let the breeze flow through, and the fan will whisk out hot air through its own flutter-shutters whenever it's on. The screened window in the top half of the door is an additional vent.

I chose the recommended size fan (10 inches diameter at 1,500 rpm) that moves 800 cfm (cubic feet per minute) of air, which is the size of the greenhouse. I hardwired it in so it's connected to a switch inside the greenhouse and a breaker in the electrical panel nearby. (They DO make fans with plug-in cords, so that's an option.) I wired in an adjustable thermostat so the fan will go on when the temperature inside reaches 80 degrees.

From a nearby faucet, I ran a hose in through a drilled hole so water would always be handy. From a nearby electrical outlet I ran a cord in through another drilled hole for a heater with its own built-in thermostat for winter. I also wired in a wall-mounted light fixture with an electrical outlet in it for convenience.

Work Benches

All went well, and it was time to build the workbenches inside. Rather than do more carpenter work building bulky table frames and legs, I decided to install heavy-duty 20-inch L-brackets (to each stud) at 30 inches high and create a 22-inch-wide workbench from four pre-stained DF 2" x 6"s attached across the tops of the brackets. I ran the workbench in a U-shape around the inside of the room and a second shelf 30 inches above the first on the high north wall.

I hung a thermometer inside but out of direct sunlight, and another thermometer outside near the door but in the shade so the difference in temps could be readily monitored. The experts say it's not the sunLIGHT but the HEAT buildup that can damage plants. You don't want to cook your zucchini on the vine, so moving and exchanging the air is mandatory.

Summers can be scorchingly hot here in southern Oregon, so I installed a roll of white reflective shade cloth I can pull down over the top on hundred-degree days.

Closing Thoughts

"Build it and they will come." Well, here they come—the plants AND the bugs—all vying for an ideal place to live and flourish, not unlike the rest of us. The nice thing about plants is they give back so much. For all that nurturing, you get to witness the wonder of life—the sprouting, unfurling, growing, flowering, maturing, and producing—right before your eyes. And to top it all off, you get to nibble and graze on what you raise.

CHAPTER 41

BEING A GRANDMA

Zane and Grandma 2013

I'm blessed to be a grandma, and I take my role very seriously—by not being very serious. Seriously. What my grandson, Zane, and I do best together is laugh. We've giggled our way through the past thirteen years—in person and over the phone—and I feel like the luckiest grandma in the world to have such a funny and witty bantering partner. He was born a wordsmith with a creative sense of humor—evident at a very young age—and his mother and I have been egging him on ever since, but it's backfiring. He now points out *our* foibles and makes us laugh harder than ever. Most kids play with toys; Zane plays with toys *and* words.

Okay, I'll admit it. Like any other grandma, I'm shamelessly in love with my grandchild, and grandparents automatically have bragging rights.

Becoming a grandmother immediately elevated my status from a mere mortal to a hallowed being, breathing the sanctified air of the nursery where the precious baby in swaddling clothes lay.

When I first held him, words cannot describe the deliciousness of the experience, and when I first heard him say "Gwamma" (with a w), it was the sweetest sound to ever grace my senses. I melted.

In short, when Zane was born I was transformed into *grandmotherhood*. With my new promotion came a whole new sense of responsibility, and I took it on with a natural ease and confidence that surprised me. I thought I'd be nervous because I hadn't been around babies for thirty-seven years. I guess handling a newborn is one of those things you never forget how to do, and for a maternal type, holding a baby is one of those precious, indescribable feelings that is unlike anything else in this world.

Grandmas come in all shapes, sizes, colors, and styles, but at the heart of each one is just that: a huge heart overflowing with love for her grandkid(s). You inherit the grandma you get, and there are no two alike. Some grandmas drink screwdrivers, and some grandmas use screwdrivers but they all have something in common—

unconditional love for their grandchildren.

My paternal grandmother, Clara, mother of five and grandmother of ten, was an iconic old-fashioned grandma who fixed her long, braided hair into a silvery gray bun and always wore a flowered apron. She was sweet, patient, and reserved. She taught me to make blackberry cobbler, biscuits from scratch, and how to brown the flour in the bacon grease to make white gravy tastier.

During one summer visit when I was six, my older sister and I unwittingly (more like half-wittingly) turned her faucet on full blast and fed her hose down into the ground like a giant snake until it was buried right up to the faucet. When Grandma came out to check on us, she put her hand to her mouth in disbelief and sighed, "Oh dear!" I'm sure she felt like strangling us! And when I wet the bed and was mortified with embarrassment, she cheerfully quipped, "Oh, I see you sprung a little leak," and left it at that as she stripped the bed. Kindness is king with kids. And who better sets the standard for kindness than a nice grandmother?

In contrast to Grandma Clara, my maternal grandmother, Rose, couldn't have been more opposite—or more eccentric. She had reared three kids by herself on a hilltop out in the country, went into town on a buckboard pulled by her horse, carried a gun, and cracked a bullwhip just for the heck of it ("you never know when you might have to kill a rattlesnake"). At night, though, during our summer visits, she'd play classical music on her piano and sing us to sleep in her beautiful contralto voice. Everybody else thought she was a tough pioneer woman, but we knew, when it came to us, she was as soft as squash.

Sometimes it isn't the easiest job in the world being a grandma, but it's always the most meaningful. There is no formula. Every child is unique and each one requires a different approach to get desired results. But there are many universal truths that work: love, praise, trust, acknowledgment, respect, acceptance, allowing a certain amount of freedom, and helping them do things themselves to earn their self-esteem. Oh, did I forget patience? That might be the crowning quality a grandma can have.

You don't have to constantly buy things for kids to make them happy. They mostly want you to give your time and attention by just being with them—reading, picnicking, cooking, tickling, wrestling, laughing, playing, or whatever.

The relationship between a grandma and her grandchild is different than between a parent and child. Grandparents offer a perspective from a different generation, and usually don't care anything about being *cool,* so a child can feel free to be him or herself and still be adored unconditionally.

We have our own special connection, Zane and I.

I'm a single grandma, and he's my only grandchild. We've been happily busy on holidays and summers creating fond memories together and learning things about country life. When he was a toddler, reading to him about farm animals was *my* favorite activity. I went for the sound effects in full-animated exaggeration to keep him (and myself) entertained, but thank goodness nobody else heard!

We spent countless hours in the sandbox, gathering eggs from the chicken coop (more sound effects) and playing in the tree house. All the while I was seeing, hearing, and touching the world anew through his eyes and ears and hands, and enjoying it to the max. Now that he's older, the activities have changed: selling mistletoe at Christmas, hanging out at the skateboard park, carving pumpkins, and going to the YMCA.

I keep his rabbit Alberta and Guinea pig Duncan fat and sassy for him to have and hold while he's here a few times a year. I also have Zorro and Pretty—the dog and cat he grew up with—and his aquatic turtle Buckwheat. He lives in a Hollywood apartment, attends a French school, and doesn't have the time and space to keep all the pets he wants, so that's where Grandma comes in.

Zane will be driving in three years. His parents will teach him to drive a car with an automatic, but his grandma (that be me) will teach him to drive an old pickup with a stick shift—the ancient truck I've had for thirty years. We'll appropriately start out in *granny low*.

Zane and I butt heads once in a while when I inadvertently cross the line into *preaching* by warning him about some of the dangers in today's culture. His rebuttal is usually, "Grandma, I *know*. Don't worry, I *know*." I say, "Okay, okay," and we both sigh. Of course he knows everything—he's thirteen! I let it go. He's a leader, not a follower, so I'm not too worried.

What I emphasize with him is honesty, empathy, and the work ethic. Good manners are a given.

Being a grandma means walking a fine line between instilling good values, expecting and insisting on respectful behavior, and doing a little spoiling along the way. Spoiling is a grandma's prerogative, and to Zane's delight, I exercise my prerogative often.

Grandmas fill a special need, such as wonderful indulging that kids may not get at home—activities we all understand are only temporary and are the exception rather than the rule. With Zane and me, during his summer stays, our special motto is, "Dinner at midnight and breakfast at noon." Uh-oh, Grandma's busted!

Nobody should ever underestimate the power and influence of being a grandmother—the senior matriarch of the family who also serves as an additional moral compass and stable anchor. In today's world of divorced parents and broken homes, family ties have never been more important for a child's sense of bonding, security, belonging, and loving.

Although an important role, Grandma plays a *supporting* role in the family dynamic and thus should respectfully defer to the parents. But a child can take comfort in knowing that no matter what happens, there's always Grandma to run to if need be. A grandma is one of the few people in the world who has known you from birth and cherishes you as your parents do.

I asked Zane what he likes most about having a grandma and he said, "I feel happy when I think about going to Grandma's house in Oregon during school breaks, and even happier when I get there." He counts the days—and so do I.

Each child is a surprise package—a unique inherited combination of everything that went before. When nature has its way, you don't know exactly what you're going to get, but you are delightfully surprised when the babies' characteristics manifest themselves, revealing more and more about them as they grow into little *people.*

I would venture to say that how a person *turns out* from a single DNA molecule into a complex human being is determined 75 percent by genetics and 25 percent by environment. I arrived at this conclusion from years of observations of not only my own kids but hundreds of others. "As the twig is bent, the tree shall grow" (old proverb).

My kids have the same parents but could not be more different in nature and talent. Eric came into this world on a piano, and Cynthia on a horse.

Eric is now a scientist and classical pianist and

composer. Cynthia (Zane's mom) is now a professional photographer and owns several horses and is active in saving the threatened mustang herds in America. They both followed their hearts and their passions.

Zane, on the other hand, is a complicated combination we haven't quite figured out yet. He's still unfurling and emerging—like a butterfly from a chrysalis. Thus far he is a fluent trilinguist (English, Spanish, French), a skilled skateboarder, a Kung Fu yellow belt, a grappling competitor, and a budding photographer. Because he has an artistic side (photographer mom, actor dad), I have a hunch he may choose to be a photographer when he grows up, but what I know for sure is that he will be encouraged to seek his own path and not be forced into any kind of mold.

Grandma represents the extended family at Thanksgiving, Christmas, and summer vacations. When it comes to grandkids, my mom's philosophy was "the more the merrier," especially on holidays. She had a dozen and wished she'd had more! She miraculously found time to lavish love and attention on each one, making each feel as unique and special as each *was*. If she had a favorite she never showed it. She was the warmest, most maternal woman I have ever known. After she reared six kids of her own, she babysat for a living until age eighty. One day she was rocking a three-year-old to sleep in her lap, and the little girl looked up and asked, "Are you Mother Nature?" Mom took that as the ultimate compliment of her *career*.

When I was only twenty-eight and my kids were seven and eight, a family friend asked me an odd question out of the blue: "What do you envision yourself doing in your old age?" It was hard to think that far ahead and project myself forty years into the future, but after a minute or so of serious deliberation I said: "I want to be a really *good* grandmother." I'll never forget his condescending reply: "Is *that* all?"

Well, it was the right answer for me, and still is. Being a good grandma *is* a noble aspiration and a very important *job*. I've worn many hats and aprons over the years, but my identity as *grandma* is my favorite me.

As our grandchildren grow and change and evolve, grandma remains the constant in the family—the consistent and steady stream of love and caring, as long as she lives and forever after; sometimes as one's little conscience in the sky.

Grown men and women get sentimental when talking about their grandmas. On stage during the Golden Globe awards, Jamie Foxx looked up to heaven with a tear in his eye, held his trophy up high, and paid tribute to his grandma. Megan Kelly, a Fox News host, says things like, "Sorry, Nana," or "Thanks, Nana," and "Happy Birthday, Nana" on national TV.

Biologically speaking, one would think that nature would do away with people past their childbearing years, but I think grandmas provide an important evolutionary service by helping to rear the grandkids when the parents are busy with survival itself.

If you don't have a grandma to call your own, there are volunteer grandmas out there wishing they had *you*. There is a surrogate grandparenting program in almost every city in the United States, just as there is the big brother and big sister program. I urge you to become a grandma to a child who doesn't have one.

Grandfathers are enormously important and influential too, but I chose to write only about grandmas in this particular essay. I had wonderful grandpas too—one who taught me at six how to use hand tools in his woodshop and how to sharpen a short pencil with a pocketknife.

How great was that! He also let me braid the few strands of hair he combed over his bald spot, and that memory is my favorite. That's when I decided I wanted to be a *beauty parlor lady* when I grew up. Who would have ever guessed a grandpa inspired that!

We all know that taking care of kids is a lot of work, and is also a mixed bag of fun, pleasure, frustration, accidents, grief, shocks, surprises, delights, and every other imaginable emotion, including pure joy, so when I told my son Eric I was writing an article on how much I love being a grandma, he teased, "Oh, you're writing fiction now?"

I'll end with a famous quote on children by the poet Kahlil Gibran (1883) because it is so profoundly wise:

> "Your children are not your children. They are the sons and daughters of life's longing for itself.
>
> They come through you but not from you. And though they are with you yet they belong not to you.
>
> You may give them your love, but not your thoughts.
>
> For they have their own thoughts. You may house their bodies but not their souls, for their souls dwell in the house of tomorrow, which you cannot visit, not even in your dreams. You may strive to be like them, but seek not to make them like you.
>
> For life goes not backward or tarries with yesterday.
>
> You are the bows from which your children as living arrows are sent forth. The archer sees the mark upon the path of the infinite, and he bends you with his might that his arrows may go swift and far. Let your bending in the archer's hand be for gladness; for even as he loves the arrow that flies, so he loves also the bow that is stable."

CHAPTER 42

A LOVE STORY

Kirt and Dorothy, third anniversary

People often ask me, "What happened to Kirt?" Well, what follows is the short story of how we met and why we parted:

He was a brawny, powerful Viking of a man, with blond curls, a dimple in his chin, and shoulders so wide he looked like he was wearing football pads. We met at the fitness center. He was easy on the eyes, but I didn't allow myself to indulge in more than a fleeting glance to admire a young man's beauty as I would admire anybody's beauty. Little did I know he was thinking the same thing about me, but his glances my way weren't that fleeting.

A Little History

Son Eric and I jogged together during a health-kick phase years ago, and started our three-mile run from the fitness center every morning. But first we'd go in and do our daily sit-ups and a light workout to warm up before the run.

One day Eric pointed out a young weight lifter in modest garb and said, "See that guy over there? Yeah, the blond guy in the baggy shirt. He's the strongest guy in here—maybe in the whole Rogue Valley. Watch him sometime; you won't believe what he can do!" Being an absentminded scientist and classical pianist, Eric isn't much of a visual person, so I figured if *he* took notice, then this guy must be spectacular. I had to admit I had noticed him before, mainly because his shoulders were as wide as a doorway. I can't help but admire symmetry and strength, so I watched him now and then out of curiosity.

He was quiet, graceful, self-assured, and moved through his workout every day with discipline and concentration like clockwork. I could tell he was serious about his routine but certainly not a show-off. Every once in a while I caught him looking at me, and his lingering glances were a little disconcerting, but I continued to feign disinterest, for obvious reasons: he was a college kid. But biology was doing its magic trick—we were both responding to the visual attractions from a distance. I saw an inverted triangle and he saw an hourglass—and spring was in the air.

I got the hint he was interested in me when he kept positioning himself at the weight machine that was closest to the women's locker room door so I would have to bump into him whenever I came out. It was just too coincidental to be accidental.

Being the friendly type, I finally broke the ice and said, "My son says you're the strongest guy in here—maybe in the whole town." He chuckled and said, "Oh yeah? I don't know about that." He was soft-spoken but his eyes were dancing, like he wished he knew what to say next but didn't have a clue how to flirt. So I kept it going with my own awkwardness because I too didn't have a clue how to flirt: "Do you work out everyday? Do you go to college?" His replies were: "Yes.... Yes...." Then I said, "Well, see you...gotta go do my jog"....and I ran off, quivering with excitement but still not believing that this gorgeous hunk was interested. I could feel the vibes, but it was too early to assume anything. I reminded myself of an old saying: "You can be an older man's darling or a younger man's fool," and I didn't want to be a fool.

The next day we accidently on purpose ran into each other again at the locker room door and I said, "Oh, hi," as nonchalantly as I could muster up, and proceeded to go over to the wall to do my leg lifts at the ballet bar. He sauntered over to do bicep curls nearby, and we talked between sets.

I finally blurted it out, "How old ARE you anyway?" He shifted from one leg to the other, and his broad shoulders swayed from side to side, mesmerizing me like a snake as we held eye contact. He said, "Twenty." I giggled in disbelief and said, "Twenty? That's impossible. NOBODY'S only twenty!" Dumb thing to say, but I was giddy. He chuckled again but was wise enough not to ask my age. I said: "How did you get this BIG in only twenty years?" Then we both laughed and resumed our workouts.

Okay, I was convinced he was smitten; there was no doubt about it. He continued to intercept my path. He was oozing testosterone from every pore, and I could feel the heat. But at the same time, he was sweet and had an almost innocent quality about him that made him twice as appealing.

It was April. I was single again, and finally recovered from a terrible heartbreak that had taken a year to get over. Like whistling in the dark, I would often sing, "I can see clearly now, the rain is gone"…for moral support.

It's in my nature to act or react when my emotions have a mind of their own, even if it's wrong. I was in great physical shape and had more energy than I knew what to do with, so the timing couldn't have been better to meet someone new.

"So now what?" I asked myself. If I left it up to him to make a move it might not have happened for a while—or ever—because I could tell he wasn't sure if I, being older, would be willing to go out with him. He told me later this was true—he WAS afraid to ask and to be rejected. He thought I might laugh in his face, or more kindly say that I already had a boyfriend; he expected the latter.

I'm a carpe diem type of gal. I'm not one to wait for anything good if it's in my power to make it happen, so although I was old enough to know better (but too young to resist), I nervously sneaked a note under his windshield wiper when I left that day. My noncommittal message was: "I'll be working at the Copper Skillet tonight if you'd like to eat dinner at a place that has really great food—Dorothy."

As Murphy's Law would have it, the other waitress called in sick and I was the only one on that night. The place was packed, with a long waiting line and an extreme noise level. My arms were loaded down with full plates, and I was rushing around like a sheep dog trying to round up the whole herd—and of course that's when he walked in. I looked up and saw an incredible silhouette barely fitting through the doorway, and I almost fainted. It was HIM! I really didn't think he'd come right away; I thought he'd play it cool. I should have known that a twenty-year-old CAN'T play it cool, especially if an attractive woman (of any age) has given him an invitation.

I don't know how I did it, but I managed to put my waitress-self on auto pilot and make it through the dinner rush and serve him a delicious meal and take his money at the register and, as he was leaving, say, "I have a hot tub, and I don't live far from here...wanna sit in it under the stars and talk tonight?" He said, "Sure!" and I said, "I get off at ten o'clock, so meet me back here and follow me up to my place...it's only three miles." He said, "Great! See you at ten."

When the moment of truth came, I was so shook up I forgot how to drive my old truck—I honked the horn and turned on the windshield wipers and ground the gears before I unintentionally laid a strip of rubber when I finally took off. (Evidently, a mature woman can't be cool either.)

He sat in his beautiful red Trans Am waiting patiently to follow me home—and ultimately, to the ends of the earth. I couldn't believe I was on a DATE—with a handsome blue-eyed hunka hunka burnin' love—and as fate would have it—it was the most wonderful date of my life and the most magical night of my life. I was willing to take the chance it might be only one date with him, but I was sure it would still be worth it. As it turned out, we would be together for ten glorious years of unwedded bliss from that night forward.

Too much, too soon? No! I WANTED too much too soon. All my life everything had been too little too late.

Every love is a first love. Suddenly I was sixteen years old again—sixteen going on forty-six, and Kirt was twenty going on forty. He said he had always felt much older than his years, being the eldest son of a pear orchard dynasty and laden with responsibility from an early age. He had saved enough money by working in the orchards to pay for his own college education. What was there NOT to like about this endearingly unpretentious guy?

This prince of a man was not an ordinary person in any sense of the word. He would continue to prove how unusual he was with every passing day, and my respect and admiration for him increased with every passing year. He turned out to be a man who, if he hadn't been real, could not be imagined.

It was no accident that Kirt and I had been so attracted to each other. We had almost everything in common but our birth date. I had never had a teen-hood, never dated, never been romanced; I was the family Cinderella through my high school years. Sweet sixteen, never been kissed. Two years after I graduated, I married the first guy who chased me, and had two kids by the time I was twenty-one. Then I worked and worked and worked—nothing but work for the next twenty-five years. Kirt had a similar background, and we shared the same values, including the big four: religion, politics, sense of humor, and the work ethic.

I had finally broken free from a one-sided marriage at thirty and started a completely new life at forty. After I ran away to Oregon like the Gingerbread Girl, I had one delightfully charming boyfriend who was lazy and unambitious, then a heartbreakingly handsome and brooding boyfriend who had an intimacy problem and withheld love—then Kirt.

Kirt was bigger than life in every way—totally healthy, stable, and hard working. He was exceedingly smart, playful, witty, humorous, and protecting—a perfect helpmate and partner. He was good-natured and patient, and he reflected back what I mirrored out: sweetness, unjadedness, beauty, laughter, and perpetual springtime love. I always felt like I was the younger woman and he was the older man—hard to believe, but true. We were both ageless for ten beautiful years. He told me daily how lucky he was to have found me, and I felt the same. We were so ridiculously compatible we didn't have even ONE serious argument in all our time together. What I saw was what I got with Kirt; there were no hidden agendas.

But inevitably—as we knew would happen someday —it came to an end. When I went through menopause, biology ruled again. I realized our time was up, our relationship had run its course, so I asked him to leave and go find a younger woman and have a more conventional life—with my blessing. It was a hard thing to do, but the right thing to do. I loved him enough to let him go. I had grown too old to be with a younger man anymore, and he deserved to start a new life and have a family. Kirt was so loyal and devoted he took an entire year to leave. We will be friends in our hearts forever. There can be no greater love and appreciation than I have for Kirt to this day. I've been alone since, by choice. I was a great one for him to begin with, and he was a great one for me to end with.

To describe Kirt in a few words and honor him properly as the man he is—which is more man than most who are twice his age—I would say: "He's all brawn AND all brain, and as legendary in the bedroom as in the forest." He deserves that compliment; he earned it—just being himself.

Kirt is married now and has two young sons, and he's a fantastic father! I'm very happy for him. He now runs the family pear orchard business, and he is also a real estate agent. He still works out as a totally natural bodybuilder, and is tremendously bigger and stronger than he was back then. Life comes full circle; he just turned forty-six (2014), the same age I was when we met.

Me? I am growing old gracefully and gratefully, and life is good.

CHAPTER 43

LOVE STORY, CONTINUED

Kirt and Dorothy, tenth anniversary

The minute Kirt left the restaurant, I called Eric and said, "Quick, quick, fire up the hot tub!" (A 6-foot-diameter, 3-foot-deep wood-fired hot tub from the Snorkel Stove Co.)

I added, "If you never do another favor for me as long as I live, do this one—hurry, fire up the hot tub! Keep putting wood in it until it's hot, okay? I have a date with that guy, Kirt—remember him?—and we'll be up in only three hours. Help! Help! Remember all those diapers I changed? It's payback time!" Eric laughed. He could tell I was out of control.

An hour passed, and I called him back: "Is the water getting warm? Stir it with the paddle! Stoke the fire! Stoke the fire!" He assured me, "I'm stokin' it, I'm stokin' it!" (Those six words became a family mantra for all future panic attacks.)

Thanks to Eric, when Kirt and I finally slithered into the nice hot water—which was a perfect temperature—it was a dream come true. The night was warm and breathless, and so was I. The submerged stove was cracklin', and Kirt was so gorgeous with his shirt off it was astonishing—he looked like a marble sculpture by Michelangelo. When we finally got brave enough to sidle up to each other, his alabaster skin over bulging muscles felt as lush and plush as velvet over boulders.

We talked until the wee hours, and the more we found out about each other, the more we fell in love. Wrapped in towels, we sauntered down the little trail to the rustic cabin I lived in, and the rest of the night wrote itself. I still call the cabin "The Honeymoon Cottage" in honor of our "wedding night."

The next morning I offered to fix him breakfast before he went to his classes at the college. I asked, "Do you like seven-grain cereal?" He thought I said "salmon-brain cereal" and answered, "Sure." That's when I knew this guy was good-natured beyond belief!

Needless to say we fell madly in love and bonded forever from that first night forward and began spending every minute together when we weren't at work or school. He quit going home where he lived with his parents, and of course they wondered why. They were good, salt-of-the earth, conventional, hard-working people and naturally wanted the traditional best for their three kids—Kirt being the oldest. He didn't know how to tell them he had fallen in love with a much older woman, so he told them he met a guy named Eric and had decided to move in with him and live in town—closer to college.

Kirt had to be on call to set out smudge pots in the orchard if a spring freeze was imminent, so he gave them Eric's phone number, which was hooked up to an answering machine (before cell phones). Every time they called for any reason, they would get Eric's voicemail and have to leave a message. They started to get suspicious. Kirt's dad told his mom he thought maybe their son was gay. His reasoning was, why on earth would Kirt all of a sudden not come home anymore and say he was living with a guy named Eric?

This was a son who, like their other two kids, had never given them any trouble. He didn't drink, smoke, dope, party, or even get traffic tickets, nor was he rebellious. Kirt was close to his mom, so the next time they talked, she told him what his dad had said. Kirt said, "Me? Gay??" He was furious (and hurt) that his father didn't know him any better than that and would immediately assume he was gay over any other options. So, on the spot, Kirt confessed everything and, courageously but unapologetically, said he was actually living with Eric's mother, Dorothy, and would continue to live with Dorothy no matter what they said. They were shocked—and horrified—but slowly and reluctantly came to accept it over the next few months, and they even warmed up a little after they met me.

Of course they wanted their son to marry a prom queen upon graduation and have 2-3 children and buy a big brocade couch and live happily ever after. Instead, he fell in love with a woman twenty-six years his senior and was living in a barn and a rustic cabin—not to mention the outhouse. His parents had to stretch and grow—or be alienated from their good son—so in silent resignation and in respect of his independence, they accepted his choice.

I totally understood their concern, but Kirt and I knew it wouldn't be forever. Considering his off-the-chart libido, I like to think I might have "saved" him from being dangerously promiscuous or impulsively marrying the wrong gal. But that was neither here nor there—we were in love, and there was no putting the genie back in the bottle. Nothing had been premeditated or planned; we were simply living life to the fullest one day at a time.

The great thing about Kirt I admired was how unruffled he was about change; he adapted to my primitive lifestyle without batting an eyelash. He switched from a mansion with a pool to almost "camping out," and it didn't bother him in the least. He took a whiz over the deck railing like he'd been doing it all his life. He never complained, never got angry, and never criticized anything we endured together on my undeveloped property. He was the most nonjudgmental person I had ever met.

Eric was living in the completed piano studio, and I was in the process of building my own house on the hill but only had the foundation in so far. Eric and I had plans to go get the logs out of the woods for my house as we had for his piano studio. When I told Kirt about that, he said, "Let's leave Eric out of the equation...I'll help you get your logs! School is out in June; when do you want to start?" It sounded too good to be true, but Kirt insisted, so we decided to gather logs as soon as school was out.

Meanwhile, from April to June, Kirt courted me in his own sweet, imitable way. A conventional courtship it was not. Instead of going out, we stayed in. Our time together was relaxed, playful, and spontaneously passionate.

One memorable day, as new lovers are wont to do, we didn't get up for twenty-four hours, except to have a snack. Kirt made me feel like the most beautiful and desirable woman in the world. I could do no wrong. And to me, he was the sexiest man alive.

On school days, every chance he got, he'd speed up to see me on his lunch hour or between classes and we'd have a picnic under the old oak tree, then go into the little cabin for *dessert*. Having to be at work at the café at 2:00 p.m. was the only unavoidable inconvenience that separated us. But without my asking, every night he came down to the restaurant at 10:00 p.m. and helped me close the place by sweeping and vacuuming so we could be back home together as soon as possible.

We were on a perpetual honeymoon and spent most of our time in each other's arms intertwined like squash vines. He said I was a fantasy come true—he had his own Playboy bunny. And for me, his masculine presence and beautiful voice heightened every sense—visual, tactile, and auditory. The alpha waves were flowing; I found myself sighing and swooning even at work as I floated around on air waiting on my customers.

We were building a relationship one day at a time as we would soon be building a house one log at a time. In June we packed up my old truck with a chainsaw, a jug of water, and some peanut butter sandwiches for energy, and off we went to tackle the forest—twenty miles up the road. Kirt had never used a large chainsaw before, but he was a quick study. He amazed me with his skill and grace in cutting up the logs, which were lying all over the forest floor—downed by the USFS in the beetle-kill area designated on my permit. We were allowed to get as many logs in any size we needed (for a personal residence) for 3 cents a lineal foot. I carried my end of most of the 8-inch-diameter logs, but Kirt had no problem carrying the 12-inch-diameter, 200- to 300-pounders on his shoulders, so we loaded up a pickup bed full of eight-footers within a few hours and headed home.

It was a great day because we each had the kind of personality and attitude that made hard work seem like play. After that first logging trip we knew without a doubt we were a perfect match.

People liked to whisper behind my back that I had deliberately set out to find a guy at the fitness center to carry my logs. The truth is it had never entered my mind when I was falling in love with Kirt. I am not one to exploit a man (or anybody) and have a hard time accepting help from anyone—ever—unless they won't take no for an answer. Kirt was a real man in every sense of the word and it wasn't in his DNA to stand by and let a woman do all the heavy work. Meeting a man of his caliber in my lifetime was sheer luck, like winning the lottery.

Knowing that some unkind people were calling us Jock and Jill and gossiping up a storm, I wrote this satirical myth just for a laugh:

Dorothy's technique for building a log house: "First choose the biggest, straightest, most beautiful tree, make it fall (in love), limb it so it can't get away, put the tenon in the mortise to make sure it's a perfect fit, repeat as often as possible, and voila! It's here to stay."

I'm of a scientific mind-set, but finding Kirt did seem almost preordained. I mean, how many women are building a log house solo, and how many men are as strong as Paul Bunyan? He was there for me like a one-man crew whenever I needed a seemingly impossible task done, and he accomplished it in short order. I had an electrical problem with my well pump, so he pulled the whole submerged pump straight up out of the well casing—single-handedly—along with 150 feet of water-filled pipe attached. We had a little help carrying the long snake out into the yard as he pulled it up, but it sure beat calling a crane operator! Within an hour, Kirt said, "There you go, honey, rewire it, and I'll put it back down in the well for you."

I was having a problem with my windmill, and he pulled up what he thought was only the pipe but ended up lifting the whole mill and motor along with it. He said, "I wondered why it was so dang heavy!" I mean, the guy was Hercules! He didn't get injured and didn't complain—or say he wished he had a "normal" girlfriend. He matter-of-factly did whatever he was capable of doing to help out. And he was unbelievably capable.

I gave back in every possible way I could. I cut his hair regularly, cooked his meals, did his laundry, tailored his T-shirts so they would go in at the waist and not look like tents, photographed everything he did to help, took body-building portraits of his anatomical "work in progress" (as he called himself), and made photo albums for him. He was so witty and funny when we worked together that I kept a notebook handy and jotted down his quotes. We were a mutual-admiration society.

Kirt loved my cooking and complimented me profusely on every delicious meal. If there was anything I knew how to do it was to whip up a great, nutritiously dense meal from scratch in record time. I wasn't a half-fast cook; I was a fast cook! That was good because he didn't like waiting more than twenty minutes when he was hungry. He expended huge amounts of energy on a daily basis in work and play. He had to eat 10,000 calories a day just to maintain his 200 pounds of muscle mass on a five-foot-eleven frame. I've always been a health nut, so I made sure he got a well-balanced diet.

Our agreement was, he would buy the food and I would cook it. A freeloader he was not. If a special dish required a long simmering time (such as spaghetti sauce), I prepared it the day before so all I had to do was heat it up. The way to a man's heart is indeed through his stomach, perhaps more than "that other place." Well, first the kitchen, then the bedroom, then the kitchen again...well...not necessarily in that order.

One time I accidentally washed all his new white skivvies in with a red rag and they turned pink. Did it bother him? No! He wore those pink shorts to the gym and deflected comments in the locker room with a chuckle. He truly didn't care what other people thought. He carried my purse when I asked him to and held his arms out like a rack to hang bras on when we went shopping for lingerie so I could try them on one at a time from the fitting room. There were a few raised eyebrows and snickers from amused shoppers, but Kirt just winked back.

When we worked out at the fitness center, he'd come over to me between sets and give me a little hug and kiss—in front of his college friends. He never spoke of our age difference and never said an unkind thing to me in the ten years we were together. We were both in suspended denial that our love affair would have to end someday, and we didn't think about it.

Eric was commissioned to compose music for the Oregon State Ballet every season because he was friends with the director and his wife and they loved his fresh originality. They were putting on The Nutcracker Suite one Christmas and asked Eric to ask Kirt if he would be the Arab. The wife had seen Kirt at the fitness center where she also worked out, and she thought he'd be perfect for the part. She envisioned him bare chested, wearing gauzy pantaloons, glittering armbands, and a turban, and she could see he moved gracefully. Kirt said laughingly, "Me in a ballet? Well, I don't know how to dance, but if it doesn't require anything but lifting the ballerina up and parading around, heck, I'll do it"—and he did. Never in his wildest imagination did he think he'd ever be in a ballet of all things. We all went to opening night at the theater (including his parents), and he was fabulous!

He was always open to learning new things. After all, he had spent his youth working in the pear orchards, learning the business, and saving and investing money, but hadn't had the free time to learn to ski, skate, and dance, so we tackled those fun things together. He had learned to play the saxophone in junior high and excelled at it, but when he met Eric and me, he was exposed to Bach and Beethoven for the first time. He took to Beethoven immediately and loved his powerful music filled with passion and energy. When we drove 300 miles to Reno to visit my mom, we listened to all nine Beethoven symphonies—full blast—all the way there, and another wild composer—Rossini—all the way back. It was crazy and exhilarating—we didn't drink or do drugs, but we were high on Beethoven! On some of our logging trips, we listened to Beethoven's Emperor Concerto all the way up and all the way back. Call us nerdy, that's okay; we'll take it as a compliment.

Oddly enough, Kirt also liked my collection of oldies but goodies from the fifties, sixties, seventies, and eighties. He didn't care about being cool—he liked what he liked and was always true to himself. No matter what we were doing—even working at the building site—when "Donna" (by Ritchie Valens) came on the boom box, Kirt would spontaneously grab me and we'd slow dance to it. How charming can a man get!

Kirt didn't sweat the small stuff. I only saw him angry a few times (at others), but he's not a guy to ever try to cheat in a business deal. Heaven help you! He might be good-natured and easy-going, but he's nobody's fool. His character was impeccable, and he expected others to be the same. He was confident, good at setting boundaries, and could never be talked into anything he didn't want to do.

Kirt continued to work for his parents in the pear orchards driving a forklift during packing season, but he supplemented his income with an odd job—literally "odd," and macabre. He was on call to pick up dead bodies whenever, wherever, and however someone died locally. He got $20 a "stiff" to put them in a body bag and unload them at the morgue (usually an hour's work). It didn't bother him at all—even the plane-crash site he had to clean up. He considered disposing of bodies as a part of life and was able to be logical and pragmatic without getting emotionally involved. He said, "Somebody has to do it." He made an extra $100 per month on average—and back in the early nineties, that was good money.

I had more building experience than Kirt did, and he gave me full credit. Often, he'd sweetly and sincerely say, "You are so smart, honey," when I worked out a solution to a building problem, and he always praised me when I did an exceptionally good job on something. His kind words blew me away—and I blossomed. I was not used to compliments and encouragement; I had grown up with criticism.

He was a dream to work with because he was a perfectionist and great with tools—hand tools or power tools—and was very patient. He was good at math and could visualize flat things in three dimensions—before they were put together—such as when we were working on mortise-and-tenon joints with logs lying unassembled all over the subfloor. He attributed his "training" to playing complicated video games!

We both worked carefully and deliberately (to avoid mistakes), but I was a lot more "animated" by nature.

He affectionately called me a "squirrel" and himself a "sloth." He kidded me in his droll way: "You can run circles around me panting and wasting energy, but it doesn't mean you get more done." When I got overly excited about something—which was often—he liked to playfully grab me and hold me so tightly against him for a few seconds that I couldn't move. He knew I'd squeal and squirm to get loose, and then we'd both burst out laughing. He had a mischievous side, but it was tempered with kindness.

My only complaint in all the years we were taskmasters together was when he left a hammer on top of the ladder and it fell on my head, and his only complaint was when I asked him to hold two pieces of wood together while I predrilled them but I slipped with the bit and drilled through his fingernail. Other than that, we were a great team. Building a log house was not easy work—it was gut-busting, painful, and intense—but we bantered and laughed while we strained and swore, and our camaraderie was deeply satisfying. My memories of working with Kirt are absolutely priceless.

We both worked full-time jobs and didn't have a lot of down time. One of my greatest pleasures at bedtime was watching nature documentaries together. I had signed up with Time-Life to get a new David Attenborough VHS tape every month. Kirt grew up watching action and horror movies, so this was something new to him, but he seemed to enjoy them in small doses and said he was learning a lot about plants and animals. After several months of it, though, he finally set his foot down—gently, of course. He said, "Honey, tonight we're going to watch something I want to watch—something scary and violent." He continued, "If I have to watch one more film about little birdies tweeting and bunnies hopping around, I'm gonna have to feel 'down here' to see if I'm still a man." And of course he felt "down there" to fully demonstrate his point. It was cute, even though the movie we watched wasn't. Freddie Krueger comes to mind...

My kids really liked Kirt. They were accepting and supportive of the man who obviously made their mother so happy. For an outrageous laugh they sometimes called him "Dad," even though they were a few years older than he was. Occasionally, a tactless person who knew I had a young son and a young boyfriend but had not met either would eventually see me with Kirt and ask, "Oh, is this your son?" I would shock them with, "Oh, no! My son is much older than this!" One woman looked too confused to be embarrassed. In this day and age, you shan't assume an overweight woman is pregnant and ask when the baby is due or assume a younger guy with an older woman is the son. In his reassuring way, Kirt would just smile at such remarks and give me a little squeeze.

But fact is stranger than fiction. If a movie of our love story was made now, Kirt could play Kirt, and my daughter Cynthia could play me, and Kirt would still be the younger man!

After we finished the second log house and got all settled in, Kirt made a habit of bringing coffee up to me in the loft in the morning. I'm not one to get spoiled—in fact, it would be impossible to spoil me—but this is the closest I've gotten to feeling totally and tenderly cherished, and I allowed myself to accept it. It is the warmest, sweetest memory I have of our life together. I had never been nurtured, served, or given to so lovingly by a man. The contrast between his size and his gentleness was incongruous—and touching.

While I was sipping coffee and waking up slowly, Kirt would say endearing things such as, "Honey, if you ever get too old to climb the stairs to the loft, I'll carry you up."

Of course we'd laugh because it sounded so silly—like that day would never come.

Another time he said, "You know what I'd do if you asked for a divorce?" I said, "What?" He said, "I wouldn't give it to you."

Even when I hiccupped he thought it was cute. He would say—like a wolf in sheep's clothing—"My, what beautiful legs you have, my dear." He loved me the way most women would like be loved: not to be put on a pedestal, but as a best friend in a natural, comfortable way. It was so easy being with Kirt; I could totally be myself, and so could he.

When the house was finished, Kirt kept surprising me with large, practical gifts: he hefted a washer and dryer—brand spankin' new—into their spots, rolled a new refrigerator into its spot, carried in a glass-top range, and then a new TV. I was shocked but thrilled to tears. I wasn't the kind of girlfriend to ask for things or expect gifts. We each handled our own hard-earned money separately, but we shared living expenses.

Kirt was wisely frugal but also wisely generous. He knew I was always struggling financially, so when he saw an important basic need, he filled it.

We worked on the log house for six years, and when it was almost done, it burned down. Kirt came home from work to no house on the hill, and when he saw the fire trucks, he realized what had happened. He was devastated and cried real tears. I respected that about him; he was man enough to cry.

The first thing he did after everybody left and we were alone and hanging onto each other for dear life was to take my hand and walk across the road to the stream. He picked up several big, flat river rocks and said, "I'm going to build you a stone house that can never be destroyed by fire." We staggered back across the road loaded down with all the rocks we could possibly carry in one trip and dumped them in a pile. I think he was still in shock, but it was a gesture that made me feel more loved than I have ever felt before. His first thoughts were how he was going to bring my house back for me.

Logging for the second house was the most amazing feat of strength and determination in a man that I have ever witnessed. As if the first time around wasn't impressive enough, the second time around was shock and awe! Kirt was a human forklift. This time he had to fell the giant trees, limb them, buck them to length, and carry each green 300- to 500-pounder on his shoulders 50 to 100 feet or more to the truck. In the real world, each log would have required two or three ordinary men to carry it, and it still would have been a struggle. We hauled 300 logs in twenty-five trips in only three weeks and lived to tell about it!

We tried to make it fun. Going back home down the steep mountain loaded with a ton and a half of logs in a half-ton pickup meant I had to stay in granny low and go very slowly with the hazard lights blinking. On one trip we were so hot and sweaty that Kirt took his shirt off, so I followed suit. I took my shirt and bra off and drove down topless. We laughed and giggled whenever people passed us and their eyes bugged out. I'd do just about anything for a laugh with Kirt. We took advantage of every opportunity to enjoy small and simple pleasures. Free fun is the best kind, and we excelled at it!

To fill in the timeline: Kirt and our newfound craftsman friend, Vadim, did all the basic rebuilding of the second house, and I did all the finish work. Then they became partners in their own construction business called Home Renaissance and ended up building forty-four beautiful high-end houses, until Kirt took over the pear orchards for his dad and Vadim took over Home Renaissance by himself.

It came natural for Kirt and me to have a good time together—we couldn't help it. We didn't only work. Every Halloween we dressed up and went downtown. One Halloween Kirt decided to be a ballerina, and it was the most ridiculous outfit I've ever seen on a guy. I was Doris Day with a polka-dot dress and a blond wig. "Oh, what a night..."

Kirt remembered every romantic occasion through the years—every birthday, anniversary, and Valentine's Day. To celebrate, he always took me out to dinner at a special (expensive) place, and our conversations were as juicy as the steaks. He gave me beautiful gifts that he carefully chose to honor my femininity. Although we worked side by side like partners in grime, to him I remained a beautiful, soft, feminine woman. Seeing that reflection in his eyes, I couldn't help but have a perpetual little smile on my face when I was with him.

Kirt wanted to go to Reno for his twenty-first birthday (December 26th), and stay at the high-rise Bali Hotel. He wanted to do something completely different and exciting on his twenty-first, and of course I agreed that he should—and while we were there, we could visit my dear mom. We left about 1:00 p.m. Christmas Day and arrived about 6:00 p.m. to check in at the hotel.

As soon as we walked into our elegant and lavish room on the twenty-first floor, the phone rang. I answered, and the caller introduced himself as the hotel security officer and stated in a deep, serious monotone voice, "Ms. Ainsworth, you are harboring a minor in your room, and it's against the law! We're coming up to press charges."

I was too shocked to even respond. All I could think of

to say was, "He'll be twenty-one in six hours," but I was speechless. After a few seconds of agonizing silence, the same caller said in a normal, relaxed voice, "Hi, Dorothy. It's me, Bill, from the fitness center. I'm spending Christmas here myself, and I saw you guys check in, and I knew it wasn't quite Kirt's birthday yet, so I thought I'd play a trick on you." Whew! The truth was, it was not against the law for minors to stay in the hotel rooms; they just can't gamble. Bill took me by surprise and had his gotcha moment; I was royally punked. I hate practical jokes (and their jokers), but all in all, we had a fabulous time in Reno. Kirt and I stayed up half the night to ring in his twenty-first year, and we even went so far as to go bowling in Bali's basement bowling alley at 2:00 a.m. Gleeful nerds again...

When Kirt was twenty-one and a half, he decided to enter the Bill Pearl Body Building contest in the middle-weight class (176 pounds). He had perfect symmetry but was too young to look "ripped" enough. The judges like contestants to look like skinned monkeys. He was natural (no steroids or drugs), so he had to really work at losing the youthful plumpness under his skin. He dieted and jogged until he lost ten pounds, but still didn't look shredded enough. He placed fourth and was terribly disappointed and discouraged. I remember him saying, "I was the best of the worst, and the worst of the best."

He inherited the tightest skin I have ever seen or felt; it was impossible to pinch him, and his muscles felt like iron. When a massage therapist student volunteered to give him a massage—her assignment required massaging a weight lifter—she couldn't press hard enough to make a dent in his muscles, so she had to pound on him with her fists and stand on his back and jump up and down to complete the job.

He decided he would never compete again except in strength contests—the reason being that after losing all that weight he said he felt "as weak as a cat" and didn't like that, and he wasn't willing to take drugs. So he put the pounds back on, and his next competition was a bench press contest where he won first place in his weight class (benched 450 pounds).

Then, on the spur of the moment, he entered a strongman contest without even training for it. He placed well in almost every category and won one event overall—in the number of times he could raise 220 pounds straight up overhead in one minute. He did it thirty-two times, beating the national champion by fifteen presses!

He hasn't competed since, but he enjoys his life as it is: staying strong, healthy, and productive, and being satisfied with setting goals, competing with himself, and doing his own personal best. As gorgeous as he always looked to me, he was reluctant to ever go shirtless in public. When I asked him why he was so darn modest, he said in jest, "Like a sculptor, I'm not ready to unveil my work yet."

When I think back about how I met Kirt, and recall so vividly our first night together, it brings to mind the old song by Dinah Washington: "What a difference a day makes....twenty-four little hours..." Indeed, my life went from famine to feast in twenty-four little hours.

CHAPTER 44

THE ZEN OF BUILDING:
Philosophical Encouragement

Gloves and drawknife after peeling 780 logs

uilding a house needn't be an intimidating undertaking. It is simply an organic process of assembling some of earth's most basic elements into geometric forms to create the microcosm we call home. Trees supply the wood, iron supplies the nails, silicon sand provides the glass, copper carries the current, wood and natural gas supply the heat, concrete is rock, and water flows freely in and out by gravity. It's all very elementary and almost primitive. It only gets complicated when we aspire to arrange these elements into a structure that satisfies our aesthetic taste; otherwise, we'd be happy to live in a hut.

The real fun of building one's own house is designing it. The rest is good old hard work, which has its own priceless rewards. My message is this: Life is tenuous, so enjoy the journey! Nature is capricious and has the ability to disassemble the whole thing in a few short minutes or hours by turning it into a pile of splintered sticks, washing it away in a flood, or burning it into lumps of carbon and melted metal—as happened to me when my house burned down in 1995—but I still believe what I said a couple of years later: "It's better to have built and rebuilt than never to have built at all."

Enjoy the work! No matter how it turns out, you will be forever changed in a positive way by the experience.

CHAPTER 45

TESTIMONIALS

Old Faithful

From: Wendell Durham

Date: April 5, 2010 2:51 PM PDT

To: dorothyainsworth@hughes.net

Dear Superwoman,

Hi. It's me. The guy you loaned the DVDs and CD to. The guy who dreams of one day building his own house of logs. The guy who also used to refer to you as Dorothy Ainsworth. Used to, until I saw the videos.

This email won't address any of the techniques, plans, details, or questions of how you did this or did that type of stuff. I'm going to start off with just my first impressions, okay? Here we go.

My mouth is still hanging open.

The articles in *Backwoods Home* and your own website, alone, just cannot convey what I saw in the videos.

I had absolutely no idea.

Mount Rushmore.

The Great Pyramids,

I'll keep going.

The entire national interstate highway system. Noah's ark.

Not that it resembles an ark at all, but the staggering amount of work that I saw with my own eyes—I'm speechless. I don't know what to say. But I will keep trying.

I don't know anyone like you on so many levels. You are truly one of a kind. Okay. Maybe not one of a kind. I'm sure in the 300-plus million in the US, I might be able to find enough people like you to, say, attempt the most-people-in-a-VW-Beetle record.

I am in awe.

You need to understand who is saying this. I'm an average forty-something-year-old man, with, I like to think, average-something intelligence and drive and determination.

The scope of your vision alone, your dream to have your own place, built with your own hands, that you don't owe a fortune to the bank for, is, in itself, awe-inspiring. Then throw in the fact that you actually carried it out, the way you did, is unimaginable to me.

I looked back in an earlier email you sent me and found this sentence: "The work doesn't have to be staggering...just methodical and time consuming." Dorothy, I am staggered.

A lot of people sit on soft chairs at work all day, drive their cars with soft seats home, and then take their spot on their soft recliners and couches, thinking they've had a "hard" day. They don't even have a beginning point, a basis, to understand what you have accomplished. I've done just enough "work" a few days in my life to understand what I've seen.

Conversations like the following have actually happened in dens and porches across America. "Do you remember that time we cut that big tree down in the back yard? Man, that was a big project. Took most of a weekend to get that cleaned up."

"And then do you remember how we had to drag the huge tree trunk to the front with a rope tied to the truck, just to be able to get to it to haul it off? Man, that was sure something. Can't believe we did that."

"Remember that time we thought we would try to patch the roof ourselves, or build a deck, or replace that broken window, etc.? Man, we sure bit off more than we could chew that time."

Those kind of events are what I call a "life event." It's something that stands out in our minds enough that it will be remembered.

You have lived a "life event" over and over, day after day. And then got up the next morning to do it again. You have had a life full of "life events."

I am so proud that you have a place of your own, unlike any other place, because you are unlike anyone else. You deserve every bit of happiness that has come your way and all future happiness yet to come.

Then when I think that you "had to" do all of this twice because of the fire...I just don't know what to say. But I bet can come up with something.

You didn't "have to." You didn't even "have to" do it once, but you did.

And then you did it again.

After the fire, after the tears, staying in a remodeled outbuilding, or staying in a travel trailer that was meant to be temporary, or having a trailer home moved in, would have certainly been understandable.

But you did it again.

Lady, you have my utmost respect and admiration.

Wendell Durham

Oklahoma City

From: Guy Fosse

Subject: Inspirational Website

Date: January 21, 2012 9:09:41 AM PST

To: dorothyainsworth@hughes.net

Hello Dorothy,

Just wanted to drop you a short note to let you know how much I thoroughly enjoyed reading through your website. While researching solar and wind shallow well pumps to assist in maintaining a bird and duck pond on some land I am purchasing, I stumbled on a link to your article in *Backwoods Home* magazine titled "Water Pumping Windmills."

Your informative and enjoyable writing style made me want to check out the other articles you had written for *Backwoods*. Within a very short period of time I was "sucked in" to your adventures and felt almost as if I were sitting on a back porch somewhere listening to a friend describe their incredible quest to build not just a house but a place where they truly felt "at home" in every sense of the word.

The fact that you tackled your projects with much more persistence, sweat, and ingenuity than with money made your story all the more interesting, but when you add in your humor and romantic vision (along with your real-life romance), the stories became much more than informative "how to" articles, they became chapters in a "can't put down" book.

Which is all to explain how a recent snowy afternoon in Northwest Montana went from a research day to a very enjoyable afternoon spent with Dorothy! By the time evening rolled around and Eric's house was almost finished I felt like I had known you "a while."

And in some ways I do think I "know you," because in many ways I think we are alike. I too am one of those souls who love going out and scrounging for materials to build with. Not always because it is less expensive (think today's gas prices) but because a lumber mill cannot turn out fresh products that can compete with what Mother Nature can do over several decades (or longer). And "shopping" outside is much more enjoyable and satisfying than inside at Home Depot or Lowe's. Nothing speaks to a successful day more than chain-saw bar oil on your clothes, wood chips in your hair, dirt from head to toe, and a pickup load full of treasures.

So I try and work with reclaimed wood as much as possible and have been lucky enough over the years to get hired by some of the fat-wallet folks that have places around here to make and install wood floors, ceilings, wall coverings, trim, stairs, mantles, doors, and so forth. Hopefully, below are a couple of photos showing the type of stuff I do. Just thought they might be a style that you would find interesting.

Well, Dorothy, I have taken enough of your time. Thank you again for sharing your wonderful story of triumph, sad loss, and "Unsinkable Molly Brown" style comeback triumph.

Your exploits will undoubtedly be an inspiration as I start on this next crazy project.

Cheers,

Guy Fosse

Flathead Lake, Montana

On Jan 12, 2009, at 10:27 AM, Ken Pagliaro wrote:

Dorothy (long pause while I virtually stare at you in awe),

I just spent the last two hours reading, looking at photos, laughing, and crying. You did a great job designing the website, but the content, your life and creativity, is/are so remarkable and inspiring that I just couldn't stop exploring it. I love the way you write. I'm immediately locked in from the first few sentences. I feel like you are talking directly to me and what you're saying isn't boring or bullshit, it's exciting and real.

Also, I have the advantage of having met the live

version of Dorothy Ainsworth so I can hear your wonderful voice in my head while I'm reading along. A plus. It's quite simply you telling your story and telling it well. And the photos, so many beautiful photos—your stories could easily stand alone with no images, but the fact that you have all of this wonderful imagery to go along with them satisfies my visual curiosities. I love it! You are truly an inspiration and a hot mama too! Some of those pics of you building...woo hoo!!

Also, I watched the videos of Eric practicing, and you can see the music flowing from his body, down his arms, and right out of his hands! Awesome! I'm actually listening to his Chopin A- Flat as I type this. I'd love to hear it live someday.

Thanks, Dorothy.

Kp

Malibu, CA

From: N. Lewis

Subject: It's all because of YOU!

Date: April 4, 2009 7:41:40 PM PDT

To: dorothyainsworth@hughes.net

Dear Dorothy,

All because of you, my muscles are aching. All because of you, I am getting ready to go outside and take another little step toward the removal of this huge boulder and tree with roots embedded in the boulder.

All because of you, I spend a lot of time covered with dirt and mud, moving rocks, digging holes, and will soon be removing trees. All because of you, for the first time in a long time, I am beginning to start to feel a true sense of self-worth.

All because of you, I am transforming myself from a hopeless, emotionally and verbally abused person with absolutely NO self-esteem into a person that is coming to realize that if I set my mind to it, I can do almost anything. That I can and will solve problems by thinking them through and handling them one at a time a little bitty step at a time, all the while transforming my body from unhealthy, overweight, and weak into a smaller one with much strength, endurance, and a sort of cheer in my step with head now high and shoulders no longer drooping with despair.

All because of you, I am taking ground that is not level, full of trees and rocks and boulders and roots, and turning it into a nice, properly graded and smooth area with a portable storage building on it with no assistance whatsoever (except possibly one person to put tension on rope while I fell a couple of large trees that need to fall in a specific area and are leaning in the wrong direction). If I can do this entire project, considering my physical and mental condition at the beginning of it, I can do nearly anything!

One day, not long ago, while in a state of anguish so great that I was seriously considering the best way to take my own life, I had planted my large buttocks in front of my PC to surf and came upon one of your articles in *Backwoods Home* (piano studio), which led me to the rest of your articles (in chronological order), which was "Day One" of the beginning of what has already become a much,

much better life for me, and I have only scratched the surface and look forward eagerly to the rest of my journey—all because of YOU!

Thank you, Dorothy!

Nanette Lewis

Madison County, Iowa

Subject: Kindred Spirit

From: Dayton's Designs

Date: Tue, 4 Feb 2014 15:12:34-0500 (EST)

To: dorothyainsworth@hughes.net

Hi Dorothy!

I am on a journey, and not sure exactly where it will take me, but have been researching for a while online, how to start a homestead of my own, and looking at land with no utilities...then I get intimidated, because I am, after all, only a woman...

Then I stumbled upon your website after researching how to build a water storage tank, and as we would say in the south...Lordy Mercy! I just wanted to send you a quick email, as l know you are probably bombarded with others, to say thanks so much for sharing your story. I have always been one that gets it done, whatever it takes, but something about taking this leap gave me pause. I now have more confidence that it can be done—even though I'm just one woman alone.

I laughed when reading your "how to" about building the water storage tank, and gunning your truck with a load of gravel, fishtailing all the way up the hill. I have my own crazy-lady stories about hauling huge things in my unconventional vehicle over the years. You are a gifted writer, and I've decided you must have really been an architect that just happened to waitress for a living, as well as all the other wonderful things I've read that you have taken on. There is so much life on your website, I am inspired.

Don't want to write you a dry, boring novel about my life and experiences, or what has caused me to want to abandon the conventional life, but just wanted to reach out to a kindred spirit to say bravo, Dorothy, bravo! You have done well with your gifts and talents. Can't wait to read more about your next venture!

All the best,

Nancy Dayton

California

From: Simone Thomas

Subject: You are my heroine

Date: March 21, 2011 8:55:12 AM PDT

To: dorothyainsworth@hughes.net

Dear Dorothy,

My name is Simone Thomas, and I am writing to you to thank you for sharing your stories with the world. You are an inspiration, motivation, and all-around angel to me. As weird as that may sound, it is true.

I am thirty-eight, and all of my life I have had this dream of building my own home. I have envisioned a log cabin home somewhere on the side of a mountain, surrounded by trees, with a view of a lake with a little boat dock where I could go out and fish—does that sound silly? My home would have a giant fireplace complete with a hearth and cooking hook to put a big cast iron pot where I could cook (which happens to be my other passion) homemade soups and casseroles made fresh with vegetables I picked from my own organic garden in a free-standing greenhouse that I have built with my own two hands.

I never in a million years thought it would be possible for me to build my own home the way I wanted until I read your story, and now I know that it is possible and I can do this. I have lived a very tough life, but I would never let that stop me from living. I look forward to building those walls, and in the process tearing down others that have held me in one place for far to long, and when I think I can't go on, I will tell myself, "Is this something that would stop Dorothy Ainsworth?", and we all know the answer to that right, LOL.

Thank you once again,

Simone Thomas

From: Jane Berlin in Texas

Date: July 10, 2014 3:41:23 PM PDT

To: dorothyainsworth@hughes.net

First, let me say I'm sorry if this is annoying!

I have no idea why I feel the need to email you. I'm sure you have better things to do with your time than reading fan mail. So I'll make sure this doesn't end as a three pager! Basically:

1) I stumbled onto your site by accident

2) I read straight through the entire story from

beginning to end

3) 6 hours later my boyfriend walked in to me bawling and laughing, hugging my laptop. It was the first time I felt alive since 2008. I can't describe accurately the immensity of experiencing a glimmer of hope through your story after fighting so hard, grasping for even a sliver of hope anywhere in my reality.

Here's the facts:

1) I have a bad attitude.

2) I was not raised like everyone else in the world. There isn't much that surprises me or impresses me.

3) I can't turn to faith when times get tough like most people, because I have believed more fervently then 85 percent of this country's pastors, priests, or preachers put together and weighed up against me. I have never met a person who knows the Bible as well as I do. I could quote more chapters of the Bible before I was ten than most Christians have ever even read in the whole of their lives. I also am not stupid, so of course by the time I turned sixteen I had pretty much figured it all out and I felt stupid for being such a zealot of a blind believer throughout my childhood.

4) I'm the oldest of eight siblings. We raised each other, and I can't say we did the best job of it.

5) In 2011 I started to give up. For the first time, I couldn't pick myself back up from a particularly bad round of sucker punches life was (naturally) hitting me with.

Opps, I'm sorry I'm babbling at you!

What I guess I'm trying to say is that I respect

you! So much! I'm in shock because I don't respect people. I can count with one hand the ones I do respect. I have never in my life respected an adult! I also never thought I'd find a ray of hope. You gave me that by telling your story.

Thank you,

Jane Berlin

Texas

From: Glen Weldon

Date: December 10, 2014

Subject: So impressed I don't really know what to say!

Well, that's not really true... I always have enough to say...er...write!

My name is Glen. I stumbled upon your website through the Forestry Forum. I own a portable band-saw mill and even though I'm fifty-two, I have dreams of building a timber-framed building. I have never been one to shy away from work and will to this day attempt to do things that other folks tell me I should pay to get others to do for me. I've never really had what I would call extra cash available. Even though I've had good jobs (I'm a manufacturing engineer without a bachelor's degree), I haven't always managed my money well, so I didn't really have any. Like many folks, I lived paycheck to paycheck...

Anyway, I'm rambling. I've never really suffered from a lack of drive or determination, and I get stuff done! That being said, I have to say that you have (had?) more drive and determination than anybody

I've ever seen!

I don't think that even in my thirties I would have attempted to do what you have accomplished! The water tank alone...what an enormous job!

The piano studio! I would be PROUD to have that structure on MY property! Oh, and the heartbreak of having to rebuild that magnificent barn home... I'm a strong-willed person, but I don't really know if I would have been able to recover! The way you described it, with detailed personality, then to wind up with a jaw-dropping "then the rag spontaneously combusted and burned it all down..." left me in shock!

It appears that "muscle-man" (John's words) Kirt was an inspiration to you all the way around. I assume he isn't in the picture anymore. I would suspect that you both knew the age difference would not work long term? I'm happy he was there for you. I can't really say enough about how impressed I am with your "drive." Women like you are rare and extraordinary! I give you all my respect. With that and a dollar, you can buy yourself a cup of coffee!

I believe you and I are kindred spirits and would have worked well together. After two failed marriages (the first one with two children who suffered greatly by the divorce), in 2007 I bought sixty acres of land in rural Alabama. It's beautiful land with hills and valleys and oaks, pine and hickory (and other trees). I started building a house similar to what you have done, but on a much smaller scale.

The house still doesn't have siding on it, but it eventually will. I'm in the process of building a metal and wood barn so that I can stop using my house as a storage building and finish it! I've got this self-sufficient mentality going on myself.

My house will eventually be supplied with a rainwater catchment system for drinking/washing/irrigation and a solar PV system for essential electricity. I work constantly on the homestead, and it is hard, enjoyable, rewarding work.

Thank you so much for taking the time to chronicle your life.

I greatly appreciate the lack of typos and the proper grammar. You are a great writer! Being the typical guy, I don't shed too many tears, but your website certainly pulled a few from me.

God bless you Dorothy...

Glen Weldon

From: Megan

Subject: Thank You

Date: January 14, 2015 8:26:03 PM PST

To: dorothyainsworth@hughes.net

Dorothy,

I first heard of you when I read your article about self-reliance some years ago on BWH's website. It resonated with me and was one I'd read over and over when I needed a pick-me-up.

I had forgotten about BWH and for whatever reason visited the website today. I found myself rereading your articles. Over the last several months, I have come to realize that your quote is true: "I learned that if you can accept your mistakes, it will free you to take more risks. Trying until you get it right is how most people learn things. Perfectionism leads to procrastination and paralysis."

I've paralyzed myself for years with anxiety about not being good enough. Sometimes I feel abnormally anxious, but reading that again today made me feel less alone and helped me remember that wallowing about my perfectionism is a waste of time.

I also noticed that you have a website, and I took a look at that. As a web developer, I am very impressed with your website. It is beautiful! I have enjoyed catching up on your articles and seeing all of those lovely pictures.

Thank you for sharing your attitude and knowledge with the world. I see you as a role model for myself for self-reliance and empowerment.

Respectfully,

Megan Bouret

North Dakota

Dorothy, 74, and still at it

www.dorothyainsworth.com

Made in the USA
Charleston, SC
03 November 2016